THE
FIREARMS
CLASSICS LIBRARY

THIS SPECIAL EDITION OF

SHOTGUNS

BY

KEITH

BY ELMER KEITH

HAS BEEN PRIVATELY PRINTED
FOR THE MEMBERS OF
THE FIREARMS CLASSICS LIBRARY

THE FIREARMS CLASSICS LIBRARY
OF THE NATIONAL RIFLE ASSOCIATION
AND ITS NATIONAL FIREARMS MUSEUM

PUBLISHED FOR

THE NATIONAL RIFLE ASSOCIATION

BY

ODYSSEUS EDITIONS, INC.

Editor's Note

"An entertaining, informative work of timeless value"

BY DR. JIM CASADA

According to his long-time acquaintance, Don Martin, Elmer Keith's writings were mirror reflections of his personality. Martin said he had a "remarkable gift for accurate, detailed observation; a prodigious and exact memory; and uncompromising honesty." These qualities shine through in *Shotguns by Keith* and loom large in making it an entertaining, informative work of timeless value. A reviewer described the volume when it first appeared as "an exhaustive, highly technical handbook," and that appraisal was as squarely on target as a shot from one of Keith's guns.

Yet while *Shotguns by Keith* is undoubtedly exhaustive, it is never exhausting, for a hallmark of Keith's writing was freshness and straightforward simplicity. That charm endures and these pages remain as appealing and compelling as they did when the book first appeared almost a half century ago.

Elmer Merrifield Keith was born on March 8, 1899, in Hardin, Missouri, the son of Forest Everett and Linnie Neal (née Merrifield) Keith. His ancestors on both sides of the family were adventurous sorts, and they moved into the Kentucky region in the Daniel Boone era before following fortune's star further west to Missouri. A maternal ancestor had been involved in an unsuccessful insurrection against the British (he was drawn and quartered for his troubles) several years before the American Revolution, and on his father's side Keith's lineage traced back to Capt. William Clark, the famous explorer commissioned by President Thomas Jefferson to charter the lands acquired in the Louisiana Purchase of 1803. In other words, Elmer Keith came quite honestly by the restlessness and love of the wild which characterized his entire life.

Keith's first six years were spent as a farm boy growing up with the prairie for a back yard. At that early stage in his life, through his father, he began to develop what would become a lifelong interest in horses. An even more compelling interest also dating from this period was Keith's attraction to firearms. As he would write late in life, "From my earliest years I seem to have been more interested in guns and ammunition than other things." Certainly his career reflected as much, because guns and knowledge of how to use them, whether as a hunter or marksman, would be a central feature of his entire life.

Most of our knowledge of these formative years comes from two autobiographical works he wrote: *Keith: An Autobiography* (1974), and *Hell, I Was There!* (1979). There are similarities between the two books but the latter varies appreciably in being more frank and a bit more personal. Together, they remain far and away the best sources for an appreciation of the man, although there are significant autobiographical elements in all of his books.

In 1905, the Keith family left Missouri, which was getting too populous for the senior Keith's tastes, and moved to the Montana mining town of Marysville. That lasted only a couple of years before they were once more back on family land in Missouri. It was at this juncture that Keith obtained his first gun, a .22 Hopkins & Allen rifle, and in short order he was supplying the family table with squirrels and rabbits in plenitude. He was a first-rate marksman from the outset, and his father contributed to this by making him account for every shot.

Interestingly, given the subject of the book being reprinted here, Keith's first experience with a shotgun was a memorable but not exactly pleasant one. He took careful aim at a fox squirrel but failed to allow for recoil. He later recounted: "What part of the gun hit me, I don't know. But it cut my upper lip clear through to my teeth and when I woke up about three hours later, there was blood all over the side of my face and the oak leaves I was lying on."

By the time the family moved to Montana for good in 1911, young Keith was already an exceptionally accomplished marksman and a fine woodsman. He was a rambunctious lad in his teens, and often with him (then and later) the veneer of civilized behavior could be thin indeed. He got into more than a fair share of scrapes and fights, and unquestionably he was a salty, contentious character. Yet, short-tempered, transparent forthrightness was also to become one of Keith's most redeeming qualities. You always knew precisely where you stood with him, for Elmer Keith was a man who minced neither words nor deeds when it came to the expression of his feelings.

Keith's teenage years in Montana saw the family live a somewhat peripatetic existence, with frequent moves, mostly to and from Missoula and Helena. Young Elmer was terribly burned in a hotel fire in the course of one of these numerous periods of transition, and he was years in fully recovering. During adolescence, however, he gained experience in a variety of areas which would serve him well in the future—broncobusting, trapping, hunting, and competitive rifle shooting.

The summer of his sixteenth year he saved money from a job feeding coal to a furnace at a large bakery and bought a hammerless double shotgun from the Ithaca Gun Company. He soon became a masterful shot with it, as was true with rifles and pistols as well.

Young Elmer did a lot of hunting, and despite the fact that after he was badly burned doctors predicted he would never live to be 21, he became a tough, seasoned young man. Montana at the time was still pretty much pioneer country, or, as Keith put it, "those were rough times in Montana in those days, and a man carried his law with him. If he didn't, he might not last too long." "Rough times" suited the exuberant and hickory tough young man just fine, and he thrived in the hurly-burly style of the times.

He was a bona fide "gun nut" by the time he reached his early twenties, and much of his earnings from a variety of jobs went towards acquiring the beginnings of a veritable arsenal. For several years, up until his marriage to Lorraine Raddall on June 16, 1926, Keith was involved in a whole host of short-lived jobs. During this period his family, after losing another son to influenza and seeing Elmer very nearly die, pulled up stakes and moved to Idaho.

For Elmer, once he recovered from flu-induced pneumonia, it was a period of being footloose and fancy-free. His interest in guns and shooting continued unabated, and in 1922 he joined the National Rifle Association. Keith was also quite anxious to get into match shooting and for this reason signed up with Montana National Guard. He made the state team in 1924 and was able to represent Montana in the national matches at Camp Perry in Ohio. Here he met renowned gun writers such as James V. Howe, Townsend Whelen, and J.S. Hatcher, although there is no indication that Keith had any inkling that his career would eventually see him tread in their footsteps.

Elmer clearly enjoyed his experiences at Camp Perry immensely. When he returned to the West, he visited his parents in their new home in Idaho, and it was then that he met his future bride, Lorraine Raddall. The next year saw him back at Camp Perry once more, and on this visit he performed well in a number of the competitive venues. By this time he had already made his first appearance in print, with a letter he had written to *American Rifleman*. While at Camp Perry he was asked to write up the 1925 matches for the publication, which he did. It was thus that Keith took his first tentative steps as an outdoor writer.

The following summer saw him married, and fittingly for a couple who joyed in the outdoors almost as much as they did in one another, the newlyweds honeymooned for ten days while spearing salmon on Idaho's Weiser River. They did a bit of ranching in the late 1920s, intermingled with a lot of hunting and shooting. During this period Elmer penned an account of an elk hunt he had taken when his partner, Bill Strong, had been killed, and he won $100 (big money at the time) in an *American Rifleman* contest for the piece.

Soon he was writing regularly for the NRA magazine, and in 1926 he sold his first piece to *Outdoor Life*. In 1930 the Keiths bought a ranch on the North Fork of the Salmon River in Idaho, and they would call this area home for the remainder of their lives.

With the depths of the Depression holding the country in a tight grip, Keith made a decision in 1930 which would guide the remainder of his life. "I had," he would later write, "decided to make my living writing and guiding big game hunters and fishing parties." One of his first outfitting trips involved two months with a large party organized by Zane Grey.

For the first half of the 1930s, guide work was the main source of income for Keith, although he was writing regularly and was well on the way to earning national recognition as a gun scribe. The year 1936 saw the appearance of his first works of greater length. Considerable controversy apparently surrounded this undertaking, and it is perhaps best described in Keith's own blunt, no-nonsense fashion:

> T.G. Samworth, who . . . operated what he called the Small Arms Technical Publishing Company, commissioned me to write three manuals, which I did. He offered me $250 down and another $250 if they sold. The first one was to be on six-gun cartridges and loads; the second one on big game rifles and cartridges; and the third on varmint rifles.
>
> I wrote the three manuals which were to sell at a dollar apiece. He never did publish the last one. He paid me $250 down on it, and $250 on each of the others. The others sold all right, and plenty good. He later sold the *Big Game and Cartridges* to the Stackpole Company and it published a lot more of them. However, I never did get the final payment on either book that he published and, of course, not on the one that he didn't publish.

There is no way of knowing Samworth's side of this, since his papers seem to have vanished, but it is interesting to note that he was at least as crusty a curmudgeon as Keith, and this literary spitting match between them is quite revealing.

The bitter taste his first venture as a book author left him notwithstanding, writing would become increasingly important to Keith and his family (the couple would have a girl and boy in addition to another daughter who died at birth). In 1936 Keith took the position of gun editor for an Ohio publication, *The Outdoorsman,* and he would continue in that post for a dozen years until he quarreled with a new editor.

Keith, always a real "character," developed a loyal following as a gun writer, and his personality and appearance in some senses added to his appeal. He favored huge ten-gallon hats, although in stature he was a small man, and he thought big not only in hats but in other ways. Probably the most famous example focuses on his devotion to rifles of big caliber, a preference which would be a source of a long-standing controversy between Keith and Jack O'Connor, who was a staunch advocate of the .243 and .270.

Although he had established a national reputation by that time, the coming of America's entry into World War II heralded the onset of some tough times for Keith and his family. Despite pulling every string he could, Keith never got to do what he wanted (some sort of active service) in contributing to America's war effort. He had to be content with an advisory position at the arsenal in Ogden, Utah. Worse still, his daughter Druzilla was badly injured in a car accident and eventually died from the effects. Keith himself was desperately ill when she died, having fallen victim to the same empyema which had troubled him as a young man.

Somehow he persevered and in 1946 brought out another book, *Keith's Rifles for Large Game,* which was published by Herman Dean of Standard Publishing Company. Dean soon sold out to Stackpole and they remaindered the book almost immediately. Today copies of the original are exceedingly rare, and those of the limited, leather-bound edition sometimes sell for more than $1,000.

Two years later he completed *Big Game Hunting,* a book which went through three editions and remains in constant demand on the out-of-print market. Meanwhile, he had given up his position as gun editor of *The Outdoorsman* and assumed one on the technical staff of *American Rifleman.* In that capacity he sometimes answered as many as 500 letters a month along with writing articles on a regular basis.

In 1950 Keith wrote the present work at the request of General Stackpole, the head of the noted Harrisburg, Pennsylvania, publishing company. Later, in 1955, he would do another Stackpole book, *Sixguns by Keith.* His final four books would come more than a decade later. They were, in chronological order of publication, *Guns and Ammo For Hunting Big Game* (1965), *Safari* (1968), *Keith: An Autobiography* (1976), and *Hell, I Was There!* (1979).

Shotguns by Keith is not the rarest of his books, but it is quite possibly the least appreciated. Admittedly, the design and to some extent even the function of shotguns have changed dramatically in the four and a half decades since the work first saw the light of day. Sporting clays was unknown in America at mid-century, and the nearest thing to the screw-in choke systems which are commonplace today was the Poly Choke. No one even thought about camouflaged stocks and barrels, and there was much less emphasis on "special purpose" shotguns than is today the case. Most folks bought one shotgun and expected it to serve in a variety of roles.

Those differences (and there are many others) being duly recognized, the fact remains that there is a timelessness to *Shotguns by Keith* which transcends changing technology and sporting preferences. You won't find deep, detailed discussion of English "bests" in this work, but you will find practical wisdom, not to mention wit, in abundance. There is none of the snobbery and elitism sometimes associated with shotguns and certain aspects of their uses, but there is simple, easily understood firearms information galore.

This work is, in short, vintage Keith, and as such it is a literary treasure which assuredly will give readers a full measure of reading enjoyment.

Before returning to Keith's later years, a few bibliographical comments on the book's publication history might also be useful. As was noted above, *Shotguns* first appeared in 1950 under the Stackpole imprint, and NRA old-timers will be interested to learn that this edition was featured as an NRA Library Book. A second Stackpole edition appeared in 1961 and a third one in 1967. The book was also reprinted in 1967 by Bonanza Books. *Shotguns* has long been out of print and comes up surprisingly infrequently, given its four editions, in the used book trade.

By the time *Shotguns by Keith* appeared, the author was well on his way to holding a venerated position among America's gun writers, and over the final two and a half decades of his life Keith was a household name among American gun enthusiasts. For the most part, these were good years for Elmer Keith. He traveled widely, making his first African safari in 1957, and would return to the Dark Continent again in the 1960s as well as hunting widely (and well) in North America and Europe.

His writing continued apace, although there were some changes in editorial positions over the years. For a time Keith served as executive editor of *Guns and Ammo,* and later he joined forces with *Petersen's Hunting* magazine. Petersen Publishing Company also published some of his later books. In 1967, he suffered a serious heart attack, and although he would live another 16 years, he lacked the stamina and drive which had been salient Keith characteristics for so many years. Still, he remained active, and just prior to turning 80 he wrote: "I have no intention of retiring. You retire, you become a vegetable and usually last six months to three years. I don't care for that kind of an end. I'd rather keep working and die with my boots on if necessary."

In 1973 he had received the Outstanding American Handgunner award, and for the final decade of his life he pretty well held center stage as the grand old man of American gunning. He obviously sensed the end lay not far distant when he wrote, at the conclusion of *Hell, I Was There!:* "Life is a fleeting thing, and one realizes how short it is only after he begins to reach old age." He ended his last book with a poem from a treasured friend, E.A. Brinninstool, and it seems appropriate to share these words before concluding our glimpse of an intriguing individual:

> If with pleasure you are viewing any work a man is doing,
> If you like it or you love him, tell him now. Don't withhold your approbations until the parson makes his orations,
> As he lies with snowy lilies o'er his brow. For no matter how you shout it, he won't really care about it.
> He won't know how many teardrops you have shed.
> If you think some praise is due him, now's the time to pass it to him,
> For he cannot read his tombstone when he's dead.

Sadly, for all his renown, Keith received less than his full due during his lifetime, thanks no doubt in part to his controversial and sometimes argumentative nature. He was perhaps closer to the mark than even he knew when he penned these words: "All my life I have tried to dodge trouble as much as possible, yet for some reason it seems to follow me." Trouble may indeed have dogged his years, but for all the tragedies and encounters which were signposts along his life's road, there is no denying that he savored his days and derived from them a degree of enjoyment few are privileged to match. Moreover, he left gunning literature a lasting legacy in the form of this book and others, and sporting posterity is far richer for his endeavors.

Jim Casada

ROCK HILL, SOUTH CAROLINA

SHOTGUNS

BY

KEITH

SHOTGUNS

BY

KEITH

ELMER KEITH

*A National Rifle Association
Library Book*

STACKPOLE & HECK, INC.

NEW YORK   HARRISBURG

To the memory of the late
MAJOR CHARLES ASKINS, SR.,
My long time friend and instructor;
One of the greatest shotgun ballisticians
Of all time, and above that, a man.

Preface

I have known Elmer Keith for twenty-five years. I first met him in 1925 at the National Matches where as a sergeant of the Idaho National Guard he was making things exceedingly tough for the Marines and others in the long range rifle matches. Elmer at that time was about twenty-five and when he was not tinkering with a shooting iron of some kind punched cows and was a horse packer for the U. S. Forest Service.

Guns were an over-riding passion with Keith and as he accumulated more and more of them it was inevitable that he should commence to write of them. His first stories appeared in the "American Rifleman" at least a quarter of a century ago. He wrote hesitantly and somewhat awkwardly at first, but as he continued to experiment and put his findings into print his ability to express himself smoothly and fluently naturally followed and the enthusiasm with which his writings were accepted made inevitable his decision to become a guns writer. The decision made, Keith bought a small ranch and there between brandings, hayings, fence building and innumerable hunting forays experimented prodigiously and wrote quite as much.

I ask you now, if you were in the boots of this Idahoan, possessed of a keen intellect, a sizeable curiosity, plenty of solitude, an assured living, ample powder and not a few firearms, what would you do? Precisely what Keith did, I suspect; and that was to become a firearms authority, and in truth such an expert as to be one of the two ranking guns writers in the country today. The other is Col. Townsend Whelen but this piece isn't written about him. Keith lived guns, ate guns, thought guns and seldom talked about anything else. Somewhere along the line however he took time away from his moulds and powder measures to persuade the local school marm to share his guns-crowded existence. Elmer got married, raised a family and made shooters of the entire Keith clan.

During the past quarter of a century the stature of Elmer Keith has steadily grown. He is known to every reader of any outdoors periodical, for he has written for all of them. He has published a small library of books and manuals and has corresponded with thousands upon thousands of sportsmen who come to him for a variety of shooting advise. Despite the literary output and the tremendous amount of test shooting Keith has found the time to tramp up and down the land, from the Arctic to deep into Mexico, hunting and guiding hunters. His has been the sort of existence Riley would have liked to have had. Elmer has been free and untrammeled and if this month he wanted to do his writing from the ranch in Idaho he did, but if the urge seized him and he hied himself away to the Yukon there has been no one to say him nay. He has killed more big game, shot away more ammunition, put in more time on the firing range, possesses more guns of every type and caliber, reloads more cartridges and accomplishes more experimentation than any firearms authority.

We have a great many pseudo authorities today, fellows who write on Sunday and sell insurance during the week. What they have learned has been gleaned from the writings of their betters. Not so our boy Keith. Elmer has killed the game, has developed the loads, has proven in his own methodical way the assertions he makes. Not infrequently he has called down upon his head the wrath of readers not yet prepared to accept his advanced thinking because he is consistently some two to five years ahead of current development.

During the late world-wide unpleasantness now usually referred to as World War II, Keith wrote to everyone whom he knew in an attempt to persuade the Army to give him a commission; despite his efforts and those of many prominent friends he was unsuccessful, but not to be denied he volunteered as Chief Inspector of Small Arms at a western arsenal and there finished the war as an exceedingly valuable civilian employee.

With some mental reservations for any shotgunning beyond 40 yards which my old amigo Keith may advocate I commend this book to you as having been written by a man who has forgotten more about scatter guns than most of us will ever know, a writer rich in the lore of his subject who you may be sure has laboriously and painstakingly proven his every point in field and marsh and upon the patterning boards before he set it here to print.

Charles Askins
Lt. Col., Ord. Dept.
82 Airborne Division

Foreword

IN 1905 my family moved from Missouri to Montana and after a three year sojourn in the Treasure State, returned to Missouri for a year while father gathered up the loose ends of his business, preparatory to making a permanent home in Montana. It was during this last year in Missouri that my shotgun shooting started. I was then a very weak, frail youngster but intensely interested in guns of all kinds, to the exclusion of nearly everything else, including school. My playmates called me "Gunny".

Dad raised trotting horses and mules and would drive the trotters to Carrolton to race them. He and Frank James were warm friends and Frank usually started the races. I still remember him well.

Most of the prosperous families in our vicinity had a good muzzle-loading double-barreled shotgun or one of the, then modern, double-barreled hammer-style "britch loaders" as they called them. The poorer folks had either a single-barreled muzzle-loader or an old Zulu musket conversion or one of the cheap, mail order, single shot "britch loaders".

Small game was plentiful and we shot ducks in the spring flight as well as in the fall. Squirrels furnished us with summer shooting, quail were abundant in the fall and we hunted rabbits all winter.

The only game law I remember was a general prohibition of Sunday hunting. Mother always made me attend Sunday School. The rest of the day was mine to do as I pleased. I used to take my .22 apart, put both stock and barrel in a flour sack, sneak out of town through the back alleys into the big woods and hunt squirrels until I could no longer see the sights.

Market hunting still continued in many sections at that time. Most of the market gunners, if they were fortunate enough to own a "britch loader", had a supply of brass shells and rolled their own. I had been hunting small game with a rifle for some time, in Montana, but had never hunted with a shotgun before returning to Missouri. My job, when spare time was available, was to keep the family table supplied with small game. That was one task I never had to be urged to do.

One day a crony and I were hunting squirrels when we met a Darky with two more boys. The colored gentleman was hunting geese along the river. He was carrying an old single-barrel muzzle-loading eight-gauge. He dared us boys to shoot his huge gun. None of the others would take the dare but I was quite willing to shoot any kind of a gun so I did. The mighty weapon was so heavy I could not hold it up in shooting position but had to find a limb to rest the barrel over. A yellow Hammer, pecking away at an old snag, was selected for the target. Putting the single brass bead on him, I pressed the trigger. Instantly I was kicked for the count, turning a complete back somersault, the gun flying out of my hands and over my head to land muzzle down in the mud where it stuck. My face was badly bruised from some part of the gun hitting me and it was several minutes before I knew what had happened. All we found of the Yellow Hammer was his beak and a few feathers. The Darky paid for his joke by having to dig a great wad of mud out of his gun barrel before he could reload but perhaps he thought it worth while.

Once in Montana father wrapped the paper case from a 12-bore around a 16-bore shotshell and allowed me to fire to at a tin can. The eight-gauge was the second shotgun I had ever fired.

My third experience with shotguns occurred when I borrowed an old Zulu conversion from a boy friend and half a dozen brass shells, for a squirrel hunt. Father advised me to stick to my rifle but I was anxious to try hunting with a shotgun. After reaching the Big Woods I soon spotted a large fox squirrel playing in the tops of some water-oaks. He saw me and hid in a leafy top where the wind swayed him back and forth. Selecting a rest for the muzzle of the gun where a small knot projected upwards on one of the down sloping, lower dead limbs of an adjacent tree, I held the stock with both hands while I aimed the single brass bead at the swaying squirrel. As he swung back toward the line of sight I pressed the trigger. The knot I was resting the gun on broke at the same time. All I remember is a blinding flash of lights and stars.

It was just after noon when I shot at the squirrel. It was nearly dusk when I came to. I had been out all afternoon. I woke up lying face down, over the gun, on the dead oak leaves, in a pool of blood, with a generous supply of leaves clotted to my face. My upper lip was cut through to the teeth and hung down over my lower lip. A white streak on the side of a water-oak six feet away showed where the old gun was pointed when it went off. I picked up the old Zulu, loaded it, and trudged sadly home. Mother managed to stick my lip up where it belonged but I had to hold it in place with one hand, while eating, for several days. The hammer spur must have hit me squarely in the mouth.

A short time after my lip healed, leaving a scar I still wear, father and I went quail hunting in the buggy. He had his double hammer gun in twelve bore and I had my .22 rifle. As we drove past a pond I spotted a duck and asked father if I could try his shotgun. He kindly stopped his high spirited trotter when out of sight of the duck, loaded both barrels, telling me to cock only one hammer when I reached the bank of the pond which was built up some four feet high. "Then," he said, "lay the gun over the bank and kill your duck." I did as directed except when I started to rest the gun over the bank the duck took off. I jumped to my feet, put the bead on the fast departing fowl, and pulled the trigger. That was more like it. The duck stopped in a cloud of feathers and skidded toward the opposite side of the pond where his momentum drifted him to shore. It was a Spoonbill and my first duck taken with a shotgun. I had killed many ducks on the water with the .22 and had once dropped one out of a flying flock with the rifle.

Father killed a nice mess of quail and we managed to annex two fat squirrels. I got a cock quail that sat on a fence rail beside the road too long, with the .22. Though I liked rifle shooting (and still do) killing the Spoonbill and watching father drop fast flying quail, put ideas in my young head that have stayed with me through the years.

My next chance to use a shotgun occurred while visiting my grand-father and uncle. Grandfather allowed me to use his fine Remington hammer double twelve-bore and taught me to reload the long brass shells. I killed a goodly number of squirrels and some ducks on a pond, then tried quail. I will never forget the first bob-white that sailed straight away and which I killed cleanly at about forty yards. Today, I cannot figure out how a frail nine year old kid could hold up that old heavy double and shoot it. I must have drawn heavily on the enthusiasm of youth to get the strength to do it.

To my grandfather and great uncles Quantrell, the James boys and the Youngers were not legendary characters. They were friends and neighbors, who like themselves, and through no fault of their own, had been caught in a web of desperate violence, wholly beyond their control. When these older relatives of mine were in a reminis-cent mood they were sure of one good listener; a skinny, small boy who hung on their words with breathless attention. As I recall their stories I can see that I came honestly by my life-long interest in firearms.

As soon as father disposed of his Missouri property we returned to Helena, Montana. At that time, in the fall of the year, we had some enormous duck flights on man-made Lake Helena. Father liked to hunt and always took me and my younger brother with him. My per-sonal armament then consisted of a .22 rifle and a heavier, and much slower, muzzle-loading squirrel rifle. I would carefully stalk single ducks in the bends of the creek above the lake and pot them with one of these rifles while father and his friends had a great time with the wing shooting. Ducks seemed to fly past them, at nice ranges, in an endless procession.

I simply had to have a shotgun. I finally managed to swap my marbles, flints and all my small property, plus a treasured Barlow jack knife, to another lad, for an 1854 Remington smooth-bore, muzzle-loading musket. In my eyes it was a great gun and I was prouder of it than I ever was, in later years, of even a best quality Westley Richards single trigger, double ejector. I used to pour two or three inches of F. G. black powder down the old gun, tamp a good section of a newspaper on top of that, then a heavy charge of No. 6 shot, probably well over an ounce, then more newspaper and more tamping, as I did not know the shot was not to be tamped as well as the powder. How that old gun would kick—and how I loved it. I shined up all the brass bands and the patch box and the old gun, as if in payment for my affection and care, always got some ducks for me.

One day I was in a blind with father and Joe Bogart. Father had his double Ithaca while Joe had a Spencer pump gun. They were watching some circling mallards when a big flock of green-wing teal swung by from our rear. I saw them coming. Jumping up, I swung that ancient Remington just ahead of the tightly bunched flock and cut loose. As the smoke lifted, I thought I had killed them all, as it seemed they never would quit falling. They were not over twenty-five or thirty yards away and the awful spread of that heavily loaded musket simply decimated the flock. I thought father and Bogart would never be able to stop laughing as they helped me gather up the dead and crippled birds. They had forgotten all about the now badly scared mallards. That was my first real success with the old gun but later I managed to do quite well when teal or snipe came by at close range.

The old musket was hopeless at any range beyond forty yards and often failed at less, on singles. I knew I simply had to have a real shotgun. Money was very scarce in those days and how a small kid was to acquire enough of it had me stumped.

I had a late Ithaca catalogue and by the time school was out that spring, had picked out a 16-bore, No. 2 Ithaca hammerless as the gun I wanted. Jobs were scarce but I finally landed one at the National Biscuit Foundry, shoveling and wheeling coal into the bake furnace fire room in the morning and gluing up the big cartons of cookies and crackers and trucking them into the store room in the afternoon. I stayed with that job day after day and week after week until my buckskin poke held the price of that No. 2 Ithaca.

I wanted the pretty Damascus barrels but the company informed me, on the receipt of my order, that they were out of them temporarily, as they came from Europe, and were sending me a No. 3 grade instead, at the same price. I was delighted with the new gun and that fall really started wing shooting. We had plenty of ruffed grouse, sharp tail grouse, sage hens, big white jack rabbits and ducks beyond counting. No lad ever had a better time.

I shot the Ithaca for seventeen years before using guns with straighter than standard stocks and then could never go back to its 1¾ by 2¾ drop. However, the last fall I shot it I managed a run of seventeen straight on chinks, including three doubles, before I missed. I also made a great many doubles from the saddle, hunting blue grouse in Oregon, after getting my horse trained to turn to the right and stand when the birds raised. Such was my early introduction to the shotgun.

Table of Contents

Page

Preface vii

Foreword ix

Chapter One
History of the Shotgun 1

Chapter Two
Double Guns 16

Chapter Three
Repeating Shotguns 60

Chapter Four
Single Loaders 80

Chapter Five
Gauges and Their Uses 92

Chapter Six
Shotgun Barrels, Chambers, Forcing Cones, Bores, Chokes, etc. 107

Chapter Seven
Chokes and Their Uses 121

Chapter Eight
Stocks and Stocking 134

Chapter Nine
Shotgun Rib and Pitch 152

Chapter Ten
Shotgun Sights 161

Chapter Eleven
Shotgun Extras 166

Chapter Twelve
Ornamentation 181

Chapter Thirteen
Modern Shotgun Shells 192

Chapter Fourteen
Shot Sizes and Their Use 204

Page

Chapter Fifteen
Buck, Ball and Slugs 213

Chapter Sixteen
Patterns 226

Chapter Seventeen
Gun Selection 242

Chapter Eighteen
Care, Cleaning and Storage 265

Chapter Nineteen
Lead and Forward Allowance 276

Chapter Twenty
Practical Shotgun Shooting 291

CHAPTER ONE

History of the Shotgun

THE HISTORY of the shotgun dates back many centuries. Some of the first hand cannons, fire- and match-locks, were used with multiple pellets as well as bolts or single slugs. No doubt some of these earliest smooth-bore weapons were used for the taking of feathered game very soon after their employment as weapons of war.

After the hand cannon came the arquebus and later the musket was developed. Scatter loads of small gravel were used first in the ancient cannon, then later in the early forms of hand weapons. Probably the old musket and the blunderbuss were used with some form of shot pellets for the taking of wild fowl and other small game. Most of the early muzzle-loading flintlocks were bored larger at the muzzle than at the breech. Constriction of the bore at the rear end of the barrel, gave them a narrower powder channel and charge, hence greater thickness of metal for safety. Some variations of boring occurred in early flintlocks, in both single barrel and double barrel, but they were largely for safety or to facilitate loading rather than any attempt at constriction of the shot charge to produce smaller patterns or greater range.

Choke boring of shotguns did not come into being until late in the percussion era in the Seventies. The English claim the invention of choke boring due to a patent taken out by W. R. Pape of Newcastle in 1866, yet we have seen no record of English guns of that time being choke bored, except a trace of taper toward the muzzle, due largely to accident. On the other hand, Fred Kimble, an unknown market hunter of Illinois, in order to get greater range for his single barrel 6 bore muzzle loader, rebored it giving the piece plenty of choke like the nozzle on a fire hose. It then shot worse than before and to bring it back to some semblance of its former patterning qualities, he started to remove the constriction at the muzzle. Before he had removed all the constriction he tested the gun again, and found that he had the closest shooting gun he, or anyone else had ever heard of. With coarse, strong black powder and an ounce and a half of No. 3 shot it would put the entire charge into a 30" circle at 40 yards and often the entire charge into a 24" circle at that range.

Kimble discovered that too much choke would scatter the charge all over the landscape, so he put in plenty of choke by boring the barrel out larger behind the muzzle, then carefully started removing the constriction at the muzzle until the gun threw the desired close full choked patterns with a given set load of shot and powder. We believe he discovered choke boring. He bored several guns this way and sent one to a Mr. Schaefer of Boston and one to Mr. W. W. Greener in England. Very soon thereafter Greener came out with his famous choke bored guns which were soon winning the English gun trials. However, Fred Kimble never received the credit he deserved for the development of choke boring.

While Mr. Pape of Newcastle may have taken out the patent and Greener no doubt went ahead after seeing and testing Kimble's gun, the fact remains that Kimble first bored and used and tested the choke system and to this day we have never been able to improve on his patterns and only in a very few isolated cases have our best patterns with modern breech loaders approached his work. To Fred Kimble, then, is due the credit for greatly extending the effective range of the shotgun, from around 40 yards to about double that range or 80 yards, with large bore guns and heavy loads of coarse shot.

Both the single and double barrel fowling piece were first developed on the Continent and in England and no doubt the Spanish, Italians and French as well as the English developed these finely finished arms about the same time. In many cases the nod seems to go to the early Spanish and Italian makers. Some of these early flintlock double barrel guns are masterpieces and really works of art. No details of wood or metal work were overlooked and the equal of their engraving and inlay work as well as the beautiful hand filing-out of the locks and various parts is today seldom seen in even the finest of modern hand production. Machine methods tend to strong, sound, mass production and our modern knowledge of metallurgy makes it possible to produce weapons with a strength of material never dreamed of in the old days, but the fact remains that the fine old hand gunsmiths attained an art in gun building that is seldom seen today and one that is fast dying out as the old smiths depart this plane.

Take many of the fine old English, French and Italian flintlocks as an instance. You will find very few gunsmiths today capable of the careful filing-out of those locks. Such careful hand filing is fast becoming a lost art. The National Rifle Association has some outstanding examples of such fine old gun building of the flint lock era in their collection at Washington.

The percussion lock aided speed of loading and surety of fire over the flint lock, also the cap lock was more nearly waterproof. Choke-bored muzzle-loaders of the late percussion era produced patterns from full choke guns that are still practically unobtainable from breech-loading cartridge guns even to this day. The powder, wads and shot were loaded into a true cylinder bore at the breech ends of the barrels. No cartridge case to jump the shot from and no forcing cone to funnel them into the bore proper, both of which, with the forcing of the crimp, produced a great many deformed shot. These deformed shot in turn were largely fliers after leaving the muzzle of the gun, hence we cannot today equal the muzzle-loading choke-bored gun in pattern performance. It had no crimp over the top wad and no forcing cone, the shot traveled straight up the bore until the charge reached the actual choke constriction, hence were delivered from the muzzle of the gun with a very minimum of shot deformation.

Breech loaders go back to the flintlock period but really successful breech loaders did not appear until the invention and introduction

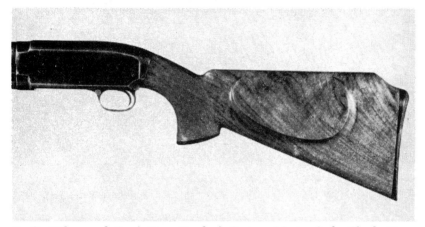

E. C. Bishop and Sons' New Standard Custom Monte Carlo Cheek Piece, Etchon Grip Stock, for Model 12 Winchester.

of the loaded shot shell, probably first in pin fire and later in the modern cap persuasion. Probably the French Lefaucheux is as good an example as any of the first successful cartridge breech loaders and it used the old pin-fire cartridge. It had a locking lever where the present foreend is situated and hinged much as do shotguns of today. Next came the under-lever actuating the bolts as made by the Germans, English Belgians and Italians. Many fine arms were made up on this system. It was and is one of the strongest of all locking systems and even today is preferred by W. J. Jeffery for their 577-and 600-bore double express rifles.

The English and Belgians next developed the side-lever, while in America the old Parker firm developed the Lifter action, with a small push button in front of the trigger guard to actuate the locking bolts. Westley Richards no doubt first invented and used the top lever and the extended rib in the form of the well-known doll's head in double gun fastenings. The cocking hook seems to be of American invention and design. Lefever and later Ithaca being mainly responsible. The Anson & Deely Barrel cocking device is credited to

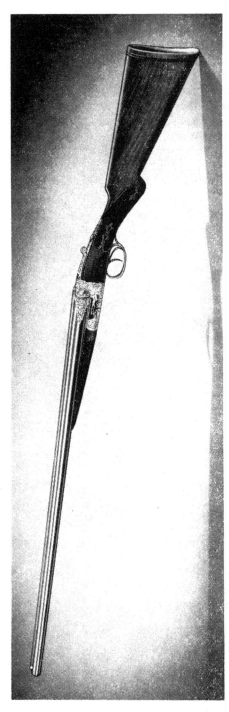

Best Quality Model De Luxe Westley Richards Box Lock with Hand Detachable Locks.

Westley Richards as they were with that firm and it was patented in 1875.

Many English firms did then and still persist in using only the double under-lugs and bolts to hold the double gun together, just as Winchester does today in their model 21. Absence of a top extension or dolls head makes for a clean breech and some claim faster loading, but the fact remains that the dolls head or extended rib with Greener cross-bolt or the American invention, the rotary bolt, is a much stronger locking system and the guns so bolted will probably stand a lot more continuous shooting without becoming loose, than will a gun with only under-bolts to hold it together.

After the advent of the good hammerless Anson & Deeley action, the hammer guns began to take a back seat but it was well along in the early 1920's before hammer guns began to disappear to some extent. In England the 12-bore became standard, and still is, while on the continent of Europe the 16-bore was and is more popular. The English went to the short 2½" 12-bore case firing only 1 1/16 ounces of shot with a normal powder charge, while the Germans, French and Belgians preferred about the same or a lighter load in 16 bore. At the same time Americans went to heavier loads in longer cases. Through the eighties and nineties and well into this century the 10-bore was about standard equipment and is still considered tops in a duck gun.

British guns were and are made very light, usually just over six pounds for a 12-bore upland gun. Continental shotguns also were very light in weight while in America, we have gone to heavy loads in long cases and necessarily to considerably greater gun weight to handle the powerful long range ammunition. Much English and European upland shooting is close-range work on driven game, hence light, fast, open-bored guns and light loads are the order of the day. The English also developed the chamberless gun; a heavy wild-fowl piece using straight, very thin, brass cases with very heavy shot charges. It is a very high percentage gun and very successful for wildfowl and all long-range difficult shooting. These guns were still 12 bore but used up to 1½ ounces of shot and the British can build as fine a heavy duck gun as anyone in a double when they desire such a weapon. When it comes to fine doubles, the British are paramount in their building, and about all the better known British makers will turn out a gun that is beyond reproach in all details. It is of course largely hand made but the fitting of barrels and actions and the lock work is like the work in a fine watch. The Germans, Belgians and French also turned out exceptionally fine weapons. The Germans especially seemed pre-eminent in the design of the over-under with their well known Kersten fastening. German steels are also exceptionally good and a great many American makers imported their barrels from Germany or Belgium for many years. Most all of the fine Damascus were made either in England or more probably on the Continent.

The better British makers also turned out over-unders and Westley Richards even made a very successful three-barrel 12 bore, with their original patented hand detachable box locks and single trigger that worked to perfection.

Combination doubles of rifle and shot persuasion date back into the flint lock period and we have seen and fired many of them, some over-unders that had revolving barrels, and one lock, but with two frizzens, while some were conventional side-by-side doubles. The three-barrel seems to be a Continental invention with Germany

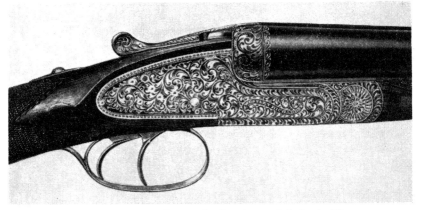

Detail View of Westley Richards Finest Side-Lock Ejector.

making the greater number of these arms. Some German makers even made four-barrels or so-called Vierlings. They were very popular in the early part of this century in this country and many were imported. In addition L. C. Smith made three-barrels and also one outfit in West Va. We have owned one of each make with double 12-bore shot barrels and the rifle barrel beneath. Such weapons are still very handy in big game country, when hunting upland grouse or wildfowl, for that occasional shot at larger game.

While the British and especially the Belgian and German makers tended toward a multiplicity of bolting, Americans turned to ever more simple but stronger systems terminating in the rotary bolt as the most advanced American system of bolting a double gun. When properly adjusted, it is one of the simplest and strongest of all shotgun bolts, but improperly adjusted the gun will kick open. We have never known an L. C. Smith to open up on firing but have had both Fox and Ithacas kick open. Some of them still did this after a couple trips back to the factory for rebolting, if the radius was not just right on the lip of the rotary bolt, and any oil accumulated in the cut in the extended rib. When the proper radius is hand stoned into the bolt, it is one of the finest if not the finest system of all American doubles and very simple.

As long as Parkers were made they stayed with the single heavy underbolt, but it was made so the wear could easily be taken up by replacing the lower face of the lug cut and did a most excellent job of holding barrels and action together.

Repeating Shotguns

Repeating shotguns were an American invention. We do not know of any pump gun coming out before the old Spencer. The Spencer was and still is a good gun if in good condition, though it was the first pump or trombone action. The model '93 Winchester and the early Marlins and the later and famous old Winchester '97 did much to popularize the pump gun in America. Later the Winchester 1901 model was brought out in both ten and twelve gauge and was quite popular with duck hunters when I was a small boy. It was never a very strong action and while it served us well in ten gauge with the older loads it was never adequate for modern progressive burning powder and heavy 1⅝ ounce shot charges. Several of them blew open with heavy loads. Likewise many of the early Marlins, whose breech block retracted back through the side cut in the frame, had their entire breech bolts blown out when first our heavy progressive duck loads were developed. Later solid-frame Marlins were much better and well able to handle any loads as were many pump guns put out by Savage, Stevens, Remington and Winchester.

The Winchester Model 12 was, and still is, a very popular pump gun and the old Remington Model '17 one of the finest pump actions of that era. However Remington had considerable patent trouble on that gun and finally dropped its manufacture, but later when the patent had run out Ithaca picked it up and developed it further in their most excellent model 37 pump gun. The only fault we ever found with the Remington, was that at times brush would trip the magazine shell holder and allow a cartridge to drop out the bottom of the magazine. With the Ithaca some of the first ones we tested and used would occasionally drop a loaded shell out the bottom in fast shooting. Evidently the cartridge retaining spring in the magazine was not strong enough.

Both are fine pump guns. One very interesting pump action shotgun in 12-bore that I saw and also shot when a small boy was made by Colts patent Firearms Mfg. Co. and was so stamped on the barrel. It had the most peculiar action we have yet seen but functioned perfectly. The pistol grip actuated the action and steel rods extended forward from the pistol grip to the action. You simply pulled the grip back and forth instead of the forearm as with conventional pump guns. It is not as fast probably as the conventional pump gun but worked very well when you became accustomed to its action. We have never seen another one and would still like to know its history.

The pump gun is probably now at its best in the latest version, the Remington Model 870 Wingmaster. Due to the fact that American ingenuity and modern machine production could produce a pump gun that would shoot as well as the finest double, but at only a fraction of the cost of said double, repeating shotguns have long been the most popular in this country. Many of the designs were due to the influence or direct invention of the late John M. Browning.

Auto-Loading Shotguns

Auto-loaders were also an American invention and Browning was responsible for most of the successful ones. Remington, Savage, Browning and others make excellent auto-loading shotguns. The early Winchester auto was never very popular and developed mechanical troubles until it was finally dropped from the Winchester line. Their later Model 40, however seemed an excellent gun and the one fault we found with it was the fact its tubular stock bolt was very easily broken off short with the action. For some reason it was discontinued and called in and exchanged for the good Model 12 Winchester. The old Savage, Browning and Remingtons, all on the Browning patent, still do yeoman service. Arthur Kovalovsky of 5524 Cahuenga Blvd., North Hollywood, Calif. is the only man to successfully alter these heavy Remington and Browning auto-loaders to handle the modern 3″ 12-bore magnum shell with one and five-eighths ounces of shot. He does a very nice job of this alteration, giving the auto-loader boys a magnum 12-bore the same as is obtainable in the Winchester heavy Model 12 duck gun or the fine double guns.

About all the older auto-loaders had very high, heavy clumsy breech actions and the Model 40 Winchester was the first streamlined auto-loader. At present the automatic shotgun has probably reached its highest stage of development in the new Remington Model Sportsman-48. This is a streamlined auto-loader that has been giving excellent service since its introduction in 1948 and seems destined to become very popular with American shooters. For the first time the weight and action of the auto-loader have been brought down to the same limitations as the more refined versions of the pump gun and the receiver has been given much the same streamlined effect.

We understand the British made one attempt at producing an auto-loading shotgun but could not compete with the machine production of the American and Belgian guns as to cost so dropped the endeavor. To John M. Browning should go most of the credit for the repeating shotgun design, either pump or auto loading. At present we consider repeating shotguns at their best in modern design in the current new Remingtons in Model 48-Sportsman auto-loader and Model 870 Wingmaster. However, the Savage auto and pump, the Marlin pump, the Winchester Model 12, the Browning auto-loader, the excellent Ithaca 37 and even the time-tried old Win-chester Model 97 are still most excellent guns in every way. The old Model '97 Winchester has been popular for over half a century and many still prefer its visible hammer to any hammerless design.

This country has long been flooded with many cheaply made pump guns with inferior materials used in the action that have, after a short period of use, given out in some part or other. These have been sold largely through mail order houses under different names

Best Quality Purdey Side Lock of Bar-Action Type.

than their manufacturers, but the better grades of repeating shot-guns have nearly all been good guns and will last a lifetime with reasonable care. We know of one Model 97 that has been in con-tinuous use for half a century.

With the present short game seasons and small bags forced on us by a shortage of game it's hard to reason why the automatic and the pump gun are in such demand when anyone should be well satisfied with the two shots from a good double. We believe it is largely due to the fact that America went all out on machine pro-duction during the war and since then has had a hard time trying to convert back to fine double gun production and so long as they can machine produce a good pump or automatic for a fraction of the cost of a fine double and so long as folks will readily buy every one they can produce there is little incentive for the manufacturer to produce double guns. The gun makers have lost many of their old workmen capable of building fine doubles, and the youngsters of this era do not seem to take kindly to the old hand-methods necessary to produce the best in fine doubles, likewise the cost of labor now makes such fine double-gun production a difficult problem. Then, too, they lost many of their best inspectors during the war, and few companies in this country are today in a position to make the fine double guns they formerly produced.

In England much the same conditions exist and those fine British makers have now lost most of their old, grey headed, custom

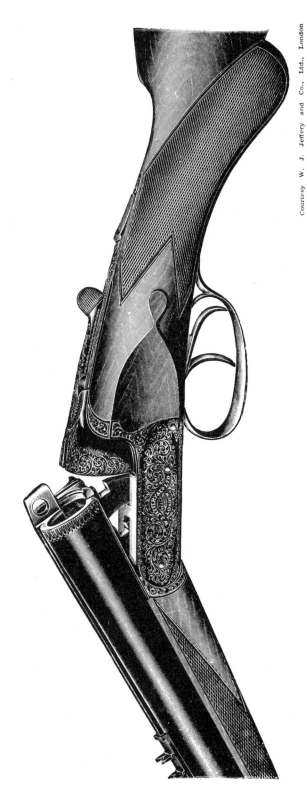

A British Side-by-Side Double Shotgun with Double Triggers.

Courtesy W. J. Jeffery and Co., Ltd., London

gun builders and they write me they have only one to three left in most of the companies and that it is problematical if they can train the youngsters before the old men who could teach them fine craftsmanship are all gone. Many youngsters today will simply not put in the time and study necessary to become top-flight gun makers for it's an exacting art and requires many years to master in even one small phase of the many necessary to produce a fine gun.

Belgium seems less affected in many ways and is again making fine guns. Italy also is producing some fine doubles that will bear very close inspection and are excellent weapons at very low cost as compared with fine British arms. The Browning Company is again manufacturing in Belgium and selling most excellent over-unders of advanced design.

The great gun builders of Germany are now largely under Soviet control so we will see very few of their fine products again except those taken during the war. While the war produced many improvements in weapons for the killing of mankind it certainly has done nothing for the custom-gun building industry that formerly produced our finest double shotguns. It is to be hoped that both here and abroad, enough companies will gather together fine craftsmen until they can again produce the wonderful weapons that were produced in such profusion prior to World War II. While the repeating shotguns are just as efficient, or more so, as the finest doubles, there will ever be those among us who appreciate the perfection in hand-made weapons of the double gun persuasion.

Single-Barrel Shot Guns

Formerly cheap single-barrel break-top guns were made in profusion in this and about all other countries. These served a very useful purpose in outfitting the youngster and giving him or her a cheap but effective single-shot scatter gun. Since the war such production has not been resumed on such a large scale.

Fine single-barrel trap guns were widely produced before the War. Baker, Parker, Ithaca, Lefevre, Smith and others produced many high grade trap guns and these are now in good demand since the companies are again producing plenty of ammunition. Most of the better British makers also produced single-barrel trap guns, with all extras, that were beyond reproach. Many of these guns are now about worn out and new ones will have to be produced as the trap game will continue to be very popular both here and abroad. While many great trap shooters have turned to the double as well as the repeater, many of the top shooters prefer the fine long-barrelled specialized single trap gun and with good reason. No other shotgun is superior for that specialized game.

On the other hand Skeet shooting has put a shot of adrenalin in the production of short barrelled upland guns and in the production of a myriad of patent chokes and compensators on the repeaters.

A Nicely Ornamented British Double Barrel Shotgun

Courtesy W. J. Jeffery and Co., Ltd., London

Both phases of the target game are excellent for the gun makers and create the greatest ammunition demand of all types of shooting.

Improvement in stock design and dimensions in this country at least, has been influenced more by trap and skeet shooting than by all other phases of shooting. German guns were usually fairly straight stocked as were most fine British guns imported into this country, but when I was a boy most commercially made American guns had far too much drop for best results in any form of shotgun shooting. These extremely crooked stocks often with a drop at heel of from 3 to 3½ or even four inches were simply a hang-over from

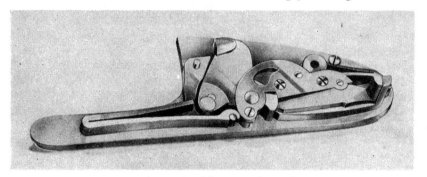

Westley Richards' Best Side Lock.

the old Kentucky rifle days. Our early Winchester and Marlin repeating rifles as well as many of our other sporting, and some military rifles, had far too much drop and too little relation between the eye and cheek bone for fast, accurate shooting. Yet with the rifle so largely in use in this country, the shotgun shooter thought he should have an equal amount of drop in his shotgun stock. Trap shooting put an end to much of that excessive heel drop, as it soon proved the fallacy of such ideas on stocking. Homo Sapiens is an adaptable cuss, and if he uses one stock for a great length of time, no matter how poorly fitted an abortion it may be, he will in time learn to conform to its shape and do fair work with it, but never will he be capable of the fine fast work he should do. Thus we see the great value that trap shooting has been to American shotgun stock design. Trap shooting also developed the Monte Carlo Comb, giving the same elevation for all angle shots regardless of where the cheek was placed, whether far forward or far to the rear. Many at first did not like the looks of it and its change in the general contour of the stock, just as later the rifle shooters looked with disfavor on my own first Monte Carlo rifle stock design, but after some use they adopted it and now it is found on practically all custom rifle stocks.

Shotgun ammunition has greatly improved over the years from the early flintlock fowling pieces to modern shotgun ammunition. However the range of shotguns has not greatly increased. Since the advent of Fred Kimble's invention, choke-boring, in his old 6-bore muzzle-loading percussion single-barrel, we have not progressed to any great extent in increased effective yardage of shotgun killing range. Today our latest Magnum ten-bore with 3½″ case and two full ounces of No. 3 Western Lubaloy shot produces only about the same 80-yard results on big fowl like mallards that Kimble's old six-bore did with 1½ ounces of No. 3 shot. But his old six-bore always put all shot in the 30″ circle and often most of it in a 24″ circle at 40 yards.

Shotguns at their best are short ranged weapons, and we have progressed from the flintlock days when the gunner had first to measure and pour his powder charge down the tube then his wadding, of whatever nature, often including a section of his shirt tail, if nothing else was available. Then his shot charge was measured or thrown from a charger on his shot pouch, after which a top wad of some sort was put in to hold it in place. Then he must look to the priming of the pan with some very fine grain powder and the adjustment of his flint so it would throw a good flash of sparks to ignite the powder in the pan when the frizzen was thrown back by the blow of the hammer or cock. Even then he had to continue to follow his bird and wait for the flash in the pan to ignite the powder and fire the gun. Modern shotgun shots would do well to shoot an old flintlock fowling piece some, just for the knowledge they would gain on swing and follow-through of their swing, while the actual firing of the piece was in progress. It's a revelation.

With the advent of the percussion cap, the lock time of the shotgun was greatly speeded up and with good guns and fast, well made locks is not appreciably slower than modern guns. The loading however took almost as much time as with the flint lock. Then came the era of the breech loader and even in hammer persuasion it was much faster than the muzzle loader, but the shooter had to save and pocket his long brass cases and also had to decap and wash them each evening and dry them before reloading. The modern brass-base paper case was the next step in shotshell progress and with the cases thrown away, faster reloading was accomplished, but ironically, as the loading of shotguns increased in speed, the game decreased in quantity.

When low-cost paper shotshells appeared in quantity, the reloading of shotshells was not so profitable and they were usually thrown away after being picked out of the chamber ends with the fingers. This in turn led to the development of ejectors on single and double barrel guns and also to the development of our repeating shotguns. Then the gunner had only to load and shoot his gun and after firing feed more ammunition into its magazine or into the chambers of the single or double.

Just what the trend will be in the future we do not pretend to know. The conservative British have always held to the double gun as the sporting weapon and are wise in so doing, and they still have as much wildfowl shooting as ever and also about as much upland game as ever as it is properly managed. Canada prohibits the use of auto-loading shotguns and with good reason, yet the auto-loader is no faster than the pump gun in skilled hands and sometimes we seriously doubt if it is as fast, for the skilled pump gun-shooter actually pulls his gun down out of recoil and also helps to poke it at his next target with that forward operating hand. With the present great increase in the number of hunters and the ever increasing scarcity of game birds and fowl, we believe shooters in general would do well to take stock of the situation as it exists today, and go to the double gun or the single-barrel trap gun for their game shooting. Hunters should well be satisfied with two shots at one raise of upland game or one flock of passing fowl. We know many old trap shots who get just as much fun from hunting with their pet single-shot trap guns as with any auto or pump gun. The three-shot repeater if it is used as it should be will save the loss of wounded birds, namely by firing but two shots on each rise of game or passing ducks and save the third always for that possible cripple. All too often however, the novice, and many veterans as well, will continue to shoot and usually cripple a third bird with that last or third shell. Some men are so fast with the repeater that we have observed many of them having three birds falling at the same time. It's great shooting and great sport, but we wonder if one could not have just as much sport when satisfied with but two shots at one time. We have found it so. Also when game was plentiful we have enjoyed just as good sport using a single gun and shooting but once on each rise.

CHAPTER TWO

Double Guns

DOUBLE-BARRELLED SHOTGUNS offer many advantages over any other shotgun design. For one thing they have two separate locks, and are really two single-barrel shotguns joined together. They will handle most any ammunition that is dropped or shoved into them providing the chambers were cut for that length of case. Paper shotshells that have been swelled from dampness or improper storage, or dropped in the bottom of a wet boat for some time, can still be used in the double gun, also in the single loader, when they would be hopeless for use in any repeating shotgun. The double gun with its two separate locks is the most reliable of all shotguns. Those two fine locks are not both going to break down at the same time, while a simple spring or an ejector or anyone of a dozen small items may break in a repeating shotgun, either auto-loader or pump and put the gun out of commission.

For this reason the double gun is the most reliable gun of all to take on long expeditions into far places. Even should one firing pin break or one main spring, you still have a good single-barrel gun. For this reason, good double shotguns are usually selected when the shotgun is used against dangerous game at close quarters or after night, such as leopard or lion, with heavy loads of buckshot. Double-barrel and single-shot guns are also much the shortest over-all for any given barrel length, hence handier in the brush in upland work or in the duck blind when decoys are used. They are also easier carried.

In England and Scotland, or on the Continent, the double gun is the only one considered, and it is there also that they have probably reached their very highest stage of development. They come in many forms by many different expert gun makers. No other shotgun has the same balance and live feel of a perfect double, nor has any other type a semblance of the beauty of a fine double. When it comes to beauty of outline, balance, the perfect fitting of wood to steel and the perfect fitting of barrels to actions, then in the slim, trim, side-by-side double shotgun, with straight grip, we have attained the utmost in perfection of outlines and symmetry. Not every one will agree with us on these statements, which is no crime, but to us the fine double appears as a beautiful streamlined chorus gal

16

compared to the usual repeating shotgun, which more nearly resembles a fat misshapen squaw.

Types of Double Gun Action

Double guns may be well divided into box-locks and side-locks, so we will take up each in turn. First some advantages and disadvantages of each type. First the frames. There is no argument but the back-action side lock leaves more metal in the frame at the angle of the breech and under the water table, hence the back-action side lock offers the strongest of all double gun frames. Next the bar-action side lock leaves more metal in the frame than does the usual box lock, hence leaves a stronger angle to the frame. We have never seen the frame cracked at the angle from a properly constructed gun, made heavy enough for the ammunition for which it was chambered, but the factories have had some come to light, and many of the lighter British double gun frames have cracked, especially when used with much more powerful ammunition than that for which they were originally built. So in the matter of strength of frame the back-action side lock is strongest, the bar-action side lock next and the box lock the weaker of the three. Yet in all fairness the good well made box lock has well stood the test of time and if properly made of proper steels almost never gives any sign of trouble.

Next is the strength of the stock at its junction with the frame. Both types of side lock remove considerable wood from the stock at this point and it is cut away until there is little but four fingers of wood contacting the frame. While the grip of the stock is the weakest point, nevertheless the side locks do not permit as much wood or as strong a juncture of wood and steel at the back of the frame as do box locks.

Next is simplicity of design and corresponding ultimate cost of the finished gun. The best box lock, the Westley Richards with hand detachable locks and hinged cover plate, has the simplest of all gun locks. Merely seven parts to their beautiful hand-detachable locks, in comparison with some 21 or 22 parts in the usual side locks. These differences are reflected in the ultimate cost of the weapon. The box lock is also at its best in the top-grade Westley Richards make with its frame showing no holes drilled through for pins at the junction of the water table and the standing breech, commonly called the angle of the frame. For this reason the best Westley Richards is no doubt the strongest as well as the simplest of all box locks of comparable quality.

In America we used to have the old Baker side lock and still have the good L. C. Smith side lock double being manufactured, while Fox, Ithaca and Parker employed the box lock. The German Blitz action which is the same as the British Dickson round action differs from the usual box locks in that about all mechanism is in-

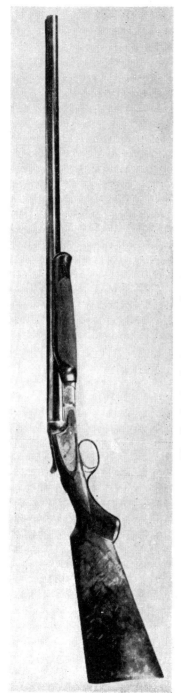

The L. C. Smith Crown Grade Shotgun.

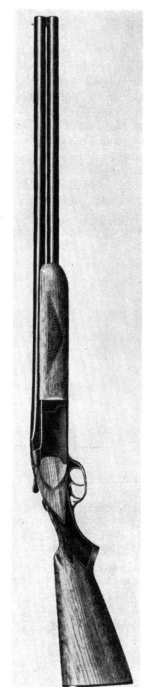

The Marlin Model 90

corporated on the trigger plate. No doubt they are both derived from the old McNaughton trigger plate action. When it comes to strength of action at the bar and angle, the Blitz or Dickson action is no doubt even stronger than the back-action side lock. The Dickson having most superior springs. It is something of a missing link between the box and side lock actions, probably stronger as to the angle of the frame than either. This action is used by most of the German makers on both side-by-side doubles and also many three-barrel jobs as well. It is a very good, simple and strong action. Trigger pulls can be adjusted just as well as the best bar-action side locks and it is more simple but does have the fault that considerable wood is removed from the stock just behind its juncture with the frame to accommodate all the action parts incorporated on the trigger plate.

Summing up the different types of action which are legion on fine double guns, we would point out that the Westley Richards Hand Detachable Lock model is probably the strongest of all the true Anson & Deeley pattern box locks. The back-action side lock as exemplified by the fine Lancaster and some Holland & Holland and other guns offers a stronger frame than does the top quality bar-action side locks such as the Purdey, Boss and others. The round action called the Blitz action in Germany and the Dickson or Mc-Naughton in Britain has a frame as strong or stronger than even the back-action side lock. The Rosson action also has a very sturdy frame. In this country the new Model Ithaca brought out in 1926 has a much stronger frame than the older Ithaca, while the Fox and the Parker have very sturdy frames for box lock actions.

Locks

When it comes to locks, the finest in British side locks is considered the best when excellence of trigger pulls is desired and in this country we have never seen gun locks even on our higher grade weapons that compared very favorably with the fine British locks. A high grade L. C. Smith lock does not compare in finish and fine workmanship with a Brazier British side lock. The intercepting safeties of fine British side locks are alone a very important feature and may prevent accidental discharge when a sear is jarred out of its notch in the tumbler. The bar-action side lock, along with the Dickson round action, also have the correct angle between tumbler and sear for finest and crispest trigger pulls. In this respect they are superior to all box locks and to about all back action side locks.

However, we consider their intercepting safeties as more important than the very slight improvement in trigger pulls due to better design of the angle of tumbler and sear. With the Anson & Deeley pattern of box lock as developed by Westley Richards workmen back in 1875, the only safety is the blocking of the trigger blade from contact with the sear tails and the gun can still be jarred off if trigger pulls are very light. In this respect of safety the intercepting safety of the fine British side lock is far superior to the safety common on about all box locks. When it comes to simplicity of mechanism, then the box lock has much the fewer parts, only seven in fact in the top-flight box lock, the Westley Richards as compared to the usual 22, I believe, in most fine side locks.

In this country the Ithaca and Fox have long advertised their simplicity of locks, Ithaca claiming a three-piece lock that operates in 1/625th of a second. Some guns have separate firing pins, some with rebound springs, while others, namely the Westley Richards and the Fox to take an example from each country, have the firing pins integral with the hammer. This we believe the better procedure and the simplest of all construction except in the making. The pressure on the fired cap is usually sufficient to drive any properly shaped firing pin back to the flush position where it will not interfere with opening of the gun. Then too the hammer is often made to retract slightly at the first part of the opening movement of the gun. This does away with the necessity for separate firing pins with their rebound springs and set screws and also leaves more metal in the frame. Separate firing pins do have the advantage that they can be bushed and can be made very small on their points as in many Brtiish guns and about all fine British double rifles. There can be no question but such small diameter pins with bushed holes that can also be easily replaced are better for the firing of powerful cartridges developing considerable pressure and even Westley Richards recognized this and while our best grade Westley Richards hand-detachable lock shotgun has the firing pins integral with the hammers as on our American Fox guns, nevertheless our three best quality Westley Richards double rifles in calibers 476, 400 and 400/360, all have separate firing pins.

For shotgun locks, we like the utter simplicity of the Westley Richards and Fox design, with firing pins integral with the tumblers. Dollar for dollar invested one can get a great deal better gun in a box lock than in a side lock if cost is a consideration. If you want a side lock then it should be of best quality only; if a bar-action side lock and if any shading from this standard of quality then the next choice might be the back-action side lock. Cheap side locks we consider far inferior to best box locks. Even in box locks we have noted much finer and more careful workmanship in British than in American guns of comparable prices and the locks of a No. 5 Ithaca we own are very crude in comparison with a box lock by William Cashmore in comparable price range. The locks of our only American side lock, the L. C. Smith, do not compare with those of top flight British makers, so if you want the very finest in a side lock gun, then get it in British make, Boss, Purdey, Holland, Westley Richards, or other first-quality British maker. Likewise, in box locks the British excell in their Westley Richards and also their fine Greeners.

Side locks offer a great deal more room for ornamentation than do box locks, but at the cost of a weaker stock at its junction with the frame. Side locks cost a great deal more and require a lot more work to manufacture. In a fine side lock gun such as the Purdey, probably 95 percent of the total cost is skilled hand work and only 5 per cent for materials.

Detachable Locks

Many of the best side locks have hand detachable locks, and this feature we like as it allows removal of the locks in case the weapon has fallen under water or has been subjected to a downpour of rain for a long period. Some like the Holland have a little screw that can be removed by hand, then a few taps on the bar section of the action with a screw driver handle will loosen them from their mortise, when they can be removed and dried and oiled. However, no detachable side lock should ever be removed more than is absolutely necessary as the mortise in the stock ears will become worn and they will not then fit, water tight. Those fitted with a simple screw fastening are even neater than the hand-detachable Holland pattern and just as readily accessible with a screw driver or as our British friends term it, a turnscrew.

When it comes to hand-detachable locks however, we have yet to see anything that approaches the simple Westley Richards design. Their locks of the box lock pattern are covered with a hinged lid, just like a fine watch case, and to remove, you simply remove the fore-end, then trip the release button and turn the lid back. Both locks can then be lifted out with thumb and forefinger alone. Since they lie in their little boxes in the bottom of the frame they can be removed and replaced as often as desired with no harm to either stock or lock. Also an extra set can be had in a small case so that on extended trips should anything become wrong with a lock or its trigger pull, it can be removed and replaced with a duplicate lock in a few seconds. We consider the Westley Richards hand-detachable locks in a class by themselves and nothing in side locks even remotely approaches them, either for simplicity and number of parts or for ready accessability. This is one reason we would always select a best quality Westley Richards hand-detachable lock double rifle for use on dangerous game or far countries away from contact with civilization or gunsmiths.

Any side lock can be easily detached for periodic cleaning and oiling. Also any box lock can also be examined and oiled by first removing one or two screws and the lock plate, but the utter simplicity and ease of removal makes the Westley Richards best quality gun superior in this one respect to all others. Tight fitting locks and lock cover plates are a necessity to keep out moisture, and Danl. Frazier,

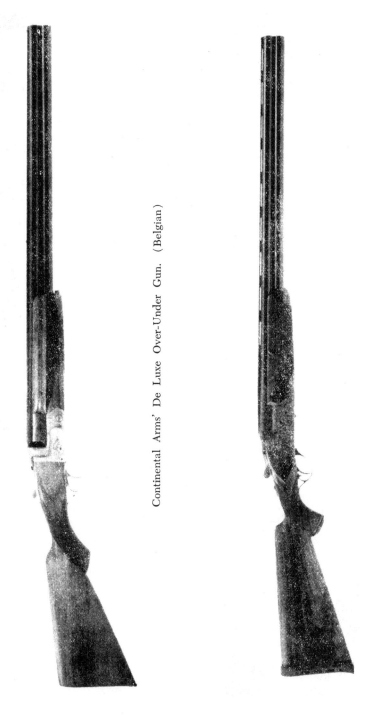

Continental Arms' De Luxe Over-Under Gun. (Belgian)

Continental Arms' (Belgian) Best Make Over-Under Gun. It is Also Made in Skeet Models. Note the Convenient Selector Button in Back of the Trigger.

the celebrated Scottish maker was unique in that he usually gold plated all parts of his box locks and also his ejector locks so they would not rust if the gun was immersed in water or in the heat and rain of the tropics. We have one double rifle by him and it shows very fine workmanship of all lock work as well as complete gold plating of the entire assembly. Though he made box locks as a rule, they were good ones.

In America we have gone to fast machine production, even of small lock parts, while in Britain, few firms have much modern machinery. They do have a great many more fine workmen capable of the finest in-hand work and while we produce a good gun at a nominal cost that will shoot as well as any in the world, our guns do not compare for fine quality of finished internal parts. In this country our better guns are all hand assembled and only our best workmen, even touch a high-grade gun. They may have only the same machined parts to work with as the workmen assembling the cheaper grade guns, but they are paid higher wages and have un-limited time to hand polish and finish fit each part of a lock, until near perfection is attained. Over about $400 the balance in cost of our highest grade guns is taken up by fine hand craftsmanship in the careful fitting of barrels to actions and the fitting of locks and ejectors and ornamentation. In England each small firm specializes more on the careful making and fitting of small parts and locks by highly specialized workmen. One may work entirely on frame and barrel fitting, another on barrel regulating and still another may only make locks, but the best British gun represents the very highest craftsmanship in the trade as regards every single part and piece of the finished weapon. Each of our big gun companies has a few of these highly skilled craftsmen and they are artists at their trade. They may work for weeks on a gun after a lower paid workman would consider it finished. They are never satisfied as they well know human limitations, but a best-quality gun either American or British will be a lasting joy to its owner. The difference between American and British standards, lies in the fact that the British as a rule work to closer standards on their fitting of nearly all parts than we do and even their more moderately priced weapons will show that same careful hand fitting, and much more hand work than will be evident on American guns. This is especially true when we examine the lock work of both British and American arms.

The Belgians, Germans and French also produced many very finely made weapons comparable to British work in many cases. However the British firms have long produced the finest weapons in side-by-side doubles. That has been their specialty for over a century. In lower price ranges however, a very fine gun for the money is often obtained from the Belgian makers. The German firms of Merkle, Sauer & Son and others, now under Russian control produced many beautiful weapons of finest workmanship. While many Belgian firms like Francotte produced both box locks as well as fine side locks, the Germans went more to the Blitz round-bottom action with all locks incorporated on the trigger plate.

American firms use long frames, while most British firms use short frames. The German Blitz action also has a short frame. Long frames with their greater distance from hinge pin to bolts should be easier bolted, but add weight to the finished weapon. British and European guns tend to a multiplicity of bolting, while American firms tend to simplicity of bolting, culminating in the L. C. Smith invention, the rotary bolt.

Some British firms, Holland & Holland for one, and most of the German firms added a strong reinforcement of metal at the angle of the frame. This greatly strengthens the weakest part of the gun frame and does much to quiet any argument against the inherent weakness of the box lock frame. The Germans even went so far as to develop the imbedded frame, wherein the barrels were imbedded nearly half their diameter in the action when it was closed. This is a very strong example of the Blitz or round action. Purdey, Westley Richards, Lancaster and many others often fitted the so-called Purdey side clips.

These are beautiful examples of hand fitting; the workmen smoking and gradually fitting the breech and ends of barrel until the standing breech and side clips fit the ends and side cuts of the barrels to an exact fit. These are supposed to prevent any side play of the barrels and lugs in the frame and certainly do just that, though the careful fitting of the lugs in their cuts in the bottom of frame through the water table should prevent any side play in a well-fitted gun. The cuts on the sides of the barrels, some argue, weaken the rear ends of the barrels. However, we fail to see the logic of this as pressures are extended much farther up the barrel over the front end of the chamber and relatively little actual pressure occurs in proportion right at the rim of the cartridge. Certainly side clips add a finished touch to an already fine gun and are superb examples of fine barrel and frame fitting. We have never seen side clips on American arms as they would add greatly to the cost, not only in the filing out of the standing breeches with their integral side clips but also in the fitting of the barrels to the action.

The nearest example we have seen on American guns was the imbedded barrel action of the inexpensive Winchester model 24 double. Remington in their fine over-under, now discontinued, used a sort of sliding breech cover that was actuated by the top lever, but was in reality a sliding cover for the top barrel, thus effectively closing and locking the barrels into the action when the gun was closed. High cost of manufacture no doubt was the reason for its discontinuance. Thus we see how the various types of locks affect the relative strength of the double gun frame, due to the various and many shaped mill cuts necessary, in the frame, for cross pins, cocking levers, springs and lock plates as well on the side lock. We believe more British gun frames have shown cracks or failures of continuity more than have German, Belgian and American due to the fact, the British have gone to such extremes to get light weight in a 12-bore gun. They use short frames and even these are cut away to such an extent to gain extreme light weight and to use such very light loads that it is small wonder some of them have in the past given way and cracked at the angle of the bar and standing breech.

Some of their weapons have been made in 12-bore as light as 5¾ to 6¼ pounds and we have a wonderful example of Westley Richards that weighs but 6¼ pounds and was proved for 1⅛ ounces of shot in 2¾" cases, a heavy load for an upland gun by British standards. Their standard upland 12-bore load contains but 1 1/16 ounces of shot, and their 2" case 12-bore handles only one ounce of shot. We never could see the horse sense in staying with a 12-bore, when such light loads were used and when only one ounce of shot is to be loaded, we would prefer it in a well made 20-bore gun, even though the larger bore will theoretically deform less shot and give a slight advantage in patterns. This particular Westley Richards gun has 26" barrels, very light ones of best fluid steel, side clips, double under bit and Greener cross bolt, yet the grip of the straight stock is very slender and the entire butt stock has been hollowed out under the recoil pad to further reduce weight. To us this seems to be beating the devil around the bush too much and we would prefer such a light gun to be a 20-bore rather than a 12; and for use with 1⅛ ounces, for which this gun was proved it should have been made a 16-bore, at least if American ammunition is to be used. We use only the 3 to 3¼ dram 1⅛ ounce loads in the gun, and it is a very fine fast handling upland gun, superbly built and engraved.

Double Gun Bolting

Next let us look at the bolting of some of the more popular foreign and American guns. Many British firms will not use an extended top rib at all, stating that it interferes with the fast loading of the piece. We never could see that an absence of an extended top rib made for much if any faster loading, but evidently others have different ideas. The best Purdeys, Holland & Holland and several other top British makers, as well as the Winchester Model 21 employ no extended top rib at all, and for our part we do not believe they will withstand the continued pounding of heavy loads, nearly as long and remain tight as will a gun with an extended top rib and either the Greener cross bolt or, the doll's-head with bite or wedge bolt, or the American rotary bolt. We have seen many Hollands and some others of best British make that were shaky and had to be returned to their makers for a periodic tightening up of the action. In sharp contrast we

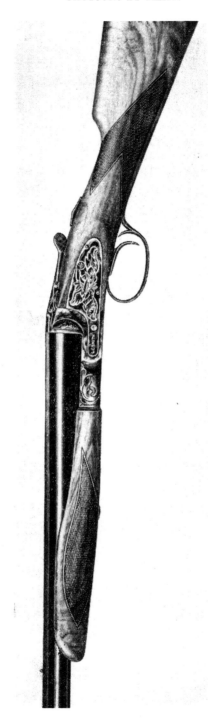

The L. C. Smith Premier Skeet Gun.

have never known of a shaky or loose L. C. Smith with its single rotary bolt through the extended rib.

Westley Richards has always maintained that the farther the bolt is from the hinge pin the stronger will be the bolting of the gun and they prefer their time-tested and well-proven doll's-head with wedge-bite in their top-snap action. This in connection with their well fitted double under-bit, produces a bolting system that we have yet to see fail. We also had a Bland double rifle with this identical bolting and it closed like a rat trap and was superbly tight. When the top lever is pushed to the side to open the gun it retracts a wedge bolt

Post-war Belgian Double Gun with Box Lock.
Imported by Continental Arms Co., New York.

that bites deep into the doll's-head. Thus when closed and the strong springs drive both the double under-bolts into place and the doll's-head seats firmly in the cut in the frame, the wedge bolt drives into the cut in the rear end of the doll's-head, the gun is closed and bolted to stay, come Hell or high water.

We have seen this particular doll's-head wedge bolt that retracts its bolt to the rear as the gun is opened only on the Westley Richards and Bland best quality guns. Many very similar systems of double under-bits and doll's-head, the latter usually with a circular cut into which some portion of the top lever turns are found on many Belgian and British guns and this seems not only a favorite system but a well tried and good one as well. Sometimes we wonder just how many of the bolts on some of these multiple bolted weapons are actually in exact contact at the same time and they would require very careful hand fitting to bring all bolts into relatively even contact at the same time. When this is done they are superbly bolted weapons.

Greener usually employs the double-under bit and also the Greener cross-bolt through the extended top rib. This exact fastening is employed on our own Westley Richards. We have never known such a gun with this bolting to shoot loose unless such looseness was due solely to wear on the hinge pin. When this fastening is also amplified with the Purdey side clips it makes a very nice and sturdy bolting of the fine double gun. The Germans went for the Greener cross-bolt in a big way, and most all of their doubles and three-barrels incorporate the Greener cross-bolt in some form, and their well known Kersten fastening also uses it on each side of the upper barrel. It would seem that a properly fitted Greener cross-bolt of more generous size would be all the bolting a double shotgun would require, yet we have never seen such a gun and they always employ the under-bolts as well as the Greener cross-bolt. Many German guns and at least one British firm have employed a square version of the Greener cross-bolt. This appears on the Jeffery Wildfowl gun, intended for heavy duck loads. However Greener stated the round bolt when properly fitted, is much superior.

Proof Marks on Darne French 16-bore Double Gun.   These Are Typical of the Markings Found on the bottoms of the barrels of European Shotguns.

It is significant, that while Jeffery makes a best side-lock double with a total absence of an extended rib, yet when they make a heavy wildfowl gun intended only for the constant pounding of heavy duck loads and heavy shot charges, then they go to the extended rib and use the Greener cross-bolt in addition to their double under-bit system. It simply shows good, sound reasoning. They also employ the Greener cross-bolt on their famous Jeffery Paradox guns and also use a doll's-head extension on all their fine double barrelled-rifles.

Double rifles, of course, fire cartridges exerting several times the breech and chamber pressure of shotguns and the fact such additional fastenings are needed on them is positive proof that the fine shotgun would also be a stronger bolted gun if it incorporated some form of extended top rib with doll's-head, Greener cross-bolt or the American rotary bolt.

The old model hammerless Ithaca employed the under bolts and in addition a bolt through the extended rib. I have never known one of those guns shooting loose. However the Ithaca company claimed that on very rare occasions the frame cracked, though I never saw or heard of one so cracking and they dropped that model about 1926 in favor of their new rotary bolted model.

Parker employed a doll's-head and also a single, heavy under bolt. This latter was fitted with an ingenious little hardened plate to take up wear and when one plate was worn to any extent a new one could be substituted for the old one, thus Parker guns have long enjoyed the name of being one of the finest guns ever built in America. They have not been made since the war, but Parkers always command a high price, and Remington should again manufacture this grand old gun. Their system of a combination of a strong and reliable under bolt with their little plate to permit taking up of all wear and their excellent doll's-head extension has proven a very reliable bolting system over many years continued usage of heavy loads.

Winchester uses a very long frame and only the under bolts in their famous high-grade double-gun, called the Model 21. They claimed all that was needed to hold their gun together during firing was a good turn of common cotton cord around the barrels and action, so dispensed with the use of any sort of extended top rib. However we believe time will prove the weapon would have been even better with an extended top rib. Their long frame gives more leverage to their under-bit bolts by giving maximum distance from the hinge pin to the bolt, but the fact remains that some form of doll's-head, Greener cross-bolt or rotary bolt, would have made it an even stronger action. They made up one double rifle on this action in caliber .405 Winchester. We would like to look that rifle over and see if it used only the under bolts without any extended top rib. A friend is now endeavoring to purchase this rifle so we may well have opportunity to examine and shoot it later. We had one Holland & Holland No. 2 double rifle without any extended top rib or doll's-head and it was, and still is, a tight, sound rifle. Also we had one Royal Grade H & H in .303 British caliber that was still tight as to breech fastening but the right barrel was completely shot out and the left chamber bulged from an overload so it seems that H & H and Purdey as well as other famous British makers, and Winchester in this country, may be able to maintain a tight action without the extended top rib in some form. Shotguns in continuous usage however, get a lot more shooting than is ever required to wear out a pair of rifle barrels and even though the rifle loads may well develop from 34,000 pounds pressure to an even higher figure in the case of the .303 British cartridge and that of the 9.3 x 74 German cartridge, still relatively few shots are fired from the rifle in comparison with the shotgun. Rigby, Lancaster, Bland and many other British makers all felt it necessary to use the extended top rib in some form of doll's-head and the Belgians nearly always employ either the doll's-head or the Greener cross-bolt in their double rifles and three we have owned and used were all superbly bolted and tight rifles.

Photo by Keith Barrette

Two of the Author's Shotguns. At the top: A Wm. Cashmore (English) 7-pound, 12-bore, Modified and Full Choke, Made For Heavy American Duck Loads. It has a Thirty-inch Barrel.

Bottom: No. 5 Ithaca 16-bore, 30-inch barrel, With All Extras. Major Askins' Old Gun—A Fine Jump-Shooting Gun.

A .400-bore Francotte we had, employed the doll's-head, while two other Belgian rifles by Jules Bury employed the Greener cross-bolt and double under-bit with a reinforced angle to frame. Incidentally these two Bury rifles incorporated some of the finest barrel and action steel we have ever seen to date. The rifles were chambered for the American .35 W.C.F. and the .405 W.C.F. and though the .35 showed considerable barrel wear in its very hard, tough barrels, it was as tight and sound as to action as the day made and weighed exactly 7 pounds. The barrels were almost as thin as shotgun tubes yet the fired cases with factory loads showed very much less case expansion than when the same loads were fired from a nearly new Model '95 Winchester lever rifle. This speaks well for the steel used in those Belgian Bury rifles as well as their fine workmanship. Many British hunters and British makers as well will tell you to steer clear of all cheap continental weapons, but we have now used and tried nearly all makes at different times noting the amount of ammunition that went through them, and the barrel and throat wear and action wear as well and we wish to take our hats off to the best Belgian makers. They knew their stuff and also their steel. They were some of the finest actions and barrels we have seen but sadly lacked the fine stocking and sighting of the British· weapons. However it must be remembered they often weighed a full two pounds less than British weapons for the same relative powered loads. A friend of ours while visiting one of the more famous British gun firms saw several cases of Francotte double rifles being unpacked. They were in the bright, not yet engraved or marked with any makers name nor yet sighted. The reader can well judge the makers name they would later bear, when engraved and finished.

The old firm of L. C. Smith, now owned by Marlin Firearms Co., has always employed the simple rotary bolt. They invented this excellent system and the Fox Gun Co. also used only the rotary bolt. Properly fitted it's one of the simplest as well as the strongest of all double gun fastenings. No under-bolts are required or needed. This makes for utter simplicity of bolting the double gun also leaves more metal in the bottom of the frame where it is needed for strength. Ithaca also went to the rotary bolt in 1926 and has used it exclusively since then for their double guns. The Smith version had two fingers on the rotary bolt, one wide one operating through a cut in the extended rib and a smaller narrow one that hooked over the extreme tip finger of the extended rib. We have never seen a Smith shoot open nor one that had developed any looseness which speaks well for the system as it has been in use now for a great many years and many of those first old hammer models are still in use and still as sound and tight as the day made.

We have seen both Fox and Ithaca Rotary bolted guns kick open and just why we do not know but strongly suspect it is improper fitting of the rotary bolt in its recess over the bottom part of the cut

Holland and Holland's Bar-Action, Side-Lock, 12-Gauge "Royal" Self-Opening Model Hammerless Ejector Gun. 26¾ or 28 inch barrels. It is made in a light game model for 2½-inch shells and weighs six pounds, six ounces. It is also made for 2¾-inch shells and weighs six and three-quarters to seven pounds. It has fine scroll engraving and is equipped with detachable locks.

Stevens Model 311 Double-Barrel Shotgun. It is made in 12, 16, 20, and 410 gauge.

in the extended rib. At any rate a friend asked us to test a fine Fox magnum 12-bore double duck gun with about all extras such as ejectors, elevated ventilated rib and single trigger. We put up a 40″ square of paper at 40 yards, loaded both barrels with 3″ case, 1⅝-ounce loads of No. 4 shot and purposely put the safety on the gun. Then taking aim at the target we pulled the trigger; that was the most automatic gun we ever fired. When we pulled the trigger, the safety went forward, both barrels fired almost together, the gun opened and the ejectors kicked the fired cases over our shoulder. Our daughter, Druzilla who was then alive, laughed heartily and said "Dad, you certainly got kicked that time". It did shove me back a couple steps as I was not braced or prepared for two of those long Roman candles at the same time. Nothing daunted, I reloaded both barrels again, put the safety back on and Dru put up a fresh sheet of paper. Again taking aim, I pulled the trigger and again the safety went forward, both barrels went off and the gun opened and ejected its fired cases while I was still back-stepping. That was enough for me, so told my friend to send the damn thing back to the factory, which he did. We carefully examined both pattern sheets and only one barrel was printed on each. Where the second barrel went, we still do not know, but probably over the target paper. In fairness to the company, we have used many fine Fox guns with the utmost satisfaction, yet that particular high-grade Fox seemed to have everything haywire with it. Shooting 3¼ ounces of No. 4 shot from an 8¾-pound double at standard high velocity is usually conductive to a bloody nose, but we experienced only a sharp rap on the sneezer with our thumb the first time.

We never experienced any trouble whatever with the older model Ithaca double hammerless made before 1926. In fact, never had one to become loose in any way though we shot one 16-bore in No. 3 grade for 17 years. Then the Ithaca Company went to the rotary bolt, and our troubles started. Both the old and the new models were superb shooting guns, in fact we have never yet seen better patterning guns, nor any guns shooting higher percentages in full choke than the Ithacas. However, we bought a 9-pound Super ten new model from my friend Capt. E. C. Crossman and he told us he had had trouble with it opening on firing and had sent it back to the factory for correction. In our hands it developed the same old trouble the first time we fired it, opening just enough from the first shot that we could feel the barrels raise and sometimes go back in place and the bolt click home again before the second barrel. At other times it opened enough that we could not fire the second barrel at all, so we wrote our old friend, Lou Smith of Ithaca, and he asked its return.

This time they did a good job on that rotary bolt and it not only stayed bolted, but proved one of the best all-around duck guns we ever used. We also bought another old Super ten-bore of the

A Best-Quality Purdey Over-Under Shotgun.

Fox Double Barrel Shotgun Model B. It is made in 12, 16, 20, and 410 gauge.

older model hammerless of Maj. Askins and this also proved a wonderful duck gun and never showed a trace of the bolts retracting during firing. Another No. 4 12-bore in the old model was, and is still, a superb shooting and handling gun. Frank Pachmayr restocked that 12-bore for us with our design of cheek piece, Monte Carlo comb straight grip stock and beavertail foreend and it was also a very good duck gun, being full choke with 32″ barrels. We had many fine days with the mallards here with all three of those guns. All three are still doing yoeman service each fall.

Next we bought Major Askins' magnum ten-bore Ithaca No. 500,000, the first magnum ten-bore ever built and largely by hand, after experimenting and hand loading for it for some time we sent it back to Ithaca and they refinished the gun and polished out more of the forcing cone for us, further improving its shooting with two ounces of No. 3 shot. However, when we allowed any oil at all on the extended rib cut or rotary bolt that big gun would open up on recoil of the first barrel. One day a big Goshawk was after the turkeys at the ranch. They scurried for the house, well knowing the big ten-bore and I would be on the job at their first frightened cries. I killed that big hawk as he came in for a turkey at very close range. The two ounces of No. 3 shot simply bored an inch hole through him in front of the gun muzzles, as we stood on the back porch. The hawk and a cloud of feathers landed right on me, the gun opened up to such extent that the barrels raised from the breech and the ejector ejected the fired case over my shoulder, all at the same time. My wife was raising turkeys at that time and the good Lord only knows how many hawks I killed with that big gun during those years. At any rate that was too much for me so we again wrote Lou Smith and again the big ten-bore went back to Ithaca for a new rotary bolt. This time it stayed put for some few seasons shooting, showing no wear whatever of the rotary bolt and the top lever still over on the right side when fully closed. When the gun was snapped shut, which we very much dislike doing with any gun, it did not open as often, but occasionally does do that dirty trick to this day and we will have to have our local gunsmith, Jack Ashurst, refit that rotary bolt before it will give the service it should. It is the finest patterning gun we have ever used, going full 93 per cent for ten-shot strings with each barrel and two ounces No. 3 Western Lubaloy shot from Western factory loads.

After Major Askin's recent death we also bought his old No. 5 Ithaca in 16-bore. It had been badly used after his death and also kicked open every few shots, so we ordered a new rotary bolt and spring and new ejector springs from Ithaca, and Ashurst refinished it and worked over the action complete, fitting the new rotary bolt with considerable radius where it contacts the cut in the extended rib. We had never seen an L. C. Smith shoot open, even old guns over 50

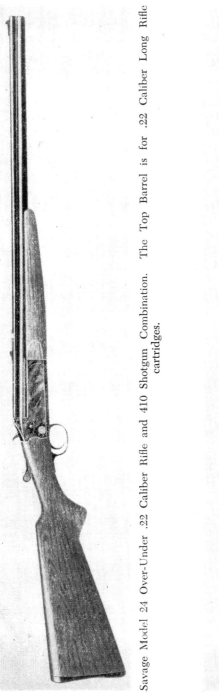

Savage Model 24 Over-Under .22 Caliber Rifle and 410 Shotgun Combination. The Top Barrel is for .22 Caliber Long Rifle cartridges.

Winchester Model 24 Double Barrel Gun—A Good but Inexpensive Model.

years old in poor condition, so finally decided that Ithaca did not stone out enough radius in the finger of the rotary bolt. At any rate this 16-bore has shown no trace of opening at all with heaviest 1⅛-ounce duck loads which we use in it exclusively.

So much for the rotary bolt. I still consider it one of the best double gun fastenings if that said bolt is fitted with the proper radius to hook over the cut in the extended rib as it should. It will not be right if it is just a straight bar where, it contacts the rib cut as were the bolts of all three of these new model Ithacas that opened up before they were worked over. It is a strong and simple fastening and leaves plenty metal in the frame at the angle and bar. Further, it is much cheaper to make and fit than a multiple-bolt system. A letter that just arrived from our friend Lou Smith, of Ithaca says that they are making 1200 pump guns per week and cannot keep up with the demand, so there is little likelihood of their ever making another double gun. This is a pity and will be another famous old American double gun gone from production, to join the ranks of the Baker and the Parker. Lefever double guns have also joined the list of those no longer made and this country is fast going pump and automatic.

At this writing it looks as though we will have only the fine old L. C. Smith and the Fox and Stevens left of our best old double gun builders, and new double guns only from them, Winchester and the Marlin over-under Model 90. The rest of the double guns used in this country will have to be imported just as are the fine Belgian Browning over-unders at present. For those of us who love the fine double shotgun, this is a sad state of affairs, but one that is to be expected from a nation, that is ever going more and more to assembly line machine production, almost to the exclusion of the fine old hand craftsmanship we once had in this country. Americans are usually in a hurry and few youngsters today would ever take the time to apprentice themselves under the few remaining fine gunsmiths we have, to learn the trade.

Ejectors

All double or single barrel shotguns should be fitted with ejectors and most of them now are so equipped, but we well remember when the ejector was less in evidence on even the high grade guns. American and German guns usually employ coil springs for their ejector locks, while most British makers and many Belgian guns as well have beautifully made and fitted flat springs. Properly tuned ejector locks are a great asset on any double or single gun and they should operate right together just after the hammers cock or at the same instant. The two fired cases should be thrown exactly the same distance from the gun and the two ejector locks should throw exactly together. If they do not do so, there is probably friction between the split extractor stems or one spring is weaker than the other or the sears do not bite on equal amount. On a properly made gun there is a joy to the shooter, when he opens the piece and hears the soft punk of the ejectors kicking the empties clear of the gun. If you do not have ejectors, you are certain to get in a hot corner sooner or later while birds raise all around you and just when you should be dropping a couple more rounds in the gun you will be fumbling with those empty cases, trying to get them out of the gun the while you watch one beautiful opportunity after another fade away on fast wings. Lack of ejectors has changed many a man from a double gun to a repeater. Ejector locks today seem fully as reliable as gun locks and seldom give any trouble at all if reasonable care is taken of the arm.

Extractors

Charles Lancaster of England was credited with the invention in 1852 of the first extractor, and later W. W. Greener improved it by utilizing the extended rib as a guide for the top of the extractor. The plain extractor is in one piece and accomplishes primary extraction by loosening and pulling the fired cases out of the chambers some one fourth to ⅜ or a half inch when the gun is opened. With ejector guns

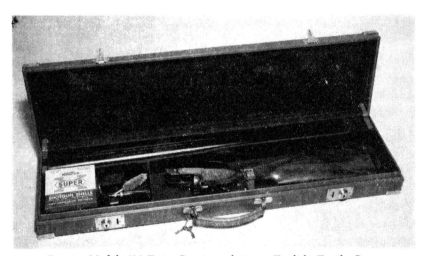

Beretta Model 411-E in Continental Arms English Trunk Case.

however, the extractor leg or stem is composed of two halves flat where they come together and round on the outside, the two forming a round leg. Primary extraction occurs just the same as on plain extractor guns but with the ejector, the split leg allows the lock of the fired barrel to kick the empty several feet from the gun, after primary extraction has been completed. Whether one barrel has been fired, or both or neither, primary extraction occurs every time the gun is opened allowing the shooter to easily grasp the heads of the shells and remove them at will. Thus if an ejector lock does fail or the spring break you still have the extractors to pull the cases back to where you can grasp the heads for final extraction.

In 1886, Anson & Deeley, with the firm of Westley Richards, patented the Anson & Deeley action, the box lock, and in 1886 obtained a patent on their fore-end ejectors. This ejector system is still in use in a great many guns to this day. The Southgate ejector, invented by a Mr. Beesley and patented by Holland in 1893 is another excellent ejector still in use and these with the Baker are the principal forms used today. The Southgate is the more commonly used as it is the simplest and probably the easiest for a gun maker to adjust,

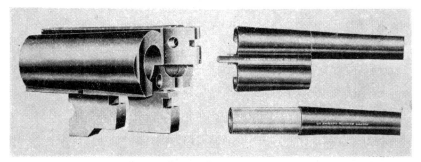

Beretta Mono-Bloc Construction.

and time, of the three ejector locks. The Anson & Deeley and the Southgate are both flat-spring ejector locks while the Baker uses a coil main spring and a different principle. The Baker ejector has one grave fault in that part of the power of the hammer or tumbler was utilized to force forward the ejector rod. Since those days many small improvements in design have occurred both in this country as well as in England and on the continent but it would fill a chapter at least to describe them all. The fore-end wood must of necessity be cut out to receive the ejector locks and this in turn slightly weakens the wood of the fore-stock, yet comparatively little trouble is ever experienced on properly made arms from the ejectors or the consequent inletting of them into the fore-stock. After many years wear, ejectors must occasionally be retuned and cleaned and oiled; but aside from this necessity seldom cause anyone any trouble. They should be a feature on all double- and single-barrel guns.

Self Opening Guns

Lancaster, Holland & Holland and others have for years produced so called self-opening guns. We had one in a Lancaster double rifle, a beautifully made and splendid shooting weapon. On firing the gun and pressing the top lever to the right, the gun simply bounced open and ejected the fired cases all in one continuous motion. These

Continental Arms Co.

Holland and Holland new 12-gauge Over-Under Gun. 28-inch Barrel, for 2¾-inch Shells, Double Trigger, Weighs 7¼ Pounds and is equipped with hand Detachable Locks.

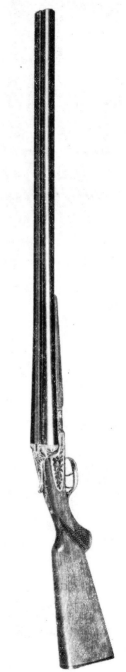

L. C. Smith Ideal Grade Shotgun.

self-opening actions do greatly speed up the opening of the gun for reloading, but my Lancaster at least, closed very hard indeed, which rather over-balanced any gain in the self-opening feature. Since my rifle was built however, these mechanisms have been greatly improved until they close much easier. They usually employ very strong springs to force the action open and in the Lancaster form at least, entailed a considerable cut in the bar of the action. However this rifle never gave me the slightest trouble in any way and I can only marvel at its perfect hand fitting. It employed a double under-bit and doll's-head extension with bite, side clips and the self-opening feature as well as back-action side locks. It was, and is, a perfect double rifle and an ejector. The self-opening feature of these fine British guns certainly adds something to the speed of opening and ejecting the fired cases, but adds something to the time required for closing the gun, entails more springs and more cut-outs in action bar or fore-end and while a beautiful example of fine gun building we do not consider it as necessary, nor highly desirable. We prefer simplicity, in shotgun mechanisms rather than complicating them with any unnecessary parts. Ejectors are a necessity, self-openers are not. It might however, be well to mention here that in the matter of simplifying an action, W. W. Greener used the main spring of the lock to actuate his ejectors and thus really simplified his gun. This Greener Unique action also has the advantage of giving about the right angle of tumbler axle, bent and sear peg for perfect trigger pulls. We shot one of these fine old Greeners for some time in 12-bore, 7 pounds weight with 30″ barrels of Damascus, and long before any warnings were issued as to the relative weakness of Damascus barrels this old gun had digested several cases of Super X heavy duck loads. It is still in tight, sound condition and is still shooting good though now used only with the lighter loads. Greeners have a well learned and enviable reputation.

Firing Order

With two triggers on double guns, the firing order should normally be your more open barrel first and your heavier choked barrel last. However in the various guns we find first one barrel or the other to be the more open. Many factories who build the cheaper double side-by-side guns will make the right barrel the more open or modified choke and that means pulling the front trigger first for the more open barrel. If the stock be a bit long the hand would normally fire the rear trigger first and that trigger always fires the left barrel. If the stock be a bit short the trigger finger is apt to be positioned just right for the front trigger and the right barrel first.

Some folks get started with a gun with the right barrel the more open and then get in the habit of shooting the right barrel first which in turn means pulling that front trigger. We started that way though our gun had both barrels full choke, and to this day that right barrel is fired first with two trigger guns unless the stock is abnormally long for us. Force of habit is the answer. Common sense tells us that for best results we should fire the rear trigger first and that left barrel should be the more open of the two in boring, then when the gun recoils it would drive the grip back through the hand positioning the front trigger just right for the finger. A great many fine Belgian guns have the front trigger hinged so it won't rap the back of the trigger finger when firing that rear trigger and left barrel. If the stock is long this is the fastest system for some folks and again it may be the slowest for others who have from habit fired the front trigger first most of their lives. Many who fire the right barrel first say they then slip the finger back to the rear trigger. That is the way we used to do it, but then we acquired a fine double 12-bore Cashmore English gun and the left barrel was modified choke and the right barrel full choke and bored and chambered for our heavy American duck loads. It is a very fine, well-balanced, fast-handling 7-pound gun and we shot it a good deal on ducks and pheasants, finding we simply had to carry the gun when expecting a bird with our finger positioned for the rear trigger and left barrel or else in the flush of the bird we would bust him with the full-choked right barrel.

Major Askins claimed he shot that left barrel with the rear trigger first and let the gun kick back through his hand so that the trigger finger was then positioned just right for the second or right barrel. We started wrong for this and simply cannot change and in the small excitement of a bird roaring up at close range will practically always pull that front trigger and fire the right barrel first, simply because we started and shot that way so many years.

Theoretically speaking the left barrel should be fired first by right handed persons, as the double gun recoils to the side slightly and if the left is fired first the gun does not recoil away from the line of sight, they claim, as badly as if the right is fired first. We never could see much in this theory as we grip a gun and simply fold our head and hands and arms down on it so that our upper torso and the gun are one unit. However, it is claimed that firing the left barrel first is the best procedure. This means pulling that rear trigger first and letting recoil drive the grip back in the hand to the extent that the trigger finger is then positioned right for the front trigger and right barrel. When firing the Magnum ten-bore or the 600-bore double elephant rifle we noticed this side whip of the gun with the big loads, but not to any extent at all with the ordinary 12-bore shotgun. The two triggers are normally spaced about ¾" apart which gives us that much variation in stock length, so again we believe all double guns should have single triggers, except possibly the so called Cape gun which has a rifle on one side and a shotgun on the other; this of course is made with two triggers for instant selection of barrels, though if it had a safety switch from right to left like the Ithaca it would work well with one trigger or like the Browning over-under, so even on the Cape gun, believe we would prefer a single, selective trigger.

With the over-under gun as made by Browning, Marlin, and about all fine English firms as well as on the Continent, Purdey, Boss, W. R., H & H, Merkles and many others, the lower barrel should always be the more open barrel and should always be fired first even though both barrels have the same boring or choke. This for the reason that the lower barrel in an over-under is more in a direct line with the gunstock and hence drives straight back in recoil with less up-chuck of the piece, allowing a faster second shot as the lower barrel recoil is not as heavy apparently and disturbs the aim over the gun less than does the recoil of the upper barrel. So the firing order of the over-under should always be lower barrel first and when used in trap shooting the lower barrel should be used at all times as it will then throw less heat waves over the top rib than if the upper barrel were used exclusively, except in doubles shooting. Many over-under two triggered guns are notorious for shooting high with the front trigger, which normally fires the bottom barrel. This is because the hand is so far forward to reach the front trigger and the thumb is well forward on the top of grip. Over-unders especially need single triggers, to eliminate this fault and the single trigger is usually placed in the rear position as it should be when the thumb comes over the rear of the grip and the gun does not then shoot high with that first or lower barrel. Most over-unders with two borings are bored more open in the lower barrel and that is the way they should be fired, first the under barrel and then the over and that is the reason the British call them under-overs instead of our American name for them. A shift of the hand from one trigger to the other does not seem to affect elevations at all on side-by-side doubles but surely does seem to do just that with the over-under guns. When both are fired by the single trigger in rear position no change in elevation is noted and they are not then high shooting guns.

For a time Browning made a set of twin single triggers on their over-under guns. These triggers permitted the use of either the first or front trigger or the rear trigger for firing both barrels and worked very well, though why the devil they wanted two of the things in one gun we do not know unless it was to give a compromise trigger position for different size men and different size hands. Suffice it to say the firing order of the over-under should always be lower barrel first and upper second and the trigger should be a selective single placed in the rear trigger position.

Safeties

Not all shotguns have safeties, most trap guns being made without any trace of a safety, so the trap shot will not inadvertently get his safety on and thus pull on a locked sear and miss his bird. Trap

The L. C. Smith "Crown Grade" Double Barrel Shotgun.

guns do not need safeties and the trap shot is better off without them, but in the field it is a far different story. All field guns should have safeties and they should be used at all times except when birds are actually on the wing. With all the old double-barrel hammer guns, one was always sure whether his gun was cocked or not, but the hammer gun possessed the distinct disadvantage of being slow to cock, that is, both barrels. Further, they were not as safe as hammerless guns because of the fact the hammers could catch on brush, trailing vines, or a wire fence and fire the gun, or at least bring it to full cock, when if not noticed it could easily be accidentally fired by brush hitting a trigger.

As a small boy living near Helena, Montana we used to hunt with an old timer who used a double hammer 12-bore of Belgian make. We were out for ruffed grouse primarily, though we usually climbed high enough before the day was over to secure some big blue grouse as well. He habitually hunted with both barrels of that old gun at full cock and would grasp the small of the stock in his right hand and carry it upside down on his right shoulder. When a grouse flushed, he had only to bring the muzzles over in an arc and the barrels fell into his left hand, pointing at the fast disappearing bird. He was a good shot, but many times when following him along some narrow deer trail in the timber, I found myself looking down those cocked tubes. One day, while going down a steep mountain trail, he was luckily in the lead, when he hooked the end of a three foot limb laying lengthwise in the trail with his right toe. He made a beautiful pole vault down the mountain, at the same time bringing the old gun over his head and fully extended in front of him as he hit the ground full length. Both barrels of the old 12-bore went off, whether from the jar, or whether he pulled the triggers we never knew, but it kicked back out of his hand and badly peeled the right side of his face with one hammer. I noticed the rest of the day he carried that gun with the hammers down. We both saw what the double charges did to a small quaking aspen in front of him, and to this day I have never again knowingly hunted with anyone who carried his gun cocked and the safety off.

Automatic Safeties

Automatic safeties which go on "SAFE" whenever the gun is opened, are a fine thing for the beginner or the man or woman who hunts but seldom, as the gun then thinks for the hunter and automatically puts the safety on each time it is opened. For the experienced hunter or shooter automatic safeties are a damned nuisance and should never be tolerated any longer than it takes to hie yourself to a gunsmith and have the link removed, making the safety nonautomatic. Safety slides should never be moved until the game is on the wing as you have ample time to push the safety slide with the

The L. C. Smith "Specialty Trap" Shotgun.

thumb, as the gun is mounted, but then the safety should stay off even though you may fire both barrels, reload and fire them both again until such time as you are through shooting at that raise of birds or the cripples from that flock of ducks. Then, and then only, is time enough to put the safety on again before resuming your march or your wait in the duck blind.

The place for a safety is on top the small of stock right where the thumb can move it instantly as the gun is mounted. Most automatics and pump guns have the safety in or near the trigger guard and this has always been an awkward, slow, safety for me to move. We have to carry the gun with the forefinger on said safety in order

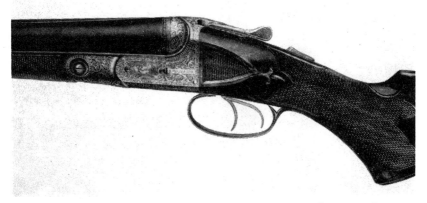

Parker Shotgun, Grade A.H.E. Parker Guns are no longer made.

to find it in a hurry as the game flushes. The old Spencer pump gun had a unique safety. It was simply a reversed trigger in the front of the guard and was pushed off by pushing forward on this trigger. It was slow for us also.

All trap guns are made without a safety in both the single trap and double trap guns and possibly with good reason. If a trap shot inadvertently put his safety on and then failed to get off a shot, or else spoiled his timing and missed, it might well lose him a lot of money in a big match, hence trap doubles and singles are made without safeties. If they are ever to be used for field work, a safety should be installed, preferably of the non-automatic variety. Pumps and automatics used by a great many of the hottest trap shots still retain their safeties and we have never heard any kicks on that score from them, so it is a moot question whether a safety should be on all guns regardless of whether for straight trap shooting or not.

My old friend, the late Major Askins, never did like a safety of any kind and hunted with them off when he was apt to flush birds. No doubt he had also formerly hunted with double-hammer guns

Photo by Keith Barrette.

Two of the Author's Shotguns. Top: A 32-inch Parker B.H.E. 12-bore With All Extras. It is a Double Trap Gun With Full Choke in Both Barrels.

Bottom: A Magnum Ten-Bore Ithaca With 32-inch Barrels. Both Barrels have Full Choke.

carried with both barrels cocked when likely to flush game until it was a habit with him. As he so often said "no gun is safe, it is the man who is using it."

Most conventional safeties lock only the triggers and the sears can still be jarred out of their notches and the gun fired. We have known several men who had lost an arm, simply by jamming a gun down on the ground while holding the muzzles in line with the arm, also some who had lost an arm by pulling a gun toward them from a car or boat or through a fence. This was a very prevalent accident in the days of the old hammer guns as the high hammers often caught on something and fired the gun.

Even when the safety is on most commercial hammerless double guns, the guns are safe only from a pull on the trigger and a hard bump may jar the sears out of the cock notch and fire the gun. We have seen this happen when a gun butt was used to jab downward on a rabbit's head to kill it. We also have seen several fine guns go off when snapped shut smartly after reloading and our old No. 3 Ithaca 16-bore once fired the right barrel when we closed the gun rather gently. All guns should be turned completely away from anything they are liable to damage when they are closed on a loaded round, just in case a sear may not have fallen into the bottom of the notch and the jar may set off the lock.

Some of the finer side-lock guns, especially the English guns with intersecting safeties, are fairly safe as this feature will usually prevent such an accidental discharge, but it is far better for the shooter to form the habit of always keeping his gun muzzles turned away from himself and friends at all times and especially while working the action of a repeater or in loading a single or double gun. Intercepting safeties are usually found only on the fine side-lock guns, either bar-action side-lock, or back-action side-lock with some variations in other models, while box-lock guns usually lock only the triggers and not the hammer and sears. We have seen many double guns with one sear notch altogether too shallow. These guns with one very light trigger pull, would sometimes go off if the gun was snapped shut or when the other barrel was fired that light sear would trip from the jar of recoil and fire both barrels. All double and single guns should be closed gently, never snapped shut, as such slamming of barrels and action together causes more wear on the locking bolts and frame and barrel fitting than many hundred rounds of actual shooting. Load your barrel and then, while holding the top lever over, raise the butt stock until the action is closed and then let the top lever gently in place. With some types of top snap action it is necessary to close the gun harder, such as many of the self opening British guns and the Westley Richards top snap action sometimes must be closed harder than with other models.

Shotgun trigger pulls even on fine trap guns should never be less than 3½ pounds as a safety feature and on two trigger guns it is well to have the first barrel, that is the one bored the more open to fire at about 3½ to 4 pounds and the second barrel to fire at 4 to 4½ pounds. So long as a trigger pull is clean and sharp it makes relatively little difference if it be four pounds or less as one soon becomes accustomed to its weight, the main thing is to have it heavy enough for safety, should the gun get a hard jar as is apt to happen if you get a bad fall, which happens to all of us hunting rough country and with our eyes open for birds rather than where we are placing our feet.

We have used many guns with the Greener side safety, and while it is a very good, reliable safety, it has always proven a very slow, awkward safety to move, when game is flushed for us at least. Most all German guns are equipped with this safety with the little button lever on the left side of the stock-ear just forward of the grip. We believe this Greener type safety, while no doubt a very sturdy reliable one, has contributed a great deal to the habit of hunting with the gun not on safe, as it is such a slow job to find and operate that Greener safety in a hurry, that most men who have guns so equipped have formed the habit of pushing it forward and hunting with the safety off.

Regardless of what type gun and safety you use, remember the gun is safe only to the extent that you keep the muzzles pointed away from yourself and friends. Remember many guns will fire even with the safety on from any hard jar, such as dropping the butt of the gun to the ground, leaning it against a tree or automobile where a wandering dog may knock it down, or closing the action of a top break double or single too smartly. The main thing is to at all times keep the muzzles pointed away from anything you do not wish to shoot. Treat all guns as loaded guns and regardless of how good a safety you have, never trust it.

There can be no question but the top-of-grip safety is the fastest of all and the intercepting safety of many fine double side-lock guns the most reliable of all safeties on double guns.

Cocking Indicators

Many German guns as well as the Ithaca doubles have cocking indicators clearly showing by feel as well as sight when the arm is cocked and these are nice. Some of the fine British side locks also had little windows showing clearly when the sear was cocked; but we always looked on these as rather unnecessary as the ultimate safe handling of any gun depends more on the grey matter and mental processes of the individual than on any mechanical safety.

Three Barrel Guns

Most German drillings or three-barrel guns are built on some form of the Blitz action. These are very useful weapons when one hunts virgin country where most anything may be on the ticket. They seldom handle as nicely as a straight double shotgun, but the

Germans have gotten their weight and balance down until very good work can be done with the shot tubes and in addition one usually has a very accurate shooting rifle barrel. Owing to the fact the three tubes are soldered together full length they are very stiff and this gives one a most accurate single-shot rifle in addition to the two-shot barrels. Nearly all of them we have examined had double underbit and Greener cross-bolt fittings. Many also had the Purdey side clips. Such weapons are very useful for taking a head of big game or a chance shot at a predator, cougar, coyote or wolf when hunting upland grouse. On the Continent they were often carried by game rangers and the rifled third barrel was often used with telling effect on poachers, as it was often a case of the game ranger killing, or being killed, by poachers. Such a weapon when it employs a powerful rifle cartridge like the 9.3 x 74 as so often made by Sauer or Merkel Bros. in conjunction with a 12-bore double, is very useful in Africa and the rifle barrel may become a life saver at times. When hunting such a country one never knows when he may be out for a mess of guinea fowl and suddenly come face to face with a lion or leopard.

Usually the "safety" operates the shift from the shot to the rifle barrels and also operates a set of rifle sights on top of the barrel through a long push rod from the slide. (The safety being the usual Greener side safety.) Such guns are certainly a great deal more than the fad that some folks think them.

Westley Richards even went so far as to make a three-barrel shotgun, all barrels the same gauge and this with their single trigger gave the owner a very fast three-shot weapon fully the equal to or better than any pump or automatic for those three shots. It was and is a peculiarly shaped weapon at the breech, but a very reliable and useful one, especially for a rapid rise of birds or in wildfowl shooting. The third barrel is also most useful in finishing off a possible cripple. The Germans even went so far as to build four-barrel guns, usually with a pair of shot barrels and a small rifle for a top rib and a heavy rifle barrel underneath. These are rather complicated mechanisms and we believe it is carrying the thing a bit far. However one such four-barrel built years ago by Fred Adolphe for our friend Harfield Conrad, was certainly a light, handy, well-balanced and very good shooting weapon.

A much simpler and more conventional design was the Cape Gun by Westley Richards and others with one rifle barrel and one shot barrel. In side-by-side type, these are odd looking but very practical meat guns and useful in far countries for getting a mess of fowl for the table and at the same time having a good accurate single shot rifle for the taking of buck and also for defense when hunting the smaller birds and meeting a lion or other dangerous game. Such two-barrel combinations we believe are at their best in the over-under design. The rifle can then be placed on top with its

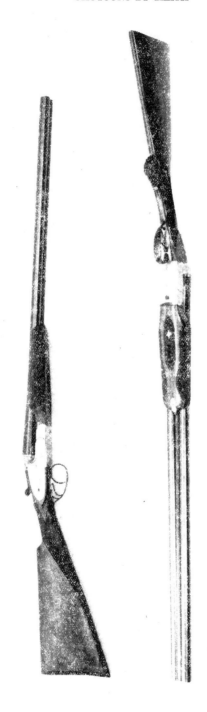

The Beretta Model 411-E. Both have Auto-Ejectors, Taper-bored Hard Chrome-Lined Barrels, Hinged Front Trigger and Built-In Gas Escape Vents.

sights and a good shot barrel underneath. They are much better appearing guns than those built on the side-by-side principle and are more easily regulated. The over-under Cape guns were most common in German makes. Another, much more common, and very practical, approach to such a problem of hunting birds in dangerous game country, is the Paradox gun built by about all the better British makers. This is a true double-barrel shotgun, built a bit heavier than standard for the gauge and with the last four to six inches of the barrels rifled with a shallow rifling. It will give the usual cylinder bore patterns when used with shot, very useful for all bird and fowl shooting at close range in wild unspoiled country and when loaded with the Paradox slug loads is a very powerful double rifle and quite accurate to a 150 yards. Slug loads in all gauges are not as potent as some would have us believe as the velocity is usually much less than rifle bullets, but in 12- or 10-bore these Paradox or ball and shot guns are very powerful when loaded, as in the 12-bore, with a 750 grain slug. Such weapons are very useful in following up wounded lion or on leopard with S. S. buck shot or the Lethal or Destructor bullets that carry several sections and break apart on impact.

These weapons are usually sighted the same as good double rifles and yet are very useful shotguns. They are made heavier and usually bolted with double under-bit bolts as well as a doll's-head or Greener cross-bolt in the extended rib. The solid pointed 750 grain slug gives very good penetration on quite heavy game and the hollow point 750-grain 12-bore slug expands readily on any game. With such heavy bullets at moderate velocity they give an excellent knock-down blow at close range, and are preferred by some to even a double rifle, for close work on the big cats. Short barrels and perfect balance make them practically as fast as a fine double shotgun and the man used to a shotgun will find them very handy on dangerous beasts such as lion or tiger at close range and with a heavy buckshot load; just the thing for a leopard in the brush. Many times when hunting birds for the table such game will be put up at close range and with the exchange of loads in these weapons the hunter is then well fixed for the larger quarry, be it buck or dangerous beast. Some hunters have even used the 10-bore Paradox guns, with hard, solid, conical bullets, for heart shots on elephant with good results.

We once tested a heavy ten-bore Paradox by H & H with 28" barrels. It must have weighed about 11 pounds and with 1⅝-ounce loads of No. 6 shot gave a very good, even spread of pattern to a full 40 yards that should have taken most all the larger game birds nicely. It seemed to spread over about a 50-inch circle at that range. Imperial Chemical Industries Limited, as far as we know, still make the various bullet loads for these guns.

"Royal" Self-opening Ejector Gun. Produced by Holland and Holland.

Courtesy Holland and Holland, Ltd., London

Over-Under Doubles

Next let us look into the over-under double guns. For many years these were obtainable only from England and the Continent and usually at very high prices. They offer a single, narrow sighting plane with the same deep fore-end as found on all pump- and auto-loading shotguns and for this reason are a very logical choice for the man or woman who wishes to change from a repeating shotgun to a double. They can usually go right to work with the over-under if it fits them. It offers much reduced recoil for the lower barrel due to the fact the lower barrel is in a more direct plane with the stock of the gun, hence drives back more in line with the stock in recoil, rather than the usual up-chuck of the side-by-side double gun. These weapons often employ very strong bolting systems, either the Kersten system so widely employed by the Germans with their Greener cross-bolt on each side of the top barrel or with side bolts as on the Woodward and other fine British guns. Practically always the lower barrel breech is imbedded deep in the frame. Fabrication of the over-under frame and lock system is usually more complicated than the side-by-side doubles and for that reason they are usually much more costly guns when of best British make. Trigger pulls are usually though not always harder to adjust and keep adjusted. The frames are most always long and deep and the forestock must of necessity be the same. In this country Remington produced a unique design in that the top of the breech slid back and forth and thus locked the barrel down in the frame as in the closed position this sliding breech went forward over the top barrel. Marlin and Stevens used a more conventional design. Today only the Marlin Model 90 and the small combinations and the Stevens and the Savage are still in production. Remington found over-unders costly to make and dropped their manufacture.

Though the over-under possesses some advantages, we could never see it in comparison with a fine side-by-side double. It is the gun for the person who must have a single sighting plane and a deep fore-end and who has been used to the repeater, but it also has many faults. It must be opened very much wider than a side-by-side double and its mechanism is usually more complicated. It also radiates heat waves to a greater extent over the barrels in continuous firing and swings harder in a strong cross wind. Some over-unders have very deep actions especially if fitted with underbolt. However, the Marlin Model 90 is a rather trim action for a low-cost gun, yet employs a heavy under-bolt. Over-under tubes are easier to regulate so both barrels shoot together than is the case with the side-by-side tubes with their necessary convergence to take care of the side whip of recoil. The over-under also has the advantage that the gun moves off the target less from the recoil of its lower barrel than almost any other shotgun known. This again is due to the fact

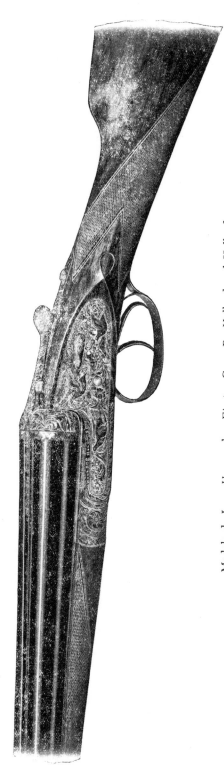

Modele de Luxe Hammerless Ejector Gun. By Holland and Holland.

Courtesy Holland and Holland, Ltd., London

that the lower barrel is nearly in line with the axis of the stock. This is a very real advantage in shooting doubles at the trap and in fast double work on game birds or fowl, as it allows the gunner to get onto his second target in faster time. In appearance, however the over-under looks like a poisoned pup that had lain too long in the sun, as compared with a neat, trim, side-by-side double. Many trap shooters use the over-under for doubles and one friend of mine, George Turner uses a Browning over-under. He claims that one barrel shoots about 18″ high, so he uses that barrel for the first target, while the other barrel shoots about that much low, so he uses it on the second bird after it has started to arc over. He seems to do right well by himself and that Browning whose barrels do not shoot together, usually winds up some place in the money.

When it comes to a reasonably priced gun in the over-under variety, then we think the new post-war Browning is one of the nicest guns of this type we have seen for the money as it sells at this writing (1950) for around $245 complete with elevated and ventilated rib, ejectors and a single, selective trigger. This gun has a short frame for an over-under and a heavy under-bolt yet it is a light, well-balanced and rather streamlined gun of this type. It certainly performs as well as any gun we have tried and shoots exceptionally well and unlike George Turner's old pre-war Browning this gun throws both patterns to the same center. At least the one we have been shooting does just that.

One peculiarity of the over-under shotgun, at least all of them we have tried, is that you seem to get different elevations in fast shooting with the two barrels owing to the shift of the hand and finger on the two-trigger models. No doubt the grip of the hand being shifted slightly when the finger shifts from one trigger to the other was the direct case, owing to the relationship of that hand with the barrel being fired. We have never noticed any difference in elevations of the two barrels when single-trigger over-under guns were used nor when shooting the conventional double barrels but this peculiarity of the over-under was apparent when patterning many different over-under two-trigger guns. For this reason we believe all top-and-bottom guns should have a single trigger.

Marlin and Savage produced the only two low-cost over-unders in this country and they were both a lot of gun for the money, but do not compare very favorably with the higher priced, now discontinued, Model 32 Remington. Nor can they compare in grade with the very fine European and British best double over-unders. The Marlin Model 90 Skeet gun was to our notion the best of these two and a very good sound, strong and perfect-shooting gun.

A lot has been written in America on the single-sighting plane and we believe that has had no small influence on the popularity, in some quarters, of the over-under gun. Personally we never could see the difference between an elevated, ventilated rib on a side-by-side double as compared with the same on the over-under. Both look alike to us. However we did notice the change in elevations when we shifted to the other trigger in the two-triggered over-unders and for me, used to the side-by-side double with its very small, shallow fore-end, the over-unders all tend to shoot high. This is due to the fact we are used to regular side-by-side doubles, and the much deeper fore-end of the over-under, pump, or autoloader all make us tend to shoot high. One unconsciously aims with his two hands and when used to one type he must consciously hold down with that left hand or shoot high. The position of the two hands in relation with the eyes becomes a habit. Lower that left hand by some two inches, in its grasp of the deep fore-end and in fast shooting that hand will automatically bring the gun up to its normal relation of the two hands and the eyes, with the result that the gun is then pointing too high. This is not so apparent in deliberate swing and pass shooting but is definitely so in the fast snap shooting which one often does in heavy cover on grouse. Just another good reason why the man used to a pump or auto and who wishes to shift to a double will find the over-under his best bet.

Likewise the pump- or auto-trained shot can always shift to the over-under even for fast snap shooting and find his two hands have the same relative alignment. He can also shift from the over-under to his pump or auto with no loss of prestige in his score ·on game, because the three types all present the same deep fore-end and position of the left hand. Over-under guns have reached their highest stage of development in the fine custom British makes and some of the better German makes such as Merkel Brothers. The makes with bifurcated lumps, usually produce a shallower frame and a better appearing gun, than those with under-bolts that necessitate a deeper frame. Practically all the better British makers turn out exceptionally fine over-unders, but some appear more clumsy, and heavier, and deeper at the breech than others and while this has no effect on the general utility of the gun it does on appearance. We particularly like the appearance of the Boss, Westley Richards and Woodward as compared with the deeper frames of some of the other makes. After having used the side-by-side double most of our life, we find all over-unders, clumsy guns, slow to reload in a hurry when birds are flushing one after another; and we never can like the extreme amount the gun has to be opened to eject and reload that bottom barrel. Personally we would prefer a fine Purdey, Holland & Holland or other good British gun of side-by-side type to any and all over-unders.

To sum up the situation, we believe the choice between over-under or the side-by-side gun to be largely a matter of personal preference, but here in America there is a surprisingly strong trend to the over-under. This in turn is no doubt due to the fact that the repeater has been for so many years almost a standard gun in this country. The man who wants a best gun in an over-under can expect to lay down a good bit more coin of the realm than he would have to for an equal grade of side-by-side double. It is the most costly of all shotguns. So, gentlemen, choose your weapon.

CHAPTER THREE

Repeating Shotguns

THE REPEATING SHOTGUN is an American invention. The old Spencer is usually credited with being the first pump gun, but whether it was developed before the first pump-action rifle, the old Colt Lightning magazine rifle, I do not know.

One of the earliest pump guns we remember was the Old Model '93 Winchester. It was and still is a good gun and oddly enough, while testing five thousand shotguns of various makes for Uncle Sam during the war, two of these old guns showed up and both still functioned perfectly, were tested, inspected and passed on for possible M.P. or other military usage. This was the fore-runner of the justly famous Model 97 Winchester pump gun, one of the most famous of all trombone-action repeating shotguns, and still one of the best liked of them all in some respects, such as the visible hammer. The early Marlin pump also was made with visible hammer, but that early model proved entirely inadequate for the present heavy duck loads and we have known of many having their breech bolts blown out the rear. This is the side-ejection hammer Marlin. The old Spencer came out in the eighties, followed shortly by the Model '93 Winchester and its improved pattern the Model '97 and these were followed by the early hammer Marlin, side-ejecting pump and the later hammerless Marlin, Stevens, Savage Remington, etc.

The old Model 10 Remington pump gun worked well for a time until that peculiar carrier would wear which usually caused trouble. At the arsenal we had plenty of trouble with that model. That peculiar carrier, or as some of the armorers called it a "flutter valve," simply had to be just right to work. This model had one mighty good feature, fired cases were ejected out the bottom of the action the same as their later and most excellent Model 17, but the Model 10 on the whole was the gunsmith's nemesis.

Another gun that was quite popular for some years was the old Model 1901 Winchester lever action. This was made in both 10- and 12-bore and with the standard loads of 1¼ ounces of shot in those days it was a very good duck and goose gun. We used one for several years on ducks when they were flying high and rather liked the old gun although it had excessive heel and comb drop and one had to consciously aim the gun like a rifle. The breech action was never too strong, and many industrious hand loaders who did not possess enough grey matter to load within reason blew them open. Major Askins had one blow up on him. No fault of the gun but of the lad who had loaded the ammunition and put in about two charges of powder. This action was never as fast as the pump guns, but was amply fast enough for making doubles by anyone raised on lever action rifles. However under the very same circumstances we have seen good pump gun men have three birds falling at about the same time.

During those early pump gun days the old Winchester Model 97 continued to be as popular as any, and with many shooters, is to this day. It is doubtful if any make or model of gun ever killed any more game in America than that time-tried old Winchester 97. The Marlin, Savage and Stevens pump guns seemed to be about equally good shooting guns and many preferred them, but over the years of continuous usage the Marlin often developed extraction troubles and the Savage and Stevens parts seem to wear out quicker than

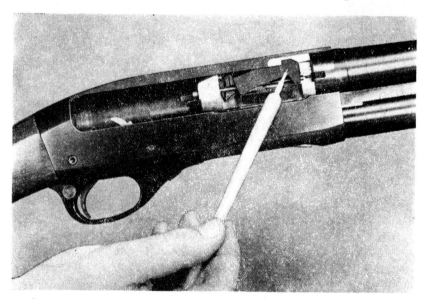

Cutaway Picture of the new Remington Model 870 Pump Action Repeating Shotgun, showing how Breech locks into Barrel Extension, an Exclusive Feature of this Gun.

did those of the old Winchester '97. Other off makes were put on the market. Some were good guns but some were not and the mail order catalogues often changed brands with the end results that one could not then get parts for the old gun and had to buy a new one. The later hammerless Marlin seemed a much better gun in many ways but never did outshoot that first old hammer model. However the new gun would handle modern, progressive powder loads while

Winchester Model 42 410-Gauge Repeater.

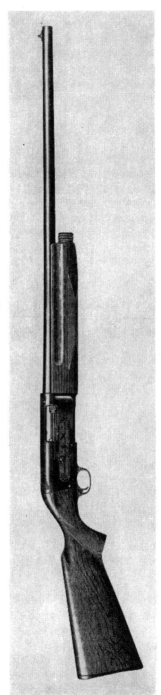

Savage Model 775 (light weight) and Model 755 (standard weight) Automatic Shotgun—5-Shot or 3-Shot, 12- or 16-Gauge, Takedown.

the old side-ejection, hammer model would occasionally blow out its breech bolt. Of all the older pump guns we much preferred the Winchester Model '97. The later Model 12 Winchester was and still is a very fine gun and popular all over this country for game as well as Skeet and Trap shooting. You can look over the gun racks at any big shoot and see plenty of Model 12 Winchesters. In testing hundreds of them we found about the only trouble that ever developed was with the recoil ring and consequent headspace. The later Model 42 Winchester in 410 bore is also a very fine little gun in every way though we never could see that roman candle 410-bore load. It is simply a case of the company trying to make a gun out of too small a bore by loading the long 3″ case and even with it, it will never equal a good 28-bore and we believe the 28-bore to be the smallest gauge that should ever be made.

The Remington Model 17 was a real gun and to my notion, in many respects, the best pump gun of all at that time. It had a solid receiver and ejected its fired cases out the bottom. However Remington got into patent trouble and rather than pay out a lot of money on two claims finally dropped this excellent model, perhaps the finest pump-gun action up to the time of its advent. My old friend Lou Smith of Ithaca waited and grabbed it up after patents had run out and the old Model 17 Remington principle is now incorporated and improved in the new Ithaca Model 37. It is one of the finest pump guns ever built and in very light weight. About the only faults we ever found with the Model 17 Remington and the first Model 37 Ithacas was that they would occasionally drop a loaded round out the bottom of the gun. Both load and eject from the bottom of the frame and are particularly nice for left-hand shooters on this account. The Southpaw doesn't have empty cases flying out past his nose with either of these excellent models. Of all the early pump guns, and aside from the excellent Model 17 Remington and the Ithaca 37, the Winchester Model 12, we still consider the old '97 superior to most of the other makes, especially when it comes to years of hard service with little or no wear of parts or necessary replacements.

Stevens made their Models 620 and 820, The J. C. Higgins Model 20 and lately the H & R clip-loading Model 500; also Mossberg has out a bolt-action shotgun in small gauges. Savage also made a very good pump gun, but none of these many models ever seemed to attain the popularity of the Winchester Model 97 and Model 12, the Remington 17 and the Ithaca 37. The Remington Model 31, however was and is a good gun and very popular, but will now probably be discontinued since the advent of Remington's latest and best pump gun, the Model 870, probably the finest pump gun ever designed to date.

The Remington 870 is a radical departure from the older conventional designs in both its take down features and its breech locking system. The new gun's breech bolt locks into a recess cut into the barrel extension, hence does away with about all trace of headspace troubles and greatly simplifies the locking system which was formerly at the rear end of the breech bolt. This new gun places the locking bolt just back of the cartridge which gives a stronger, simpler method of locking the breech bolt in every way. The 870 also has the simplest of all take-down systems. You merely unscrew the magazine cap and pull the slide back, then lift the barrel with its extension out of the receiver. It is also one of the lighest of all pump guns and we predict it will soon be the most popular pump gun ever made. The receiver is more streamlined than that of former models and the gun 12 gauge weighs only about 6½ pounds with a 28″ barrel and a steel receiver.

The company also furnishes a long, heavy plug of solid steel to slip in as a magazine plug and thus increase the weight to 7¼ pounds when wanted. We cannot see this heavy hunk of pig iron from any angle, as it simply ruins the balance and fast handling of an otherwise perfect pump shotgun. The pesky thing throws the balance of the gun entirely too far forward and it then has lost its live feel and general fast handling qualities, so for us at least, this long hunk of iron or steel that Remington gives away with the Model 870 had just as well be kept at the factory and melted up for parts, for we would never tolerate one in a gun of ours. This new gun has two push rods, one on either side of fore-end to preclude the possibility of any cramping and is one of the fastest, slickest pump guns imaginable and the easiest working gun we have seen since the Remington 17 and the Ithaca 37. Remington has come a long, long way in the design of this Model 870 and other companies are going to have to bring out new and improved designs if they are ever to compete with it successfully on the open market. Its utter simplicity, as well as its reliability and greatly streamlined receiver, all add to its salability. Its forward breech lock alone puts it far ahead of mist designs, and when combined with such an easy take down feature, is bound to make it very popular. It operates as slick as the finest hand stoned Model 12 Winchester or 17 Remington or 37 Ithaca, just as it comes from the factory in standard grade. It is also one of the easiest of all pump guns to load. At its present low price it is also going to make tough competition for all the mail order guns as well as the cheaper grade pump guns like the J. C. Higgins and the Western Field Model 60 and the new Winchester Model 25.

This latest Model 25 solid frame Winchester pump gun incorporates some simplification over the older Model 12 but in the main offers little that is new or much of an improvement. It is simply a bid for the low price field by Winchester, and while an excellent gun for the money in every way, we doubt if it becomes ever as popular as the new Remington 870. We also fail to see how the Savage-

Stevens line can compete with the new Remington or the Ithaca Model 37.

Now that ducks are no longer in such profusion as in former years and the bag limit has been cut to five fowl per gun per day, there is no longer the need for the heavy pump gun of former years, necessary to absorb some of the recoil of continuous shooting in the duck blind or pass. Likewise the pump gun is now more of an all around gun for upland as well as duck shooting and the modern choke devices make it quickly adaptable to any sort of shooting.

Since starting this chapter we have learned more about that ancient Colt repeater we used when a boy, with the pistol grip operating the action. A Burgess patent pump gun operated by the pistol grip was made in Buffalo in the early 90s and as Colt also made a lever action rifle under the Burgess patents, no doubt they made that gun we used under those patent rights, before it was finally brought out as the Burgess gun in Buffalo. We still remember hunting jack rabbits with the owner of that old gun one bitterly cold day in Montana. The mercury stood at 20 below and the wind was howling with fine hard snow driving with it. We were hunting across the wind and having a hard time just to keep from freezing and had jumped and killed but two of the big white Montana Jacks when my partner walked up to a deep cut bank or wash.

Instantly two big coyotes jumped out right in front of him. They had been bedded behind the cutbank out of the wind and when jumped were not over six feet from him as he walked out to the lip of the cut bank. Grasping his mitten in his teeth he peeled it off and killed those two coyotes before they went 10 yards. The top of the first one's head was blown off completely and the second one received the charge of No. 4s in the back of the neck. He certainly could work that old gun and we have also seen him have three sharp tail grouse falling at one time when using it.

We nearly froze our fingers, getting the pelts off those two Ki-dorgs in the cold wind, but found enough shelter under the cut bank to enable us to finish the job.

To John M. Browning goes the credit for the design of the Model '97 Winchester, also the Model 1901 lever action, but Browning and Winchester agreed to disagree before the Model 12 Winchester was brought out. Browning probably influenced the design of more guns of repeating persuasion, both rifle and shotgun, as well as pistol, than any other living man. He was an inventive genius.

For the man who wants greater range and a bigger shot load for duck and goose shooting, the Model 12 Winchester is in a class by itself as it is made in the heavy model to take the long 3" 1⅝-ounce shell. For long range duck and goose shooting, this feature has long made the Model 12 heavy duck gun the most popular of all pump guns. It handles the standard Super 10 bore load perfectly

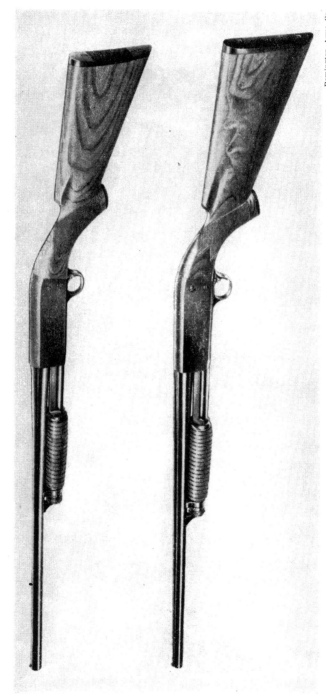

Top: Ithaca Model 37 Standard Repeating Gun. Bottom: Ithaca Model 37R, Solid Rib Grade Repeating Gun.

Remington Arms Co.

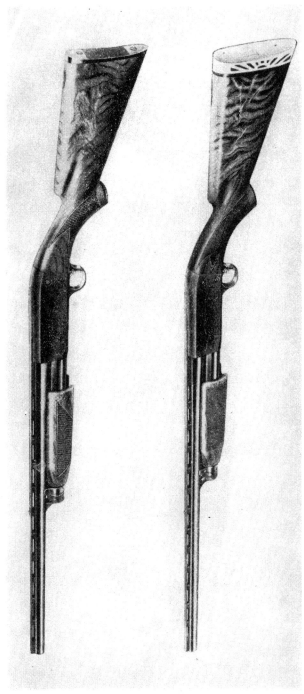

Top: Ithaca Model 37S Repeating Skeet Gun. Bottom: Ithaca Model 37T Repeating Trap Gun.

High Grade Remington Model 870.

A Parker Single Barrel Trap Gun.

and while theoretically it should deform more shot than a 10 bore handling the same charge, we never could detect much if any difference in the field. We thoroughly tested one of the first of these fine guns on both ducks and sage hens, finding it superior in every way to all other repeating shotguns for long range difficult shooting. The big load seemingly added 5 to 10 yards effective range to the 12 bore standard load. It was an efficient duck killer to a full 70 yards with 1⅝ ounces of No. 4 shot. Many a wise old mallard that thought he was well out of range, folded up and skidded to the ground or water when I was using that fine heavy Model 12. It is still very popular among the duck shooters.

Right here is a good time to mention the fact that owners of all the old Heavy automatics for the standard 12 bore load, Brownings, Remington Model 11s, and presumably also the good Savage made under the same patent, can have them remodelled to handle the magnum 12 bore 3″ shell with 1⅞ ounces of shot. This alteration is accomplished by Mr. Arthur Kovalovsky, of 5524 Cahuenga Blvd., No. Hollywood, Calif. He thoroughly tests every arm he alters and guarantees his work. Though most magnum 12 bores are over-bored for the big load, he has found that standard boring seems to handle the load just as well with the new and improved wadding now currently loaded in the 3″ magnum 12 bore loads. This alteration puts the auto loader in the same class with the Model 12 Winchester heavy duck gun and also the magnum 12 bore double guns and the Super 10 bore as well, in double gun persuasion, as a long range duck and goose gun.

Advantages of Pump Guns

For the price involved, it is very doubtful if any other shotgun will ever be made that will approach the pump gun for real value per dollar invested. It will shoot as well as any gun, last as long as any other gun, and can be fired accurately just as fast as any automatic. Some may take exception to this statement, but it is true nevertheless.

In skilled hands, the slide handle is operated while the gun is in recoil and actually aids in pulling the piece down out of recoil and also in pointing it at the next target as the slide is pushed forward. For accurately aimed, or pointed, fire the pump gun will deliver its loads just as fast as will any auto-loader. The pump gun, as well as the auto-loader, can be fitted with any of the excellent variable chokes, making it useful for about all types of shooting from short range skeet, grouse, or quail shooting, to long range difficult duck or goose shooting. It can also be fitted with all types of compensators if they are desired.

Thus the pump gun user can have any desired degree of choke, as well as greatly decreased recoil if desired, but the latter only at the expense of much increased muzzle blast as all compensators

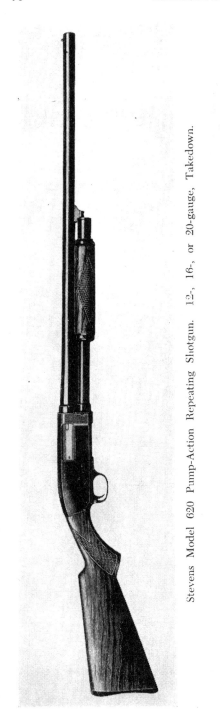

Stevens Model 620 Pump-Action Repeating Shotgun. 12-, 16-, or 20-gauge, Takedown.

Winchester Model 25 Pump-Action, Solid-Frame Repeater

we have seen and tested throw the muzzle blast back in your ears and a few shots with any of them about deafens you for a day or so. We prefer the full use of our ears without any plugs or cotton, when hunting, to any and all compensators.

Pump Gun Disadvantages

Next, their faults. In the older models you had a fairly heavy gun, but today light-weight models are to be had in all popular gauges from 410 up to 12 bore. Next you have a long receiver extending from stock to barrel and there is no way of overcoming this feature. It does offer ample room for plenty of ornamentation but also greatly increases the over-all length of the gun as compared to any good double or single barrel. Then you have the long tubular magazine holding five shells without plug or two with plug. As these loads are fired the gun is constantly changing balance slightly, but hardly enough to be noticed. Forestock wood is usually thin and more susceptible to damage than the forestocks of double or single guns.

The long receiver and overall length of the pump gun is an advantage in difficult long range pass shooting but a distinct disadvantage for short range brush hunting. Even with a 26" barrel, about as short as barrels on shotguns should ever be made, the gun is several inches longer than a corresponding length of barrel double gun. Although the big receiver makes ample room for all kinds of engraving or inlay work in game scenes, the pump or out loader can never be given the clean lines of a fine double because of that big receiver, the tubular magazine, and the big fore-end so necessary for fast work. In spite of these faults it is a very efficient game or target buster in either pump or automatic type.

Now that we have such small bag limits, I can see little need for the extra shell in the pump gun and have always believed that anyone should be satisfied to fire a couple rounds into one rise of birds or one pair of passing ducks. However if that third shell is used as it should be to kill a possible cripple, then the extra load in the pump or auto can be made to pay dividends. All too often however it is thrown after a bird that is by then out of range and he is only wounded and lost. When one is killing crows or similiar pests then the full magazine is a very great asset and at one time L. L. Bean I believe furnished full length magazines to hold about ten rounds and these would be still better when in the thick of a well loaded crow roost or flight.

Selfloading Shotguns

Next we have the auto-loaders, very efficient guns from every viewpoint. They are a bit more expensive than a good pump gun as a rule and no faster, if as fast, on game when in the hands of an experienced shooter. They do eliminate any manual work except loading the weapon. Many of the faults of the pump gun also hold true with the automatic, namely the long heavy receiver and the big deep fore-end necessary to cover the tubular magazine. The large forestock is usually very thin and also fragile but it does not rattle when carried as is the case with the fore-ends or slides on some pump guns. Receivers of the older models were still more ugly and ungainly than the usual pump guns and looked too much like a machine gun to us. The auto loader shoots just as hard as any other shotgun, the answer to a question I am often asked.

I have tested and used all makes from the first heavy Brownings, Remingtons and Savages all made under the Browning patents and quite similar in quality and action. Also the Winchester Model 11 which we believe was not made under the Browning patent. This latter gun was more or less a failure, lost the Winchester Company a lot of money, and was finally discontinued. The action was actuated by pushing or pulling back on a knurled section of the barrel forward of the forestock. When properly adjusted it did good work but was prone to develop more faults and defects than any other auto-loading shotgun we have used. A common fault with this gun we noticed, when testing a great many for Uncle Sam, was the fact it would cut the cases in two at the front of the brass and spatter our forehead around the shooting glasses with burning powder and pieces of paper case.

One day while testing shotguns at Ogden Arsenal, a peculiar and very painful accident happened to one of our helpers named Buck Lee.

Lee and Mrs. Brockway were loading the various makes of guns and passing them to me from a truck while I did the test shooting, keeping them both busy. Buck was an ex cow-poke from southern Utah. Just as I finished testing a gun and started to pass it back to them and reach for another gun to test, Lee, in his slow southern drawl, asked, "Keith when you get time will you please help me get this damn rat-trap off my thumb?"

Looking around we found that Buck had gotten his right thumb into the ejection port when he pressed the release and the breech block had gone forward with a bang driving the long extractor right through the thumb nail and nearly through his thumb as well, bone and all. He had been using his thumb nail to reflect light in the bore and make sure it was clear before loading the magazine according to my orders, but had forgotten to remove his thumb in time to clear the slam of that breech block and extractor. We had the devil of a time getting that extractor out of his thumb as the hook on the end of it, undercut to hold the rim of the shell case, acted like the barb on a fish hook. With Alta Brockway helping we would jack the gun open, only to have it carry Bucks thumb back to the rear of the ejection port when he would let out a yell as his thumb hit the rear of the ejection port and the extractor hook really started tearing. We finally had to hold the breech block about half way back and literally kick his thumb off that hooked extractor. Buck was out of commission as far as work was concerned for some days from the badly torn and bruised thumb.

In spite of the many action faults this Winchester like all of them was a good shooting gun when it did operate. The Company dropped its manufacture long before the advent of their model 40, the first streamlined auto loading shotgun.

The early, heavy Remington, Browning and Savage autos were, and are still, all good guns and very efficient game killers; too efficient to our way of thinking. Their big square receivers with their abrupt overhang in front of the grip did offer a most excellent eye catcher in lieu of a rear sight and they not only fitted most men well but shot very well indeed and were exceptionally fast guns on a target for their weight. Remodelled for the 3″ magnum 12 bore shell by Kovalovsky, they are still today the most effective long range auto-loading duck and goose gun in existence. The actions do not open until the charge is out of the barrel, and when properly adjusted as to the friction rings are very pleasant to shoot; but if the said rings are set for light loads and heavy loads used in the gun, they can kick about as hard as any shotgun for the gauge and load. Cracked fore-ends seemed to be the most common of all breakages with these excellent guns.

We tested a great many at the arsenal and occasionally found one whose sear had been filed until it would machine-gun the five rounds in full automatic style. The first of these we hit we were standing to the rear of a big canvas covered army truck shooting the guns while two girls remained in the truck, checking the bores to see that they were clear and then loading five rounds into the magazine of standard 00 buck. This auto loader went full automatic and in spite of our best efforts to hang onto the thing it nearly tipped us over backwards, and we almost shot the rear hoop off the truck cover with the last round.

Just for the hell of it we decided to learn to shoot that gun full automatic and did so with the help of one of the girls. The girl would stand behind us and push hard on each shoulder with her hands while we got on the target and turned the brute loose. It seemed to have a very high rate of fire and with a bit of practice and someone to push hard and steady on the back of our shoulders we learned to keep the five loads of buckshot well on a man target at 50 yards. This stunt surely surprised the natives and some of the officers about the post, as we kept the gun hid out for a time and used it for demonstrations. However before long the armorers would mischieviously fix one up for us to go full automatic and we soon had plenty of them in that condition and new parts had to be fitted be-

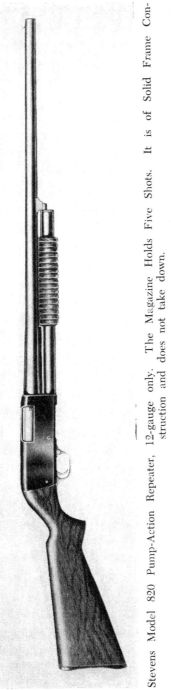

Stevens Model 820 Pump-Action Repeater, 12-gauge only. The Magazine Holds Five Shots. It is of Solid Frame Construction and does not take down.

Winchester Model 12 Pump Action Repeater.

fore some would stop machine-gunning on us. After that first one, however, we never did let one get away from us nor tip us over backwards again as we habitually leaned well into them from then on whenever an auto loader came up for test. As we tested 5000 in one lot alone and shot steadily for over two months, Sundays and all, to the tune of a case and a half to two and a half cases of those buckshot loads per day, and all from the shoulder, we learned a lot about the merits and shortcomings of the various repeating shotguns. At the start of this testing and when time permitted as we got ahead of the shop force on repairing them, we would have one helper throw empty cases as high in the air as possible and thus got in some wing shooting of a sort. Also occasionally a hawk would fly over the range and we would get him if close enough, and an occasional jack rabbit would also barge across the range at times and get in the way so to speak. We had several jacks do this and even with the ten shells from two guns poured on him he would miraculously escape any damage although the dust raised continuously all around him from the continued pounding of those heavy buckshot loads. These were some of the bright spots on what would otherwise have been a very tough job of hard work. We were working under General J. S. Hatcher who then headed Field Service of the Ordnance Department.

We believe the General would have forgiven us for these few breaks in the monotony of continuous shotgun testing had he been there, but the officers soon ruled out all aerial shooting as the Hill Field military planes took off and came directly over our testing range. We did have some fun by taking out each new batch of Junior officers who arrived at the post and letting them shoot some shotguns while we watched for defects in the functioning of the weapons. Some of them had shot before and would test four or five guns before recoil blacked their shoulders, while others would quit after a couple of guns with five rounds each. They all found that shooting at a stationary target was a lot different from wing or trap shooting, and some of them were bruised up until they did not report for duty for a week after a test session with those shotguns. The shop foreman and the officer in charge thought they would soon kill me off, but when the 5000 guns were completed, we were still calling for more guns to test.

We remember one time an M. P. outfit had to be equipped with the short pump riot guns by a certain time so they could entrain for their embarkation point for overseas service. The night before their departure, we tested guns far into the night, with the girls loading in the glare of the truck headlights and the fire flying in long streams from the gun muzzles. We stopped only for a quick meal those two days, but got the M. P. outfit on the road completely equipped on schedule. Needless to say both the armorers on the benches in the

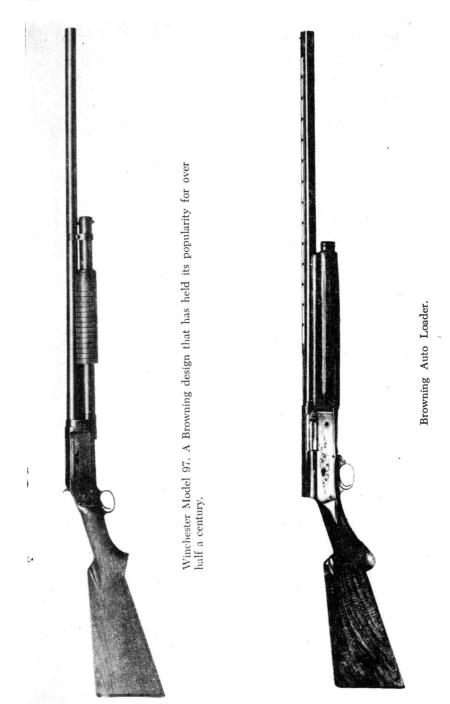

Winchester Model 97. A Browning design that has held its popularity for over half a century.

Browning Auto Loader.

small arms shop and my little test crew were entirely bushed by the time the job was finished.

Right here is a good time to point out the value of a shotgun for military use. For jungle fighting, close range trench fighting or night raiding of enemy lines it is extremely doubtful if there is a single weapon in the military service half as good as a short pump or auto loading shotgun and a haversack full of buckshot loads. The average American soldier is entirely familiar with pump or auto shotguns and used to shooting them prior to military service and when in a tight corner after dark, he will shoot them well by feel alone. The spread of 9 pellets of 00 buck is large enough to be rather certain on an enemy soldier up to 40 yards and sometimes beyond that, while at close range of a few feet the devastating effect of a charge of buck is not equalled by any other shoulder weapon. Many of my friends who fought through the Pacific show claim the pump or auto shotgun the best tool of all for much of that jungle fighting and particularly for night work. Some of them actually got as many as three of the enemy at one shot with the spread of their pattern. Night fighting is a dirty business and usually at close range. In the final analysis we believe a squad armed with pump or auto-loading short barrelled shotguns and plenty of buckshot per man will do more damage than a squad armed with any other small arm excepting of course an emplaced machine gun, in short range night fighting. A charge of buckshot at short range is rather final, to say the least. The shotgun is also a natural pointer.

Getting back to that Model 40 Winchester. It came out just before the war and as far as we were able to tell was well liked. We tested a good many of them at the Arsenal, as well as doing some shooting with one belonging to a Winchester Representative and found no functional fault with the gun whatever. It also was a natural pointer and shot very well. The receiver was the first to be really streamlined and had more the appearance of a good pump gun than the older auto-loaders we were then used to. The only serious defect we found in them at the Arsenal was the fact the stock bolt was a thin piece of tubing and prone to break off at the grip and at its junction with the frame in rough usage. Many came in for new tubular stock bolts. We still believe there must have been some way of remedying this serious defect in the design. However since the war Winchester has been calling them in wherever possible and replacing them with good Model 12 pump guns, so there must have been other reasons for their discontinuance. At any rate this first streamlined auto loader was destined to go the same way as the Model 720 Remington rifle, which appeared just before the war and then went out of existence.

A real improvement in auto-loaders is the new Remington model 11-48 and its twin the Sportsman 48. The former has a full five shot magazine and the latter a two shell magazine, making with one in the barrel a legal waterfowl gun with three shot capacity. This to our notion is the finest auto loader ever produced. We gave it every conceivable test in all kinds of weather down to 20 below zero and it still functioned perfectly.

The receiver is streamlined to the last degree and at a casual glance it appears to be a pump gun, not an automatic. Recoil is also greatly reduced over former models due to the fact the spring is flat in its contact with the magazine tube rather than round and being of square cross section, acts greatly to the shooter's benefit in cutting down recoil.

There is no high protruding hump in front of the grip on the Model 48, and the trigger guard is sloped into the receiver at the forward end. The breech block locks into the barrel extension just behind the cartridge and like their excellent model 870 Wingmaster pump gun the Remington -48 is a very simple easy gun to take down. Both 26″ and 28″ barrels are furnished and with about any degree of choke desired. Also any of the patent chokes or compensators can be fitted and used. It is furnished in standard, Deluxe and also in about any grade of fancy arm. The receiver and all parts are good sound steel and they have cut the weight to 7¼ pounds. Stock dimensions seem to fit a majority of shooters and we have yet to see a good shot who could not go right to work with a Remington Model 48. It is also made in 16 bore at 6½ pounds and 20 bore at 6¼ pounds weight. Matted or elevated ventilated ribs are to be had as well as any degree of engraving or ornamentation desired. Altogether, we believe the Remington 48 and the Sportsman 48 are two auto-loaders that will take a lot of beating.

Savage also made a bid for a more streamlined auto-loader in their excellent models 755 and 775. The rear end of the receiver in front of the top of the grip is nicely rounded off and these Savage autos have always been very fine performing guns. The 755 is a long range duck gun with a weight of about 8¼ pounds. The 775 is an alloy receiver light weight gun intended for upland work and a weight of around 6¾ pounds. Both models are to be had with various barrel lengths and in 12 and 16 gauge. Some few of these guns were made before the war, but with the start of hostilities this great company went on full war production of machine guns and British 303 Enfields.

Repeating shotguns are legion in number and we have made no attempt to cover all the later ones, as such a treatise would fill the book. Mossberg and Stevens both have bolt action clip loading repeaters in the smaller gauges and J. C. Higgins has a cross bolt repeater that look like an automatic. In the main these freak designs as well as the bolt action shotguns are all slow guns to operate in comparison with the conventional pump or auto loader, so we have not given them much space. They do fill a distinct need for the youngster and at a low price, enabling him or her to have a repeating shotgun and a good sound safe and good shooting gun at very low cost.

Just after World War I, the Germans manufactured a lot of 12 bore bolt action guns from their old Mauser service rifles. The receiver was hollowed out to take the larger barrel and the bolt had a false face added. These were never very successful and the bolt head was continually coming off as well as the extractors breaking. They were such a failure in comparison with the American Mossberg and Stevens as to need no further mention here.

Although the American seems to be going over more to the repeater, thank Allah, the English, Belgians, French and Italians still make and prefer fine doubles, so we will not be likely to see any shortage of double guns for those who prefer them. In this day of small bag limits and greatly decreased game supply, we believe all shooters would do well to fire but two shots at any rise of birds or passing flock of fowl and save that extra shell in their repeater for a possible cripple.

CHAPTER FOUR

Single Loaders

THERE ARE JUST TWO general classes of single shot shot-guns, the highly specialized and finely made trap gun, with every conceivable extra that will in any way help break more targets, and the cheap single shot for the youngster.

Fine trap guns in single barrel design are made by a great many gun builders over the world. In this country, L. C. Smith, Baker, Parker, Lefevre, Ithaca, all made fine trap guns and some of the lesser lights, such as Iver Johnson, Stevens etc., turned out creditable one barrel guns. In Britain, most of the better gun builders made fine specialized trap guns, and on the Continent the same is true. More money is put up and more wagered in trap shooting than in any other form of competitive shooting today, hence it has a following of well-to-do sportsmen, able to pay for anything their hearts desire in the way of the trap gun, and if they can think of anything whatever that will add a couple dead birds to their score they will have it.

Trap shooting has also furthered the building of other fine guns. the development of better ammunition and the utmost efforts in gun boring, chambering and choking of said bores.

Trap shooting has also greatly influenced stock design. Many of the extras we use and enjoy today can be traced directly to the art of trap shooting, such as the elevated ventilated rib, the Monte Carlo trap comb, the check piece on American guns, the double ivory sights, the ejectors and to some extent at least the single trigger as well as the recoil pads.

Trap guns take an awful beating as they fire many thousands of rounds per year. They must have the most perfect of bolting to withstand the constant strain of firing as well as the greater strain of being snapped shut. Though no double or single loader should be *snapped* shut, that is the way a great many shooters close their gun with consequent wear on the bolts and hinge pin. Much also has been learned of shotgun bolting as applied to all single and double barrel guns, due to trap shooting. The trap gun takes more of a beating as to its bolting and locks in one year than most game guns will receive in a lifetime. This in turn has taught the gun makers a great deal of what is necessary to make up a fine and lasting arm. Trap shooting has also taught the gun makers more of stock fit, as well as rib and stock pitch than any other form of shotgun shooting today. So all of us who like to shoot the shotgun owe much to the trap shooting game. Sure, it's just a game, but a very highly specialized one, and he who would compete in it has much to learn of gun handling and fit before he will become proficient enough to win any money.

Professional trap shots early learned the necessity of individual fitting of their guns, hence the wide variations one sees today in the dimensions of trap gun stocks, boring, trigger pulls, and sights, as well as rib and stock pitch.

Most fine single trap guns have long barrels, as long barrels give more accurate gun pointing. Many of the best trap shots stick to the 34 inch barrel. Long barrels not only give a long sighting plane and aid accurate pointing but also hold the charge of shot together for a greater distance. As modern shotgun powders usually burn in the first foot, or a little over, of the barrel, pressure, and especially the muzzle blast is greatly reduced at the muzzle of a 34 inch barrel over that of a gun with less barrel length. Hence patterns are less affected by over-powder wads being driven into or through the charge at the muzzle. Gas pressures which are less at the muzzle of a long barrel also further good patterns to some extent, hence the long barrels on the professional trap shot's favorite single gun.

As such guns are mounted and the head dropped forward on the stock just so, each and every time before the bird is called for, they are as a rule far too straight for game guns. Likewise most trap guns have sufficient rib pitch to throw the pattern 8" to 10" high at 35 yards, to automatically take care of fast raising targets. For these reasons they seldom make good game guns. However, when a trap gun is not stocked too straight and does not have excessive rib pitch it is usually a very fine gun in standard 12 bore for pass shooting. We once had an ancient No. 4 Ithaca old model single trap 12 bore that was a whale of a good shooting gun and we used it on pheasants a great deal. Also for some pass mallard shooting and the only fault found with the gun was the fact it had no safety at all which we did not like in the field.

Trap guns are made without safeties for the very good reason that should the shooter ever accidentally put the safety on, in a match and fail to push it off, he would no doubt miss his bird, and also all chances for any prize money in that match; so practically all trap guns come without safeties. The gun is supposed to be broken and left open until time for the shooter's next shot, a very good ruling. Such guns if fitted with a safety and not stocked too straight for field use make one of the most delightful guns imaginable for single bird shooting in upland work, especially fairly long range pheasant shooting. We once knew an old trap shot who had such a 34 inch barrelled Ithaca, who was one of the most deadly pheasant shots we ever have seen; for we never remember him missing a pheasant or sharp tail grouse within 50 yards to 55 yards range. He simply killed them all.

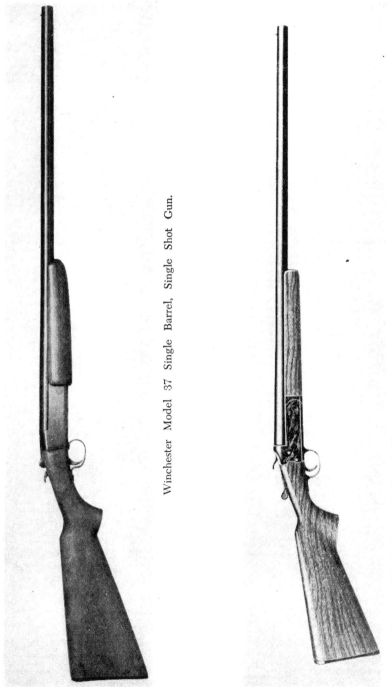

Winchester Model 37 Single Barrel, Single Shot Gun.

Stevens Model 94 Single Barrel Shotgun. It is Available in 12, 16, 20, and 410 Gauge, Takedown.

He was not a particularly fast shot, but he was absolutely deadly. He shot entirely by the swing and lead methods he had employed at the trap and after the bird season was over he simply removed his safety slide and used the same gun for his trap shooting. He won plenty of money with that old long tom.

Many trap shots are as finicky about their stock fit as an old hen with a single chick. Some of them are continually changing the drop at comb or at the heel. Many trap stocks have been cut down and built up again and again cut down or cut into until they resemble a piece of inlaid veneer furniture. Some of them, when they have a bad day, lay all blame on their stocks and immediately lower or raise the comb or change the pitch or the heel drop. Then they usually have some more bad runs and wind up by having the stock put back about where it was in the first place and probably by the glueing on of another comb and also a piece of wood glued on the butt under the pad. Such stock butchery adds nothing to the appearance of a fine gun, and very often little to the score of the shooter and it is a much better procedure to select a comb and heel drop that is right in the first place by trying out several different guns, then stick with that stock and really learn to shoot it.

Many trap shots are just as finicky about their trigger pulls and will have them changed time and again; so all told, the trap shot is the gunsmith's meal ticket. Just the same they have brought about most of the improvements in shotguns for many years, just as the rifle crank has developed most of the new items in rifle cartridges and rifle stocks.

They also experiment just as much with their forcing cones and chokes at times. What they want is that even 30 inch spread of pattern with no single hole in it at the average range at which they break their targets and they will go to any amount of work or expense to get just that. Some fine trap shots will want the very utmost in patterns for handicap shooting. Out at the longer yardage they need the ultimate and then their work is well justified. Some will have a few thousandths of the choke ground out and shoot it a while, then they decide they need more choke, so will have the barrel recess choked to give it smaller and tighter pattern and so it goes.

Our friend George Turner has another trap shooting friend with an old No. 7 Ithaca from which about all the forcing cone has been removed by draw boring and polishing. That is the craziest shooting 12 bore we ever have heard of, as George has seen it repeatedly put the entire charge in a 30 inch circle at 40 yards and for a full 100% and sometimes in a 24 inch circle at 40 yards and usually the 24 inch circle takes in most of the pattern. George Turner, who is known as the Bandit from New Mexico, as he usually garners in his share of the dinero, says that is the finest shooting shotgun he, or anyone he knows, has ever seen; and of course no amount of money could buy it. It has the long 34 inch barrel.

Lock time is a very important item in the fine trap gun. Ithaca claims their lock operates in 1/625th of a second. Certainly trap gun locks are made to operate as fast as possible and with as clean a trigger pull as money and ingenuity can produce. Joe Heistand's long record run on registered targets should well indicate their claims as being correct. Whether the Ithaca lock is any faster than other good trap gun locks, or as fast, for that matter, we do not pretend to know, but if records mean anything, then their claims seem well substantiated. There can be no question but that a very fast lock does cut down the amount of lead necessary and also furthers the breaking of the targets at closer ranges. Even more important in all probability is a clean breaking uniform trigger pull. Trap gun locks are usually polished like the works in a fine watch, and with good reason. Thus we see the demands of the professional trap shots have had a great bearing on the development of better shooting shotguns, and better patterning ammunition.

Although patterns and chokes will be taken up separately, we believe all prospective trap shots would do well to borrow a single trap gun that fits them that is equipped with a Poly Choke. Then they should shoot patterns with that gun with the various degrees of choke and compare them with the known ranges at which they usually break their targets and thus find out exactly what degree of choke best fits their individual speed of swing and lead on the clays. This pattern shooting will also teach them much of the normal elevation of the pattern as well as the spread of the charge. They can set the device to give them about anything they wish in spread at any given range. Such experimenting will enable them to order a trap gun that will not only fit them but which will be bored expressly for the range they wish to break their targets. While the things add nothing to the lines and beauty of a gun, they are very efficient devices and enable the trap shot to change his choke at will, at an instant's notice.

Thus if he has been shooting 16 yard targets and wishes to move back to a longer handicap range, he can set his Poly Choke to give him a closer pattern at the new range.

This practice shooting will also help the new shooter decide whether he wants a straight or a pistol grip stock, and in the absence of a good stock fitter is the next best way to find out such things before buying the gun. Although a great many fine trap shots use pump, auto loading or double barrelled guns for standard trap shooting, we believe the highly specialized single trap gun will always have a place on the gun rack at such shoots and will also always be among the top shooters in such events.

The cheap single barrel shotgun is the one best gun for most youngsters to start with. It will often shoot about as well as any shotgun, is light in weight, and the youngster soon learns that he or she has but the one shot and must kill with it or lose the game. When a person knows that but one shot is available, he is soon apt to make the best possible use of that single shot. This results in careful gun pointing. The single-shot is also the best gun for the youngster from the standpoint of safety.

Whether the gun be a hammer or hammerless model makes little difference. Sometimes we think the hammer model is the safer as they can see instantly if the gun is safe or cocked. On the other side of the picture is the fact that the safety slide can be moved from safe to fire or back with no danger of an accidental discharge, while with the hammer models the trigger must be pulled while the hammer is held by the thumb and let down to safe. This fact causes many accidental discharges not possible with the hammerless models. The hammer models may also cause some accidental discharges by having the hammer catch on a fence, brush, or trailing vines where the smooth hammerless gun would not catch at all.

We were once in the hospital at St. Paul, Minn. at the same time a boy was brought in with only his upper right arm left from pulling such a hammer single out of a boat by grasping its muzzle. Although that happened 36 years ago, the Stevens Arms Co. was even then furnishing most excellently balanced and designed hammerless singles with automatic ejectors. Though dangerous gun handling caused the accident, nevertheless it would not have happened with a hammerless gun.

What such a 12 gauge single can do to a man at close range is a caution. Not long before the war we had a gunfight in the Pahsimeroi valley. Three men involved, all friends of ours. The Swede named Hanson had gone berserk over his wife's leaving him, and took up station in the house with a single barrel 12 bore shotgun. Young Bradley was with the late Julius Maelzer as they walked unknowingly toward the house. The Swede met them in the door and fired point blank at Bradley's head but he twisted just enough to save his life, though the charge peeled his scalp away from the skull the full length of one side of his head, dropping him in a pool of blood in the door yard. The Swede dropped the empty 12 bore single and grabbed up a 22 caliber repeater as Julius ran a few yards and threw himself into an irrigation ditch for cover. Julius had a Colt Woodsman in a shoulder holster for jack rabbits. A very poor gun for use in a gun fight, but as it was all he had to save both his own and Bradley's life he did the best he could. The Swede sniped at his every movement in the grass of the ditch bank from the cover of the door jam, but Julius Maelzer finally managed to pink the Swede through the arm, making him drop the rifle, then jumped up and got the drop on him. As he was taking him out through the corral, young Bradley regained consciousness, followed them and grabbing a pitch fork, crowned the

5E Grade Ithaca Single Barrel Trap Gun.

Swede with it, using a round house swing which put the Swede to sleep for some time. They both required some patching up after the sheriff got them to town and a stay in the hospital. A much happier ending than most gun fights in this country.

Many of the earlier single barrel cheap shotguns were choked by simply swaging down the barrel, the actual amount of choke often being a mystery. Some of them with excessive choke would kick like two wild mules but threw cartwheel patterns. We remember one boy friend who while crawling up on a bunch of mallards with us managed to fill his gun muzzle with mud. We jumped up as the flock of ducks rose and each picked a duck. We killed our greenhead alright, but noticed a peculiar report from our friend's gun. Turning around we found him sitting in the mud with some six inches of his gun muzzle simply gone. Just how he was to keep his folks from learning of the accident we did not at the time know. However we found a hacksaw in the blacksmith shop and cut the barrel off clean and smooth at the muzzle. It then scattered shot all over the scenery about like my earlier Remington musket, so he drove the muzzle of the barrel down into the hub of some sort of early buggy, that he found there, thus giving it some choke. Then a gunsmith friend drilled and tapped the barrel and fitted a new front sight and strange to say the old gun shot about as well as ever. His father noticed the shortness of the piece but though he looked at us with a critical eye at times when we again went hunting he never asked us what had happened. We believe however, he must have known, for he found the old buggy hub and the piece of two by four we had driven the barrel down with after removing stock and foreend. At any rate we noticed him pick them up and then glance at the shortened shotgun.

I suppose he believed we had learned our lesson and there was no use to say anything further on the subject.

Those early single barrel days bring back some of the most pleasant memories of our youth. Thirty-five years ago the Helena Meat Co. paid 20 cents each for cottontails and forty cents each for the big white Jackrabbits in season, so after the duck and grouse seasons were ended and winter had set in, we would spend all our time Saturdays and Sundays when out of school, running a trap line and hunting rabbits. A kindly neighbor had two shotguns. One a very fancy fully engraved 12 bore Marlin side ejection hammer pump and the other a cheap Monkey-Ward single Long Tom, with a 40″ barrel in 12 bore. He would always loan us the old Long Tom, so I used it a lot. To this day we have never seen a 12 bore gun that would throw as close a pattern of No. 2 shot as that ungainly weapon. It was our Jackrabbit gun. The big hares would feed at night, then dig out a bed under a sage brush and hole up for the day and when jumped they simply bounced into full flight and how they could run. We early learned to pick them up and swing and lead them as we shot and when the charge of No. 2 shot which we used exclusively for them, caught up, and the big bunny would start to roll into a ball and turn somersaults, it was a thrilling experience.

They were very heavy, running from eight to twelve pounds and two or three of them were always a load for a skinny youngster, but 40 cents was a lot of money in those days. Sometimes we hunted them with a model 1890 Winchester .22 Special and still remember the first one we turned over in full flight. The rifle was much lighter to carry and better for the cottontails and we soon learned to make it very hot for the big John rabbits with the rifle regardless of their speed, so quit borrowing the Long Tom for rabbits from then on. If we wounded a rabbit, we would methodically trail him up and jump him again on the snow and finally add him to the bag, then trudge the long ten miles back to town with our kill.

One day a friend was hunting with us and carrying a 16 bore hammerless Stevens shotgun. He jumped a big white John rabbit and bowled him over in great style but the bunny was caught too far back with the charge of shot and was still alive when we caught up with him and pulling himself along with his front feet as a wounded elk or deer would do. My friend ran up after reloading and with the gun in one hand brought the butt of the stock down hard in a tamping motion on the rabbit's head. It killed the rabbit alright, but the gun went off as he had no doubt pushed the safety ahead again and the charge took one side of his cap out and also some of the hair from that side of his head just back of the right ear. No shot touched his skin, but he was well blackened from the black powder load and learned his lesson. He threw away the remains of his cap and bound his ears in my silk scarf for the rest of the hunt. We kept absolutely mum about the accident and this is the first time it has been mentioned to a soul, though it happened over 35 years ago.

Another time, Father hitched up the trotting mare to the old spring wagon and with a friend, Dick Tinker, then also a youth of Helena, we drove out around the Scratch Gravel hills for sage hens and jackrabbits. That day we did not jump any of the big sage grouse in range but did jump plenty of John rabbits and made a killing as we had only to pack them a short distance to the spring wagon. Dick's father, who survives him, had just given Dick a brand new model '97 12 bore pump Winchester and he was very proud of it. Both father and the writer made many clean kills on the big Jacks that day, but Dick managed to miss every one, seeming always to be shooting behind them. As we were spread out at 200 yard intervals, walking back toward the spring wagon for the cold drive home in the gathering winter dusk, Dick suddenly stopped, spread his long legs on either side of a big sage brush and slowly pushed the muzzle of his long full choked pump gun down into the bush. Then he shot and out kicked a big white bunny, sans head and ears.

Dick said he intended to make sure of that one so shoved the gun down within two inches of the Jacks neck and let her go. Just why that fool rabbit thought he was still hidden will ever remain one of the dim mysteries.

Another fall day, in late season, after the lake had frozen, but the warm pot holes were still open, two other lads and the writer had hiked down to the warm sloughs above the lake. The ducks were flying in great style, from one warm pot hole to another and enough hunters were about to keep them moving. Again we were using that Long Tom 12 bore single and did right well that day with it on those high flying ducks. Though we did most of the killing with the Long Tom, the three of us were well loaded with ducks and completely tired out by the time we reached the N. P. Railroad yards. We had unloaded our guns and were just passing a brick residence of some railroad man when a huge English bull dog ran out and made a dive for the seat of our pants. Our two companions took off in a great sprint, but never being any shakes as a runner, we had no chance and the huge dog was soon on us. Whirling around, we rammed that Long Tom down his throat just as he sprang for us. Then pushing as hard as we could we continued to drive that long barrel down into his tummy. He finally backed off the gun, sat down and coughed a couple of times and turning around walked slowly back to the house. When we arrived home we found 16 inches of froth frozen on the outside of the gun barrel. Afterwards, that dog never made another run at us, though we passed his residence many times on the way to or from the lake.

After moving to Idaho, we did considerable pass shooting on Mallards along the Snake river. The big fowl flew high and well out but we had a little brown Irish spaniel that would dive in and get them and finally drift out a quarter mile below. We tried many guns on those ducks. They had been shot at enough to know to a nicety the range of a standard 12 bore gun and though we killed some with our old 16 bore Ithaca and more with our brother's Model '97 Winchester we simply could not reach them in most cases. Finally we swapped for an English 10 bore single with a very heavy twist barrel 36 inches long. This piece we hand-loaded with 1½ ounces of No. 3 shot and enormous charges of black powder in the long brass cases. It did the business and we killed many mallards to a full 80 yards. If we got the lead right a duck had little chance at 70 yards. That shooting taught us much of pass shooting in general.

One day a big grey bird came along that we supposed was some kind of a goose, so swinging with him and then on ahead we cut loose with the big ten bore and he pitched into the river. The little spaniel finally made it out and grabbed him by the neck, after which she wisely drifted with the current and angled to the shore with the big bird. Immediately we saw his head was different than any other goose we had seen and soon decided we had killed a loon. Thinking to have some fun, we packed him home and told Mother we had killed a goose.

She immediately picked up her wash tub to save the feathers, spread a newspaper over her lap and started to pluck the bird. She had no luck at all, the feathers simply would not come out from her best efforts and she said "Elmer I don't believe this is a goose at all,— I never before saw a goose I couldn't pick." We told her then what it was. Taking it out to the orchard where we had a pet brown bear on a chain, we gave it to Bobby. The little bear rushed up and grabbed the loon with a growl. Biting deep into the breast he put a paw on that tough fowl and pulled with all his might. His teeth simply clicked together and he didn't even break the skin. Nothing daunted he placed a fore paw on each end of the fowl and proceeded to bite and chew until he got a good hold on the bird's breast, then he tugged upwards with all his might. Again his teeth clicked together and only a feather between his teeth rewarded his best efforts. In utter disgust, he gave the fowl a slap with his left paw that sent it sailing away and stalked back into his barrel and went to sleep.

Formerly a great many cheap single barrel shotguns were made in this country by Savage-Stevens, Hopkins & Allen, Iver Johnson, Harrington & Richardson, and many others. They served a very useful purpose in teaching the kids of that time to shoot and to handle a gun safely and we still believe they are the one best gun for the youngster. Some are still made in this country, by Savage-Stevens, Winchester in their model 37, H & H, Iver Johnson, Western Field etc. The Winchester model 37 is one of the best of them all if not the best. For the youngster, or the man wanting a good shooting gun at a minimum of cost they are still the best bet. Often big game expeditions want a cheap shotgun along for birds for the pot and such a cheap single will usually fill the bill, also the pot, very nicely and when taken down rolls up in the bed roll. If a pack horse rolls on it and damages the gun you are not out much and if said nag rolls into a river and is lost the gun is no great loss.

The Germans made many fine single barrel shotguns of the top-break variety and this country has also produced some in bolt action persuasion like the new 185 model Mossberg, which however is also a repeater with a clip magazine, complete with patent adjustable choke and compensator, a very good shooting low cost gun to sell at under $30. However such bolt actions are slow to reload and are not much advantage over the single gun, except that the next round is readily loaded by the stroke of the bolt and while they are faster to reload for the second shot, they are usually too slow in manipulation for a second shot at the same bird, should the first miss.

The English have made some fine singles, usually with better workmanship than machine-made American low cost singles. They also have a folding single barrel gun, sold by W. J. Jeffery & Co. of London, that is very handy for long trips as it can be rolled up in the bed roll. It simply folds up as the barrel can be tipped on over and folds back against the stock.

In these days of small bag limits one can soon fill his limit with the single loader if any birds are about and the youngster is not now so badly handicapped with one as formerly when a great deal more game was to had. They also give the game a fair chance for its life and a lot of fun can be had with a good single. Practically all are now made with automatic ejectors and one can reload very quickly. They offer a good shooting gun at a very minimum of cost. They are also suitable for installation of the Poly or other patent chokes making them useful for about any type of shooting if of a suitable gauge.

Along the East Coast poachers still use very heavy large bore punt guns, illegally, for flock shooting of rafted ducks for the market (or black market, we should say). Some of them are of enormous bore, but now thanks to Federal law they are becoming ever more scarce and such duck poachers should be given life sentences when caught at such depredations to our fast diminishing wild fowl. In England such guns are still in use they tell me and the English still have about as many fowl as ever. However in England only the higher classes have the opportunity or money to shoot to any extent, hence the reason for their continued wildfowl population. Such swivel guns when mounted on the bow of a boat or raft and loaded with from a quarter to a half pound of heavy shot were very destructive to the ducks. The boats or rafts were camouflaged with reeds or grass or cattails and allowed to slowly drift down on a raft of sleeping or feeding fowl and when in certain range the poacher fired them into the flock killing and wounding hundreds of fowl. Such poachers are beyond comprehension.

CHAPTER FIVE

Gauges and Their Use

TIME WAS, when the 10-bore was considered the standard shotgun gauge in this country and everyone had to have a ten bore to amount to anything in society. The ten bore was popular as a muzzle loader and still more so in the eighties and nineties, and well into this century, as a breech loader. At that time this country was alive with all manner of waterfowl and on the prairie grass lands the prairie chickens simply swarmed. Turkey were also plentiful in many sections and geese as well. Market hunting was the order of the day for many, and for those that did not shoot for the market, the table had to be supplied. In those days the shotgun or rifle, or both, supplied most of the families with meat as they moved westward and pushed the Indians back, gradually settling up this great country. A good gun was then a necessity for every family to supply most of the table meat and for many who market hunted to supply the city dwellers.

We well remember our uncle, Olander Beery taking us out of the house one evening and pointing up in a huge tree that stood in one corner of his Missouri yard. He said he had fired both barrels of his old ten bore muzzle loader into a flock of passenger pigeons in that tree and he and aunt Mary had picked up and dressed over 30 of the birds from that one double discharge. He was an old Confederate veteran and had fought under Quantrel. He was finally wounded and invalided home at the battle of Lexington. Said they were rolling cotton bales toward the northern fort, two men to a bale. He had just reached up above the bale of cotton to start a bullet down his old muzzle loading squirrel rifle, when a Minnie ball took him through the shoulder. He hunted for the market for a time and later went into the livestock business. To Uncle Lander as we called him, anything but a ten gauge was simply a pop gun.

When I was a small youngster, in Missouri, most hardware stores carried black powder and all sizes of shot in bulk and you could buy as little as a nickel's worth of each if you wished. The Darkies usually had an old single barrel muzzle loader of some sort and they very often bought in about that quantity. They would await a large flock of ducks or geese on the pond or bend in the river and crawl up to short range, then simply decimate the flock by ground sluicing them. The idea seemed more to kill as many as possible with the least expenditure of ammunition, than any thought of sportsmanship. It was simply a job to be done, and they hunted in both spring and fall on the waterfowl population.

Even today if one had much duck and goose shooting to do the present version of the old ten bore would be one of the best possible guns to use if you preferred a double. In the old days only 1¼ ounces of shot comprised the standard ten bore load but most muzzle loaders were loaded heavier. Today that 1¼ ounces is simply our standard 12 bore load. However our present Super Ten bore load with 1⅝ ounces of shot is about the best all around duck and goose gun possible to procure. If the shooter prefers a pump or automatic then he can get the fine Winchester Model 12 in Magnum 12 bore using the 3″ shell with the same shot load or have Arthur Kovalovsky remodel a heavy Remington, Savage or Browning 12 bore auto loader to handle the long 3″ shells.

That is the proper load for all-around duck and goose gun where the shooting is at heavy well feathered birds and often out to 70 yards range. Those one and five eighths ounce loads of No. 4 shot for ducks and twos or better threes for geese will kill more of the fowl cleanly than will any smaller gauges or shot loads, if we had plenty of shooting as was formerly the case. Even with our tiny five bird bag limit at present, more fun can be had by bagging those five birds and no good pass with a ten bore or Magnum 12 than with anything smaller.

As an all-around gun the ten bore, also the Magnum 12 as well, are now replaced by the standard 1¼ ounce 2¾″ 12 bore. However if you want an all-around duck and goose gun then nothing smaller will equal the Super ten or the Magnum 12 with 1⅝ ounces of shot.

For pass shooting alone, both the Super ten and the Magnum 12 must take a back seat to the big Magnum ten bore throwing a full two ounces of shot, size No. 3 preferably. This big gun, the largest allowed by Federal law, is the finest tool for pass shooting we have ever used and we have been shooting one now for a good many years. It will take passing single ducks out to a full 80 yards with the above load, something no smaller shotgun can ever do regularly and more fun can be had killing a few birds at such long range than by killing triple the amount of ducks over decoys at close range. It is the tool for the finished wing shot who loves long range pass shooting.

The gun is heavy, usually a minimum of 10½ pounds, and some weigh up to 13 pounds and the barrels are long—from 32 to 34 inches. Such a gun is not for the poacher as it is too heavy, has too heavy a recoil and the report can be heard for miles. Ammunition is also expensive, but by picking out and killing singles or occasionally a double at long range, more fun is to be had from the big gun on ducks and geese than any smaller weapon will produce. It is a gun for the finished shot and a very sporting weapon, but is too heavy and slow for jump shooting and throws entirely too heavy a charge for average shotgun work. Where turkeys, geese or long range ducks are the order of the day nothing else will equal it or afford as much keen pleasure. Every man who likes long range waterfowl shooting and is good enough shot to master the big gun, should have one or a Super Ten or Magnum 12 for such work. Used as it should be for pass shooting and in a sportsmanlike manner it will not wound and lose a fraction as many ducks as will the average gunner trying to pound the birds out of range of a standard 12 or smaller weapon.

The big ten bores and the Magnum 12 should always be had in full choke persuasion and bored to throw the closest possible patterns with two ounces of threes in the Magnum ten with its long Roman candle loads of 3½" case, and 1⅝ ounces of fours in the two smaller guns. These are long range guns and should be used as such. For geese and turkeys the two ounce load might as well be No. 3 shot and never larger than No. 2 and for the 1⅝ ounces loads No. 3 would probably be the best of all for the big birds or at the largest No. 2 shot. There is no horse sense in loading these big guns with any smaller shot. If these big loads could be standardized to the extent of loading with just No. 2 and No. 3 shot in the two ounce load and No. 3 and No. 4 shot in the 1⅝ ounce loads cheaper ammunition might be the end result.

Next we have the standard 12 bore with 2¾" case and loaded with either 1⅛ ounces or 1¼ ounces of shot. This is the best all around bore. The English will have nothing else and even go to such extremes as loading a one ounce load of shot in a 2 inch case for the 12 bore and making guns as light as 6 pounds in double barrel guns. We never could see this crazy fad of such an extreme light weight 12 bore, or for that matter, such light loads. If one is to use only an ounce of shot then the 20 bore gun is big enough to handle it and if he wants but 1⅛ ounces then the 16 bore gun will do all with it that any 12 bore will do. Some may take exception to these statements, and theoretically the larger gauge should deform less shot but based on many hundreds of patterns run and carefully counted we would take the lighter weight one ounce load in a 20 bore and the 1⅛ ounce load in a 16 bore and we have yet to see any 12 bore throw higher percentage patterns than two Ithaca sixteen bores we have used with 1⅛ ounces of shot.

We believe only 1⅛ ounces and 1¼ ounces of shot should be loaded in the standard 12 bore and these all in the standard (in America at least) 2¾ inch case. Thus the 12 bore man has a choice of a light 3¼ dram powder 1⅛ ounce load for light or average shooting and the heavier 3¾ dram equivalent with 1¼ ounces of shot for harder or longer range shooting or larger birds. The standard 12 bore gun with 1¼ ounces of shot size five or six will kill ducks or grouse or pheasants to a full 60 yards in full choke regularly and with the lighter loads is also an equally good killer on all smaller upland game to about 50 yards, sometimes to 55 yards. For our own use we would standardize on one shot load and that to be 1¼ ounces only. This shot load will always give better patterns than the 1⅜ ounce load and we believe the latter should be left to the 16 bore. Of course trap loads are now standardized at 1⅛ ounces, which calls for a terrific amount of this shot charge to be loaded by the companies, but we still believe the 12 bore gun should be loaded with 1¼ ounces only for game shooting. If a man is to pack a 12 bore gun all day then he should have 12 bore loads for it, not necessarily all heavy loads by any means for when the shooting is under 50 yards the low base lighter powder load is equally effective on most game except on tough birds like ducks and pheasants. For these the heavy duck loads will always prove best, if shots are to be taken beyond 45 yards. Under that range the lighter powder load is ample for any feathered game we are likely to shoot. Time was when the trap load contained 1¼ ounces of shot and it was a better patterning trap load than has ever been produced in the 1⅛ ounce charge.

For most decoy and cornfield shooting, the 3¼ dram powder load with 1¼ ounces of No. 6 shot will kill all the fowl any man is allowed in short order. We well remember, when the duck limit was 20 birds, a certain cornfield near the Payette River in southern Idaho. Only mallard appeared but they were in such large numbers that we shot only greenheads. Those birds simply could not be driven from that cornfield by one dog and gun and we had no trouble killing a limit of greenheads. We used only the low base 12 bore load with 1¼ ounce of sixes and 3¼ drams of powder and that was all the load anyone needed for that shooting; in fact a 20 or a 16 bore would have been ample and have done equally well. The birds came in for their corn, come Hell or high water, and though the corn patch was blanketed with a six inch fall of snow the fowl had used it so long they were determined to have their corn. One flock after another would swing in for their evening feed from the river. We have never seen better duck shooting. Two days on the field produced all the ducks we wanted to eat that season. The shooting was usually at about 35 to 40 yards range and we killed one limit of 20 greenheads with just 26 shells, and really should have done better as it was the easiest duck shooting we have ever enjoyed, but at that not half as much fun as killing five or six out at long range on a good pass with the big ten bore. There were no cripples as we picked out greenheads only and only those out on the edge of each flock and killed a double and then waited for the next flock to come in. Those we missed were fast turning birds that had seen us but we should have done better shooting at such short range.

When the shooting is at such close ranges, there is no need to pound the birds with heavy duck loads; they should be saved for the long shots.

Peters Cartridge Co. used to load a cheap yellow paper case low base trap load with 3 drams bulk powder and 1¼ ounces of No. 7½ shot. That was the best load we ever used in a standard 12 bore for quail, doves or snipe and we fail to see how it could be improved on for that small bird shooting. It was cheap and we bought it in case lots and the recoil was negligible. From that full choked No. 4 Ithaca we then used it took all birds to a full 50 yards with a good hold and often a bit farther out on doves. It would, however, throw the entire pattern under the spread of my hand at 20 yards, so birds had to be waited out with that gun until they had reached the 35 yard range at least. Later we used the same load on doves from a Poly Choke equipped 12 bore and then by opening up the choke to improved cylinder it was just right for all small bird fast close range shooting. The big pattern made hitting much easier and birds could be taken before they could dodge around some clump of brush. We would cheerfully use that load against all others for such small birds the rest of our lives in a standard 12 bore, if we were content to use that gauge.

Light to moderate bulk powder loads are all that is needed for most shooting to 45 yards, from there on out to 60 yards the progressive burning powder heavy duck loads should be the order of the day. More 12 bore guns are in use than any other gauge and it is probable that more 12s are used than all other gauges combined. That fact is one reason why we have such a prolific list of 12 bore loads available. The standard trap and live pigeon gun has long been the 12 bore. The old load was 1¼ ounces, however, and just why the 16 bore has not come in for standard trap shooting since the change to 1⅛ ounce loads we do not know. As long as one is restricted to 1⅛ ounces of shot we would take the 16 bore gun and believe when properly bored it will do the job just as well as the 12 bore with that shot load.

12 bore trap loads are available at all shoots hence the 12 bore is commonly used but if 16 bore loads were used and available we think many shooters, especially small men and women, might do just as well or better with the 16 bore. Though of course the light 1⅛ ounce 12 bore trap load would in turn become the heavy duck load for the 16 bore. Long strings at the traps would produce of course less recoil with a heavy 12 bore trap gun than with a light 16 bore gun, but given an equal weight in a 16 bore trap gun it should produce about the same results with the same shot load. Standard trap shooting recognizes only the standard 12 bore gun and load but Skeet recognizes the smaller bore guns and each is classed separately even down to the little .410 bore. While

1¼ ounce loads in the 16 bore would require the heavy progressive duck load, the same load in the 12 bore is a light one. Just another reason for its continued usage as a trap gun and load.

When the 12 bore man turns his attention to ducks and geese and long range pheasants, he needs the heavy duck loads as shooting is very often out to a full 60 yards. If he uses a repeater, he can well fit it with a patent choke such as the Poly Choke and make the gun equally useful for quail at short ranges or ducks at long ranges, simply by changing from improved cylinder or modified to full choke and the use of the light trap loads for quail and heavy duck loads for the long range game shooting. Thus the standard 12 bore becomes a very versatile weapon. The double gun man can have one barrel bored more open than the other and also have a very good all around shotgun. He can use it on any type of game to a full 60 yards with proper loads, or can go right into a registered trap shoot with the same gun if he so desires. Thus for the man who wishes but one shot gun and who may do diversified shooting all the way from quail and snipe or woodcocks and ruffed grouse as well as duck and pheasant shooting and possibly some trap work as well, the 12 bore is the gauge to choose.

For long range ducks, pheasants or sage hens, only heavy duck loads of 1¼ ounces should be used and the shot sizes needed are fours, fives, and sixes. No other sizes are required and we could get along very well with these three sizes and No. 7½ for trap and small birds for everything up to geese and turkeys. When the standard 12 bore is to be used on such large powerful fowl, we believe the load should usually be No. 3 shot rather than No. 2 as threes make so much better pattern for the 12 bore standard load and will carry pellet energy even on big birds out far beyond the patterning range of any standard 12 bore gun. Why threes are not loaded for geese in the 12 bore more than No. 2 is beyond us for they are a better load from every standpoint for the 1¼ ounce gun. Any man doubting this need only fire ten shots at pattern paper at 40 yards with each size and count up the percentages and also note the density of his pattern to know the truth. The 12 bore standard goose shooting is about all done at 60 yards anyway and threes will give him a fairly dense pattern for the big birds where twos are much thinner in pattern and far fewer shot will register. You can cut out goose silhouettes and nail them over a pattern paper and measure off 60 yards and shoot with both sizes of shot and if this is done we believe most shooters will demand No. 3 shot for their 1¼ ounce goose loads.

The poor or average shot will do better work on game with the 12 bore and a more open boring than he can possibly do with a smaller gauge gun with tighter boring. All of us like to kill when we shoot at game and for this reason, if the beginner has the strength to carry and handle the 12 bore, he will by using an improved cylinder for quail or a modified choke for ducks and pheasants be able to hit and kill far more birds with a given number of shots than he would with a smaller gauge gun and a tighter choke necessary for the same pattern density. That wider spread of pattern will help him no end to make clean kills where his aim or point is a few inches off the flying bird. This is just one good sound reason why 12 bore guns are placed in a class by themselves in the Skeet shoots. They are more deadly on account of the larger pattern permissible for equal density at a given range. The 12 bore will give the novice a spread of pattern commensurate with his degree of skill, better than will any smaller bore gun.

The 12 bore 1¼ ounce load is also a more effective load than anything smaller for off season crow and hawk shooting. All hunters should indulge in such work whenever possible and thus help their game supply, and at the same time improve their shotgun pointing for the serious game shooting to follow in the fall. One pair of crows or magpies can very easily destroy a whole nest of mallards or pheasants and thus cut down on your game supply, so shoot the devils at every opportunity. In England the crows are called rooks and used for food but we seriously doubt if they will ever look or taste right to the American palate. We have seen one pair of goshawks clean out all the pheasants, quail and cottontails from a long mountain stream during one winter and the snow carried mute evidence of their depredations. They and the big horned owls should be shot at every opportunity. Both are tough birds to kill unless you can get in certain range and getting in range of a goshawk often takes on the same aspect as goose stalking.

While the 12 bore is still the accepted standard gauge shotgun in this country it is losing face in many sections, notably so in the deep south where quail are shot more than other game, and there the smaller gauges are coming into their own as standard guns. We would not be surprised to see the 16 bore take over as the standard gauge ere another decade is past were it not for the fact that trap shooting employs only the 12 bore and the 12 bore is also standard equipment used by Uncle Sam in training aerial gunners. It is doubtful if the English will ever accept anything but a 12 as a standard gun.

This brings us to the 16 bore, perhaps the nicest of all upland guns and a very useful gun for average range duck shooting as well with the heavy 1⅛ ounce loads with progressive powders. We have shot a 16 bore all our life and use it more than any other gauge. For all upland shooting, we have never felt in the least handicapped when using the 16 bore against all manner of 12 bores, for where our hunting partners have about three to a maximum of five yards range on us with the best shooting 12 bores, we gain about that

Son Ted with a Goshawk and Author's 10-Gauge Magnum Ithaca. This
Photograph Was Taken in 1944.

yardage in faster gun mounting and can see no real difference in
actual shooting results on upland game. However, we have never
used the lighter ⅞ ounce loads nor the one ounce loads at all and
always stick to the heavy duck load. Formerly we used only Peters
Ideal, but now use any and all makes of heavy duck 16 bore loads.
Our old No. 3 Ithaca double had 30 inch barrels and both a full
choke 80% with No. 5 shot; and our later No. 5 Ithaca, Major Askins'
old gun, is also 30 inch full choke and goes a full 90% for both
barrels with No. 6 shot heavy loads. Very few 12 bores will throw

such patterns as these two guns will, and we have yet to see the 12 bore that would duplicate our No. 6 shot 16 bore patterns with the same 1⅛ ounce loads. No doubt there are guns that will do the trick but we simply have not run across them.

The 16 bore gives one a lighter gun to lug all day afield and the ammunition is also smaller and lighter and one comes in fresher at the end of the day than if he packed a heavy 12 bore. True, light 12 bores of equal weight can be had, but we have used the 16 so long and know its range so well that we prrefer it for all average upland work. Our guns however are far too close shooting for usual work on quail or woodcock or ruffed grouse, but the season has long been closed on these birds here and our shooting is mostly pheasants, Huns * with some ruffed and blue grouse and sage hens, so we do not need a more open gun here; but if we were shooting quail regularly, especially little Bob White then we prefer about a 50% choke in both barrels or a 50% first barrel and a 60% second barrel for that work. We do still have dove shooting but that is often long range tough shooting anyway and the 1⅛ ounce heavy load of 7½ shot is just the ticket for that work as it is also on Huns. Those fast flying little sage bullets break cover and fly more like quail than any other bird and are bigger, faster and far tougher, so the full choked 16 bore is just the ticket for them. Few dogs work them very well and they often break at 30 yards or more from the gun and are notorious for twisting and dodging around tall sage brush. When wounded or winged, you need to hit them again if at all possible as you can simply run your legs off trying to catch one if you haven't a good dog to do so for you.

Our first 16 bore double weighed just 6¾ pounds, 30 inch full choked barrels, standard stock, foreend and rib. This No. 5 however weighs 7½ pounds and is complete with elevated ventilated rib, beavertail foreend and cheek piece stock. It is the most delightful gun for upland work we have ever owned. For average pheasant shooting, jump shooting of mallards along creeks and sloughs, Huns, big blue grouse and sage hens it is a hard gun to beat and we fail to see how it could be otherwise than a fine trap gun if the 1⅛ ounce No. 7½ shot heavy loads were used. It was also Major Askins' favorite for such shooting for a good many years. That gun comes up on the mark wherever we look and fits like an old glove. The weight is just right for us for fast work and for all shooting of such game from 40 to 55 yards, our usual ranges, we fail to see where a 12 bore is any better if half as good considering weight of gun and ammunition. Certainly we have used it in the field along with some very fine fast shots using 12 bores and always were able to get as many birds for ammunition expenditure as the 12 bores produced.

---

* Hungarian Pheasants.

The 16 bore gun is our own preferance for all such shooting. It is also a most delightful gun for the woman of average strength. For the quail shot a lighter 16 bore with 26 to 28 inch barrels, bored improved cylinder, 45% and 50% would be a hard gun to beat and can be had in a weight of 6½ to 6¾ pound nicely; or even lighter if desired. For the woman or man who prefers the repeater, either pump or auto, the gun can be fitted with a patent choke, making it ideal for all upland work from quail and wood cock to pheasants by simply turning the choke sleeve for the desired pattern. What it won't kill within that 55 yard range limit in full choke is not to be killed with any weapon on birds up to and including mallards or pheasants or grouse. The repeater with Poly Choke set at improved cylinder, with 1⅛ ounces of 7½ shot is perfect for quail shooting, and closed to modified or full choke is also about perfect for snipe shooting. In full choke it is a most excellent dove gun, also an equally good duck gun for use over decoys and corn field shooting. Wherever the shooting is to be at under 55 yards, we do not feel handicapped in the slightest with the 16 bore and in fact prefer it to the heavier slower-to-mount 12 bore. Of course the 12 bore can be had in the same weights in either a double or a repeater in the new Remington Wingmaster or the Ithaca 37 as well as many other good makes, but we have yet to see the 12 bore that would do any better on game with the same weight of shot charge and we believe the 1⅛ ounce load belongs to the 16 bore gun. For straight duck shooting, it can never equal the 12 bore with its 1¼ ounce load, or for shooting beyond 55 yards, but under that range its a most delightful gun to use, light to carry and fast to mount and swing on the mark. The ammunition is also lighter than 12 bore ammunition and less bulky in the pocket.

Our American Heavy duck loads in the 16 bore throw a heavier charge than do many of the 12 bore standard British loads with 1 1/16 ounces of shot. Their upland shooting is very often driven game that comes over fast but at close range, hence the typical light British loads; some as light as one ounce of shot in the 12 bore. In the nature of things, this inherent tenacity to the 12 bore by the British amounts almost to an obsession. Certainly the 16 bore will do all that their light 1⅛ ounce or lighter loads will do on any game. When they skeletonize and hollow out the stock of a gun and lighten the frame and barrels as much as possible as well to give them about a 6 pound gun and then fit big 12 bore barrels for use with a two inch case and one ounce of shot, we simply fail to follow their mental processes. Such short chambered, extremely light weight 12 bore guns, when they do get away from England are potential death traps and altogether too many men in this country, who do not know about these light short chambered British guns, are apt to drop a heavy duck load in them if the chamber be long enough and then blow their gun and themselves up in great style. It has happened and can happen again and many youngsters and tyros at the shooting game naturally suppose any 12 bore gun should take any factory loaded 12 bore shell. We have even run onto several shooting 3 inch Magnum 12 bore loads in a 2¾ inch chambered modern American pump gun as a singleloader and they can thank their stars it was a good honest sturdy built American gun. Otherwise they would probably have already journeyed to the nether regions, or be practicing on a harp for St. Peter's choir.

We have received a surprising number of letters from ex G.I.'s since the war, who wanted to know why their light British and Continental shotguns developed excessive pressures when fired with American heavy duck loads and on checking found their chambers were too short for the 2¾ inch case. There is an old saying, "the Lord looks after fools, drunks and babies." Only by the grace of Allah are they still with us, and not floating around on a pink cloud the while they grow and try out their new wings.

We believe the British so called 12-20, which is a 12 bore gun in the usual weight of a 20 bore, would have been a far better gun if they had fitted it with a pair of 16 bore barrels. When they build the gun for a 2¾ inch case in 12 bore and proof test it for 1¼ ounce loads then that is O.K. and makes a mighty good weapon in a double for upland game, but when the British fad of extreme light weight 12 bores, extremely light shot charges and short cases is carried to the extreme, we fail utterly to grasp their reasoning. The British build fine double guns, none finer, but we believe they would do well to confine their efforts and wonderful workmanship to a properly chambered gauge, commensurate with the weight of the gun and stop building 12 bore guns for 20 bore loads of shot and powder. If they want a lighter gun than their usual 1¼ ounce 12 bore then they should not be so stiff necked and come down to the 16 bore or even a 20 if they wish to use but one ounce of shot. We like fine British double guns, when built for proper 12 bore loads, but can see no horse sense in trying to scale a 12 bore down in both weight and shot load to the 20 bore level. The British can build and do build very fine 16 and 20 bore guns and these should be the order of the day when loads lighter than 1¼ ounces of shot are the regular bill of fare.

On the Continent the 16 bore has long been the standard shotgun gauge, and more German, Belgium and French guns will be found chambered for the 16 bore shell than any other gauge. They have found it well answers their upland game shooting problems so build most of their output for local consumption in that gauge. All British and Continental guns should be checked for chamber length before firing unless they are plainly stamped on the bottom flats of the breeches what case length they are chambered for.

Usually this is the case but some have not been so proof marked, usually of Continental manufacture. British guns are almost always proof fired and marked for the load of shot and also the case length, at least all that we have seen and used, and the owner has only to take the gun down and read the proof stenciling to know for what case length his gun is chambered.

For the man or woman who wants a very fine upland gun that is light enough to carry all day and will regularly kill large birds like pheasants to 50 or 55 yards, we believe they need look no further than the 2¾ inch chambered 16 bore gun. With its heavy 1⅛ ounce load of a suitable size shot for the birds hunted it will do all that is needed and they will come in fresher in the evening than if they had lugged a heavier 12 bore and 12 bore ammunition all day. It is also questionable if the heavier slower-to-mount 12 bore will give them any more game for the number of shots expended, unless they are very powerful men and women.

In the deep south, the 16 and 20 bore guns are now becoming far more popular in many sections than the 12 bore. They shoot a lot of quail down there and the smaller gun is all that is needed for such work. We will get around to writing a chapter on patterns one of these days and endeavor to show just what can be accomplished with a good 16 bore gun.

Next we have the little 20 bore. A very popular gauge in the South for quail shooting and it is probably the finest little gun of all for straight quail shooting. With an ounce of No. 7½ shot the 20 bore will kill quail, doves, snipe and all such small game nicely to 40 yards and very often to 45 as well, if in full choke. It can be had in a weight of 5¾ pounds to six pounds in either double, pump or auto loader, is light to carry, fast to mount and the ammunition is also light. There is no use in heaving a big 1¼ ounce shot load at one little bob white when an ounce will do the work just as well. It is also hard to find a better gun for ruffed grouse and woodcock in dense cover. That one ounce load is, we believe, the one best load for the 20 bore and it will do nicely for all such reasonably close range upland work. It will also kill ducks regularly at 45 yards and often out to 50 with exceptionally good shooting guns. No. 7½ shot are just right for teal and No. 6 for larger birds in the 20 bore and we see no reason to use heavier shot in the 20 bore than No. 6, unless one is trying to kill a goose with it. We do not consider the 20 bore as a duck gun at all nor for long range difficult pheasant or Hun shooting, but it will take all these birds very nicely and steadily if they are shot within 45 yards from a full choke gun or at from 20 to 35 yards with a more open boring and for short range quail shooting the 50% boring is very good.

One must remember, they are using a small bore gun and that all small bores are most deadly in full choke if the ranges are at or near 40 yards. While the one ounce load of No. 7½ shot will take quail and similar birds regularly at 25 to 35 yards, you need a closer boring for the 20 than for a 16 or 12 bore gun. For that 20 to 35 yard quail shooting we like at least 50% boring; and the improved cylinder going 45% while wonderful on quail at 20 to 30 yards needs a bit more choke for pattern density for longer ranges. If the birds are laying well and a good dog is used, the shots are usually well within this range and the spiteful crack of the little 20 when properly pointed will come as near filling a quail limit as any gun. If the shooting runs from 30 to 45 yards nothing less than a modified choke is called for and when you wish to extend the range of the 20 bore out to 45 or a possible 50 yards then only full choke will deliver the goods even on large ducks and pheasants and grouse. We have killed about all game birds except geese with a 20 and often marvelled at the effectiveness of the little gun. One has to point closer with a 20 than with a larger gauge where more shot are employed. Thus the 20 bore is more a gun for the expert than the novice.

We also believe the 20 bore the smallest gauge that should be used for really serious shooting. We shot a double 20 bore one season on blue, ruffed grouse and the big sage hens. It was a swell tool for the grouse when we had high mountains to climb and the birds would usually raise at 15 to 20 yards and the little gun was so light and fast we could handle it almost with one hand, making clean kills very often before the birds were over 30 to 35 yards. For such shooting it seemed nearly ideal, but when we turned to sage hens something was lacking in killing range that we badly needed. Many of the big heavy birds we had to pound with one barrel after the other and then they often sailed off to fall in a cloud of dust. Though we killed several limits of sage hens with the little gun, we found it lacking in range for such game, and all too often we had to whip in that second barrel to effect a kill. The 20 bore is more of a light bird upland game gun for use at short to very medium ranges in the main and so used it will give a lot of pleasure and satisfaction to its owner.

Try to stretch its effective range a few yards and you will lose many cripples and soon become disgusted with the 20 bore. It definitely is not the gun to choose for the heavier Western shooting of pheasants, ducks and Huns that raise at longer ranges in open country, and while a fine little gun to start the boy or lady with, we believe they should also be graduated to a 16 bore for the more open Western hunting. On the other hand in the East and South where many shore birds and ducks are shot in the dense cover as well as grouse, woodcock, and quail the 20 will give a good account of itself. The main thing is to use it within its effective range for the size bird hunted. If this is done many will continue to like the 20 bore. If the game can be shot regularly under 40 yards then the

20 bore will do the trick nicely and with a very minimum of gun and ammunition weight to carry all day.

The 20 gauge is not the gun for anyone to select as an all around shotgun, nor for the one gun man, but the expert shot or the person who wants to project around with a light, fast and deadly little weapon and who will shoot only when he can take his game under 40 to 45 yards preferably, will find the 20 almost as deadly as the larger bores. If he keeps a record he will probably find his kills average within about ten percent of the amount killed with the larger bores, particularly in quail, ruffed grouse, or woodcock shooting.

This brings us to the two really small bores, the 28 gauge and the 410. The 410 bore really measured that calibre, while all other gauges are taken from the number of balls to the pound that the bore will accept with a good fit. Thus the eight bore takes a two ounce round ball and the ten bore round balls go ten to the pound, the 12 bore twelve to the pound down to the 20 with 20 balls to the pound, but the 410 is taken differently and is measured by thousandths same as rifle bores.

We never could see much if any excuse for a 410 bore gun either in the 2½ inch which is about worthless or the 3 inch magnum 410 which throws ¾ ounce of shot. Such guns may be useful for the taxidermist to kill very small birds for mounting at very close range and we have patterned 3 inch 410 bores with No. 7½ shot that would take birds like grouse and ducks to 35 yards regularly and had one Marlin over-under Model 90 that would put four or five pellets on such big birds to a full 40 yards if No. 7½ shot were used, but it was an exceptionally good shooting 3 inch 410 bore. This gauge is used more by the poacher than the legitimate shooter and except for its class in Skeet we believe it a mistake to ever arm anyone for game shooting with a 410 bore. The 28 gauge is a far better weapon and throws the same ¾ ounce of shot and even it is the gun for the oldster who can no longer handle a heavier weapon and yet who is an expert shot and desirous of killing a few birds at close range. We played with one fine Parker 28 bore for a season on ruffed grouse and it would kill them nicely in the dense timber where shots were at very close range. Also we saw an expert use this same little gun on jacksnipe with very good effect. It had 30 inch barrels and was full choked. We believe all 410 and 28 bores should be full choke as the shot charge is just too light to permit much spread of pattern and still retain a killing density. For quail shooting to 30 yards or possibly 35 yards on ruffed grouse the 28 bore will kill nicely when in the hands of an expert shotgunner, but with its small full choked pattern it will have to be pointed right and no mistake in aim can occur and secure clean kills. Some folks recommend the 28 bore as a ladies' gun but we have watched a good many women shoot over the years and nothing is more detestable to them than wounding and losing a bird to die a lingering death and we would never recommend any gauge smaller than a 20 even for ladies' or boys' use. We consider the 28 more a gun for the finished wing shot to be used on rare occasions for very close range precision work on such small birds as quail and woodcock or close range ruffed grouse.

No. 8 shot will give a denser pattern for the 410, 28 and even the 20 gauge for close range quail shooting and if the shooting is under 30 yards, the smaller No. 8 shot may well be a bit better and it is only in these small bores that we would ever use or recommend their use. When snipe are laying well to the gun and jump at very close range, the expert wing shot can have a lot of fun with a 28 bore but he will kill far more birds with a 20, day in and day out on any game he shoots.

CHILLED AND DROP SHOT

Size No.°	Chilled Shot No. per ounce	Drop Shot No. per ounce	Diameter (inches)°
9	585	568	0.08
8	409	399	.09
7½	345	338	.095
6	223	218	.11
5	172	168	.12
4	136	132	.13
3	109	106	.14
2	88	86	.15
1	73	71	.16

°Disregarding the decimal point, the diameter in inches added to the size number equals 17. Thus for No. 5 shot, 5 + 12 = 17.

BUCK SHOT

Eastern Size No.	Approximate Number to the pound	Diameter Inches
4	341	.24
3	299	.25
2	238	.27
1	175	.30
0	144	.32
00	122	.34
000	103	.36

Shotgun Barrels, Chambers, Forcing Cones, Bores, Chokes, Etc.

TODAY, shotgun barrels are made by boring out round bar stock and finish reaming. Then the bore is purposely left with considerable constriction at the muzzle for the choke. Modern shotgun loads demand the finest in fluid steels and modern heat treatment. Formerly many of the finely figured twist and Damascus barrels were made in Europe and imported into this country where they were finished. These were made by twisting and welding thin strips of iron and steel together and then welding same around a mandrel. They were literally hand forged from many long thin strips of alternating steel and iron and hand welded also around that mandrel to form the beautiful pattern when finished and browned. Such a system was very expensive, had to be done by the finest most expert craftsmen or flaws were liable to occur in the weld and the tensile strength of the finished product did not compare with modern forged bar stock drilled and reamed from one solid piece of best steel. The soft iron used in the alternating strips of the twist and Damascus barrels also was much weaker than modern steel. A shotgun barrel is only as strong as its weakest part and Damascus and twist barrels should have gone out of the gate with the introduction of smokeless powders.

Just the same, when properly finish ground and polished and then blued by the cold rust browning process they were by far the most beautiful barrels ever put on a shotgun, and likewise the weakest. In all fairness however, we must state we have never known a Damascus or twist barrel in perfect condition inside to blow up with a normal modern factory load. Others have had this experience and have written it up many times but to date I have never seen it occur without an obstruction, rust pits, or heavy grease in the bore. Some early cheap shotgun barrels were also made by wrapping a strip of sheet metal around a mandrel and welding the seam. This also produced a very poor barrel that was liable to open and sometimes did just that from an overload. Such cheap construction was in no manner as strong as the twist and Damascus barrels.

Longitudinal flaws have also occurred at times in modern barrels and under heavy pressure they have split longitudinally.

Formerly Whitworth Fluid, Krupp Fluid and similar steels were considered the best and most modern of all but today many steel mills both here and abroad produce even harder and finer grained steels of much greater tensile strength, that go into the barrels of our modern shotguns. Modern metallurgy has made great strides in the past decade, both in alloys used and also in the modern system of heat treatment.

It is a moot question if the heaviest in modern loads develop any higher breech pressures than the older heavy duck loads produced 20 to 35 years ago, such as the U. S. Ajax, Remington Arrow, Winchester Leader or Peters Ideal. However, modern progressive burning shotgun powders used in the heaviest loads today are much slower burning and thus extend the pressure peak farther up the tube where it is much thinner and less able to take the strain of heavy pressures. This fact alone puts the finger on the use of modern heavy duck loads in the older twist and Damascus barrels as well as all older cheaply made steel barrels of relatively low tensile strength. Before all loading companies and the Sporting Arms & Ammunition Manufacturer's Institute issued warnings on the use of any smokeless loads in the older Damascus and twist barrel guns, all the very heaviest loads were universally used in them and with mighty few blow-ups. None to my credit or under my observation, which speaks well for some of those fine old craftsmen who thus welded those thin strips of iron and steel together so that the whole barrel was simply one continuous weld. After many years of age and neglect, so that rust pitting often ate away the soft iron in those twisted strips and thus weakened the welding, it is no wonder that some of them blew up under modern shotgun pressures.

Today only best modern steels are used, of great tensile strength, and alloyed to prevent rust as much as possible. These modern steels come in round bar stock and are centered and drilled, then finish reamed, leaving a constriction of .040″ or more for a 12 bore and .045″ or more constriction in a ten bore. In the 12 bore they are reamed and polished to as near .729″ as possible for the bore up to the choke constriction. The whole tube is polished highly, chambered and the forcing cone also cut with the long reamer. The chambers and cones are in turn polished and then the barrel is ground down outside to even contour on large stones, after which it is polished on the outside and blued. After fitting to the action the gun is shot for pattern and nearly always some of the choke is reamed or ground out until the gun gives the desired even spread at a given range for a certain degree of choke.

Some folks think that an extra strong or heavy choke will make the gun shoot closer; and this is usually all wrong, for too much choke usually means cart-wheel patterns with an open center and too much choke is far worse than too little. Fred Kimble discovered this fact many years ago when he discovered choke boring and bored and choked his first old 6 bore muzzle loader.

Today the usual procedure is to leave plenty of choke, then grind or ream it out until the right percentage, with standard loads, is secured and this is the way most companies do the job. Practically all gun companies put some amount of choke in their barrels; even so-called cylinder borings usually have a little choke to round out their patterns, and give an even spread. A true cylinder is the most worthless of all borings and will almost always have holes in its patterns and be irregular both in density and shape. No gun company wants such barrels out under their name so for this reason they almost all put some choke in the gun. Gun companies today will guarantee you a 70% full choke pattern, but it is a mighty poor gun that will not do 75 to 80% and some even better with modern loads, yet the companies want to be on the safe, conservative side and with good reason.

In boring shotgun barrels we will take the standard 12 bore gun as an example. Both here and abroad, most all companies have standardized on a bore of .729" for the 12 bore gun. This may vary a few thousandths of an inch from gun to gun in the boring, reaming and polishing operations and it's virtually impossible for the compaines to cut two tubes exactly alike. The bore proper of a 12 gauge may run anywhere from .725" to .735" and of course forcing cones and chokes vary a like amount in actual diameter but must be in proper relation one to the other for any good results; 12 bore chambers usually run to a taper of about .0047" per inch from rim to front end of chamber or beginning of the forcing cone. Thus 12 bore chambers will run as a rule from about .800" at rear end just forward of the rim cut to possibly .816". At the front end of the standard 2¾ inch chamber the diameter of the chamber will run from about .796 inch minimum. All things are relative and doubly so, when we get to shotgun bore, chamber and choke measurements.

Some companies cut their chambers a trifle short, from 1/16" to ⅛", so that the cases will lap that much in the cone but the general practice is to cut the chamber proper to the exact full length of the unfolded paper case or in the case of the 12 bore, 2¾ inches. Chambers should never be longer than the case for best patterns, as such a longer chamber as in the case of a 3" chambered Magnum 12 bore using standard 12 bore 2¾ inch cases, may allow some gas escapage past the over-powder wads into the shot charge and also a spreading of the shot charge at that point in front of the chamber proper, when they must again be constricted into the cone which in turn will deform more shot than necessary or desirable.

Hence the longer-than-necessary chamber tends to deform more shot or allow gas escapage into the shot column, either for a loss in pattern percentages. With the latest modern cup seal over-powder wads and the American standard of a long wad column between the powder and shot charges, the chamber should be exactly the same length as the cartridge case. This in turn gives a minimum of chamber pressure when fired, while a short chamber with the paper case lapping up to an eighth inch in the forcing cone, while it furthers good patterns, also raises pressures. Three inch Magnum 12 bore loads should never be fired in standard 2¾" chambers, (though some folks have done so) as pressures mount greatly. While some pattern loss is to be expected when the standard 2¾" cases are used in the long Magnum chambers, pressures will be very low.

Chambers should be smooth and well polished to further easy and free extraction and with enough expansion to relieve pressures somewhat. Too large or loose a chamber tends to cause head cracks, in the brass heads, or undue expansion, and while some experimenters have purposely enlarged their chambers to give the shot column some cushioning effect at the time of discharge we do not favor such procedure.

The Remington corrugated paper case is however a step in the right direction, as it allows some cushioning effect to the shot column when the initial pressure hits the shot charge, as these corrugations are ironed out by pressure in the chamber. This effect also favors easy extraction. The purpose here is to hold the shot charge in place and form as much as possible during initial combustion and then to move it as gently as possible into and through the forcing cone into the bore proper. This should be accomplished with a minimum of crowding of the shot column. The thrust of the powder gases is hard enough on that column of shot without augmenting it further, by allowing the shot to expand into an oversize chamber and then be again funnelled into the forcing cone. We believe normal or minimum chambers of exact case length best to deliver the shot column into the forcing cone with a minimum of shot deformation.

Where it is desired to use short shells in long chambers such as standard 12 bores in guns chambered for the 3" Magnum cartridge, then the longer and more gradual the forcing cone the better, at least with modern American wadding. We had an old model Ithaca double 20 bore with 3" chambers and that gun also had a short abrupt forcing cone and never would deliver better than a 65% pattern from its full choke barrel with standard 1 ounce 2¾" shells. On the other hand my Magnum ten bore Ithaca No. 500,000 chambered for the 3½" Magnum ten bore case has very little forcing cone left and even that cut on a very long taper and it shoots standard Super Ten Bore loads in 2⅞" cases very well, some patterns running as high as 85 to 90%.

Generally speaking long chambers with the usual abrupt short forcing cone will give a reduction in pattern percentage of 5 to 15% when used with short shells. The shot naturally expand to fill the front end of the chamber in front of the paper case on discharge and then must again be forced from a diameter of some .796" to a diameter of roughly .729" in the short length of the cone. This causes considerable jamming and deformation of the shot, more by far than are ever deformed in the choke of the gun.

The British usually use less wadding between powder and shot charge than we do, hence it is more liable to allow gas to escape past the wadding when short shells are used in long chambers with resultant shot balling and blown patterns. Modern American cup seal wads or expanding wads and their long column of wads is pretty certain to seal off all the gas even when the charge must be jumped from a long chamber into the cone. For this reason the man using a Magnum 12 with its 3 inch chambers for wildfowl shooting, can usually get a very good upland pattern with the same gun by using the standard 2¾" shell. If the gun runs around 80% patterns with the big 1⅞ ounce loads it will usually shoot 65 to 70% patterns with the 2¾" case and very often this is just about the pattern desired for upland work on pheasants and similar game. One of the most experienced game shots in this country, Nash Buckingham, uses a Magnum 12 bore a lot and the long shells for the difficult work and the standard loads for average shooting. This Magnum 12 and his big ten bore duck gun do most of his shooting and it is doubtful if any man will ever again have as much game shooting experience with the scatter gun as he has behind him now.

Thus we see a chamber that is oversize at the front end does not further best patterns and a short shell in a long chamber also cuts down on pattern percentages, while a short lap of case into the cone when a long shell is used in a short chamber improves and furthers good patterns but in turn raises pressures and tends to shred the front end of the paper case. We have seen bits of a torn case lodge in the front end of the chamber, where succeeding loads simply glued them in place; then the gun did not do its best until these bits of case were cleaned out. A rough chambering job is also an abomination.

Next let us take up forcing cones. Chambering reamers are very expensive and only the best tool makers can properly cut and hone a reamer so it will do its best work, a smooth even-cut chamber and cone. The longer the cone the more expensive the reamer, hence the factories do not grind long reamers nor cut long tapered forcing cones. With many of the lighter loads that abrupt forcing cone helped no end in balancing the load and helped in powder combustion, while with a very long gentle cone the powder must be balanced more against the weight of the shot and wad column. The heavier the shot load and the longer the shot column, the more necessary is a long gentle forcing cone, for best pattern percentages. With modern oversize expanding or cup seal wads we can get away with a long cone nicely, while with the older wads, that did not expand to fill instantly, the powder was apt to escape past the wad column into the shot charge when long forcing cones were used. Thus modern American wadding goes a long long way toward making the use of a long cone feasible and an improvement in shotgun performance.

More shot have always been deformed in the cone than in the choke of the gun, hence the reason some of the old muzzle loaders patterned higher than was possible with most breech loaders. The muzzle loader had no chamber and no forcing cone. The charge lay in a smooth barrel and the wadding already fitted the bore tight on top of the powder load. When fired the charge simply drove forward up a smooth even bore until it reached the choke. That is the reason Fred Kimble obtained such exceptional patterns from his old 6 bore muzzle loader with only 1½ ounces of No. 3 shot. The nearest we have attained to equalling the performance of that old single six bore is the Magnum ten bore with two ounces of No. 3 shot. Our own Magnum ten Ithaca, the first one built, by the way, and for Major Askins, has had the cone and bore worked over three different times by the best men at the Ithaca factory and in so doing the cone was largely removed. This gun now has very little cone at all, just a gradual taper from the front end of the chamber forward for some six inches to the true bore diameter and with Western Super X two ounce loads of No. 3 Lubaloy shot has consistently fired the highest counting patterns we personally have ever run. It has made its run of ten shots with each barrel for an average of 93%, and some place in each ten shot string, was a pattern that exactly duplicated the performance of the other barrel. Never before or since have we found any double gun that shot so exactly alike.

George Turners' friend's old No. 7 Ithaca single trap is another case in point where the forcing cone was gradually worked out by draw boring until little remained and that also is the highest patterning trap gun of which we have ever heard. It practically always places the entire charge in a 30 inch circle and George claims they have actually shot 100% patterns with it at 40 yards and very often the bulk of the charge is in a 24 inch circle at 40 yards. It's a real handicap gun and its performance is largely due to the removal of that forcing cone and also made possible by the latest developments in shot shell over-powder wadding.

Reamers, polishing tools and abrasives are nearly always turned in a lathe and even though the chamber and cone and bore appear highly polished, if one could cut out a section or split the barrel full length, the fine reamer marks and cross marks of the polishing compound or tool still would be visible, at least under a glass. These in turn abrade the shot charge and cause more deformation of the in-

GAUGE	BORE	A	B(a)	C	D	E	F	G	FULL J	FULL K	IMP. MOD J	IMP. MOD K	MODIFIED J	MODIFIED K	IMP. CYL'R SKEET J	IMP. CYL'R SKEET K	CYLINDER J	CYLINDER K
10 / 10 MAG.	.775	.841	.8379	.933	.8554	2.875 / 3.500	.074	.026	.739		.748		.757		.766		.775	
12 / 12 MAG	.729	.798	.7968	.886	.8118	2.750 / 3.000	.072	.026	.693	$2\frac{1}{2}$	.702	$1\frac{7}{8}$	.711	$1\frac{1}{4}$	.720	$\frac{5}{8}$	.729	0
16	.662	.732		.820	.7458	2.750	.065	.026	.636		.6425		.649		.6555		.662	
20	.615	.685		.766	.6988	2.750	.060	.024	.589		.5955		.602		.6085		.615	
28	.550	.614		.688	.6284	2.875	.060	.022	.530		.535		.540		.545		.550	
410	.410	.463		.537	.478	3.000	.060	.020	.390		.395		.400		.405		.410	

Diagram (T-113): 55° — INCLUDED TAPER .005" PER INCH — MINIMUM CHAMBER — 5°30' — dimensions G, F, E, K — Ø

Title block:
ITHACA GUN Co, Inc.
ITHACA, N.Y.
STANDARD BORE, CHAMBER & CHOKE FOR SHOT GUNS
T-113

| A | .8379 WAS .838, .7968 WAS .797 | n.d.d. | 11-6-45 | n.d.d. 3-10-39 | | | | | 1"=1" |
| REV. A | REVISION | BY | DATE | DRAWN BY | CHECKED BY | TRACED BY | LIMITS OK | MATERIAL | SCALE |

dividual pellets laying on the outer edge of the charge and are in turn more apt to become fliers when fired.

When a forcing cone is largely removed by draw boring and the whole shotgun tube is highly polished by that process any minute scratches or cuts in the steel are longitudinal, not cross-wise of the bore, hence do not abrade the shot charge. The more a shotgun is fired the higher the polish of the cone and bore will become and the better patterns it will shoot. In time the shot and wadding smooth up the entire bore until the finest patterns will be the end result. In testing thousands of shotguns, I have noticed that almost all of the best shooting guns were those that had been shot a great deal, usually trap guns.

The nearer one can come to elimination of the forcing cone through draw boring, and the higher the polish of the cone and bore, the better patterns will result. This elimination of the cone in turn is made possible through the modern expanding over-powder wads and would not have worked at all with many of the older wads formerly used as gas would then have escaped past the wads into the shot column while it was forcing the cone into the bore proper.

The English for a time used chamberless guns for wildfowl shooting. These guns had no regular chamber or forcing cone as we know them; simply a rim cut in rear end of barrel, and they used a long paper thin brass case with oversize wads that sealed off the powder gas from the shot charge. They in turn had to use very heavy shot charges to balance the powder load and absence of the forcing cone. These guns are claimed to have given very exceptional performance with 1½ ounces of shot, 12 bore on long range waterfowl. Sir Charles Heath did considerable work with them and no doubt Major Burrard also worked with them. The brass cases were harder to make and much more expensive than paper cases and these guns seem to have about died out, but the fact remains the principle was right and if they had had our latest expanding wads and found a cheaper method of case manufacture the chamberless guns might still be in vogue for long range pass shooting.

English powders were probably not as well adapted to such loads as are modern American progressive burning powders, or their results might have been even better.

At any rate it was the first and probably the only attempt to use modern shotshell in a chamberless gun bored like the old muzzle loaders, and results secured indicate they were on the right track. However modern shotgun shells are made of paper and this is necessarily much thicker than the thin brass case used in the chamberless guns. This in turn necessitated a wad that was either well oversize or would expand to seal off the pushing gas from the shot charge. With modern American wadding we believe such a gun entirely possible today with paper cases, and heavy shot charges such as the 1⅝ ounce 12 bore Magnum load or the two ounce Magnum ten bore.

Gun makers have long sought to standardize everything as much as possible, and with good reason, for only by such a system can they in turn put out enough guns to hold manufacturing costs down. Thus our chambers and forcing cones are pretty well standardized today. Few men have the ability to use an 80 to 90% shotgun and still fewer need such a gun anyway, so why should an enterprising gun company go to all the trouble to build such a gun.

If the finished weapon is to be sold at a nominal price, that means mass production and standardized boring tolls and chambering reamers. Likewise the gun maker wants his gun to shoot well with any make of load, either domestic or foreign, that the customer is likely to put into it. For this reason a highly specialized weapon built and regulated for a certain shot load and case is neither necessary nor desirable from the manufacturers standpoint. About all they can gain from such a gun is prestige in the shooting world and at the cost usually of considerable expensive hand work.

Bore diameters are now well standardized for all gauges and little need be said of them other than that the higher the polish the bore attains through shot smoothing from long useage with perfect care, the more perfect shot will it deliver at the choke. Some bores are smoothed by lapping and others by burnishing reamers and others by draw boring with a burnisher. Very experienced barrel makers claim that a smoother higher polish can be attained without lapping than with lapping, as the compound they claim becomes impregated into the steel where it acts as an abrasive for a considerable length of time and is very hard to wash out. No doubt when any form of emery is used this is the case but with softer polishing compounds it is a question.

Powdered pumice stone, rouge and other such polishing compounds can only help smooth up the bore. Such very highly polished bores lead very little or none at all and usually shoot the highest patterns. They are also the easiest to clean and keep clean. Regardless of what some makers say about cleaning the gun and that cleaning is unnecessary, we still prefer to properly clean every gun after using it.

Condensation can alone cause rusting of the bore and if properly cleaned and all traces of lead removed the gun is then safe, otherwise you may someday find it has rust pitted if traces of leading are allowed to remain in the bore.

We have come a long way since the bell-mouthed blunderbuss of the Pilgrim Fathers. Thanks to Fred Kimble, chokes are now well standardized as to amount of relative constriction of the bore. The length of the choke varies greatly from maker to maker, some claiming a long tapered choke best while others seem to get just as high a pattern percentage with a very short choke. Of the two we favor the longer more moderate taper.

Curiously enough that first choke bored muzzle loader of Fred Kimble's was also about the finest performing full choked gun I have ever heard of with the one exception of the above mentioned No. 7 Ithaca singletrap gun. That is the only modern cartridge gun that we have ever heard of that threw 100% patterns at 40 yards most of the time in a 30 inch circle. Possibly if the gun makers would measure and study its chamber, bore and choke they could improve present guns but it would entail long cone reamers and that would increase cost too much.

Like the bores, chambers and cones, shotgun chokes are cut by a rotating cutting tool and the polishing process is also done by a rotating tool. Though the polishing is supposed to remove all traces of the cutting tool it seldom does entirely eliminate them. While factories do not lap shotgun barrels, we believe all portions of cone, bore and choke should be draw polished so that any microscopic tool or polishing marks left would be the length of the barrel and not cross hatched marks left by a rotating tool or polishing device.

Many fine guns as they come from American makers today, will plainly show that a rod with emery cloth has been rotated in the muzzle of the choke to take out some of the choke and these marks are clearly visible from the abrasive used.

We have not seen such marks on fine English guns and believe the English are more careful of the finish of a better quality gun. In time sufficient shooting will polish away these microscopic marks in the steel and hard shot will polish a bore quicker than soft and Lubaloy even faster than chilled.

Some guns, notably those made 30 to 40 years ago, in full choke persuasion are nearly all over-choked for our present progressive powder heavy duck loads. More constriction was needed in those days, with the powders then available, than at present and many of those older pump and auto loaders that were then gored modified choke, now throw a most excellent full choke pattern with present heavy American duck loads. Bob Ward of Missoula, Montana, has for years made a business of measuring up and later removing some of the choke in these older weapons nearly always to the improvement of the pattern and also to the pellet count in the 30 inch circle.

I have seen chokes that started a full six inches from the muzzle and also chokes that were barely an inch long. Remington seems to favor very short chokes and they seem to shoot just as well as longer ones. In the nature of things, it would seem that a longer more gradual taper to the choke would deform less pellets, but it must be remembered that when a shot charge reaches the choke portion of the barrel that velocity is well up, yet internal pressures have dropped off sharply. For this reason the shot do not suffer so violent an action in the choke as they do in going through the forcing cone where pressures are at the absolute maximum.

Many companies favor giving the barrel more choke than necessary or desirable, then grinding out a bit of the choke at a time, at the muzzle, as they shoot the gun for patterns. We have seen many Ithacas and Winchesters that plainly showed this had been the procedure and they shot like the devil by any standard.

No set amount of constriction can be given a certain gun. It must be relative to the actual bore diameter which in turn may vary a good many thousandths even in the best shooting guns. Some 12 bore guns may run an even .730″ throughout the bore proper with a constriction of 40 thousandths in the choke to a diameter of but .690″ for a full choke gun. Other guns with larger bores, say .738″ may have as much as 48 thousandths choke and be equally good shooting weapons.

No doubt you have many times heard gun owners state that their choke was getting shot out. This is seldom the case but the older soft barrels did wear considerably and in time some of the choke was worn out, leaving slightly less constriction. Very often this was to the betterment of patterns, had they tested the guns for ten shot strings on the pattern board.

Holland & Holland standard chokes for 12 bore run from .005″ for improved cylinder, .010″ for one fourth choke, .020″ for ½ choke, .030″ for ¾ choke to a full .040″ for full choke, but no doubt they like all other makers vary the amount in relation to the actual bore diameter and even then may vary it still more when they regulate the gun to get the best patterns out of it. Larger bore guns will stand more choke in full choke persuasion and the Super ten bore can often handle as much as .045″ choke. Smaller gauges need less constriction down to from .030″ to .033″ for many full choked 20 bore guns and some even less.

Trying to measure the choke in a gun with a dime is all applesauce and the dime has no bearing whatever on the bore diameter of that particular barrel. Choke gauges, while they do give the measurement of the choke at the muzzle, are a very unreliable method to use as only inside mikes or a star gauge can tell you just what you have in the way of bore and choke dimensions.

Many guns that were originally bored improved cylinder with about .005″ constriction are later recess choked to give much higher percentages and some makers even favor a recess or jug choke on all guns. When the recess choke is used, the bore is enlarged at a point anywhere from an inch to several inches just back of the choke and may be enlarged as much as .005″. Then the choke of course is just that much heavier when the charge reaches it and will of course give a greater degree of choke. Many barrels are too thin for recess choking but we have seen many so choked that a tightly patched cleaning rod would enable you to feel them as you shove it up the bore.

Recess choking is about the only method of adding choke to a gun, short of over-boring the whole barrel, and the tube must be heavy enough to permit either over-boring or recess boring to strengthen the action of the choke. Cylinder bored guns can thus be easily changed to improved cylinder or 45% guns and improved cylinder guns to 50% choke, or modified to improved modified or 65% guns and sometimes to full choke when desired. A lot depends of course on the thickness of the tubes at the point just back of the choke and whether such metal is thick enough to permit the jug or recess choke boring.

This is about the only known method of increasing the choke of double barrel guns, and we would much prefer to have the bore of the gun run a true exact diameter from the end of the cone to the choke, as with all recess chokes, the shot charge is allowed to expand to fill the recessed portion, then must again be constricted in the choke and we believe the less jamming around of that shot charge the better, if even uniformly round pellets are to be delivered at the muzzle of the gun.

Many makers believe in bringing the choke right to the muzzle of the gun with the closest constriction flush with the muzzle while others believe in having the last one half to one inch of the barrel a true cylinder and the exact diameter of the choke at its extreme constriction. We much prefer the latter system. It enables the shot to sort themselves out and become chambered in the bore again before leaving the muzzle. Such a barrel with the last inch running a true cylinder of the exact dimensions as the closest point of constriction, also leaves the gun maker with the easiest possible way of later removing some of the choke, should it be found that the gun overchoked; as simply polishing out some of this last cylindrical portion of the barrel, right back into the choke will regulate the gun for any given load of powder and shot or any make and load of cartridge.

Any gun maker can regulate the choke to fit a given cartridge and size of shot, but what all strive for is a barrel that will shoot every load well, even though none of them may reach as high a percentage as is possible if they fitted the gun to one load alone. We had Ithaca fit this Magnum ten bore No. 500,000 to one load, Western Super X two ounces of No. 3 Lubaloy; and Ithaca's work well shows what can be done when the gun owner specifies one load and one size shot. That big gun will only throw 85% for the same make cartridge with two ounces of No. 2 Lubaloy and only 80% with two ounces of No. 4 shot, but it shoots the two ounces of No. 3 Lubaloy for a full 93% which is the best we personally have ever obtained from any gun in that small a shot size. We firmly believe pass guns should be ordered direct from the maker to use one make of cartridge and one shot load and also give them the size shot as well, then if they have the time and inclination to put a good barrel man on the job and let him play with that barrel or pair of barrels, he can often fit the choke to that exact load to give crazy results, but put in another make of cartridge or a different size shot or different amount of shot and you may find your high percentage pattern has fallen off from 5% to as much as 20%.

By hand loading we used to fit a load to the individual choke of the gun. It required a lot of time and work and was not always successful. But it did teach us a great deal about shotgun chokes in general.

A true cylinder barrel is usually worthless as the patterns will nearly always have holes in them through which you could heave the family cat. They are usually irregular and may be square or any shape but round; but put in about .003 to .005″ constriction at the muzzle and you have an improved cylinder pattern that is usually round and also an even spread and the most useful of all patterns for close range work on woodcock, ruffed grouse or quail. This for shooting at from 20 to 35 yards range, or for Skeet shooting.

Very few gun makers will bore a true cylinder any more and none in this country that I know of. If you have a variable choke on a single barrel gun, then you can easily get the full cylinder pattern and look it over, usually to your utter disgust

The English formerly did bore a lot of true cylinder barrels but in later years we believe they nearly all put in a few points of con-striction to round out, shape up and even their patterns. They would be utter fools if they did not do so.

Most gun makers could very easily give their guns a little more choke than is now their current practice, and such procedure might make the gun deliver a bit higher percentages with a given load and certain size shot, but would be almost certain to fall down with other loads and shot sizes.

For this reason they try to cut a choke that will perform say 70% or better in full choke with about all loads likely to be shot in the gun.

We once had an old model hammerless No. 4 double 12 bore. The bores were well shot, smoothed from much shooting yet had some very slight pits in them from neglect. Just the same that old gun would pour both barrels of a cheap Peters trap load with 1¼ ounces of No. 7½ shot with 3 drams bulk powder under the spread of my hand at 20 yards and do it all the time. It also patterned the highest with those cheap trap loads, or any trap loads, of any gun I ever patterned at 40 yards, but put in any of the current heavy duck loads with either sixes or fours and it would not do better than 70% and was plainly overchoked for the heavier loads. It could have been relieved a bit at the muzzles and would then have given higher per-centages with the big duck loads but just as it was it was the most wicked shooting gun I ever used on jacksnipe, doves, sparrow hawks and similar size birds and would kill them most of the time even with those small shot to a full 60 yards. It was also the best magpie gun I ever shot. A Handicap trap shot would have been in Heaven with that gun, and load.

As a rule the longer the choke and the longer the taper the more constriction it will stand for a given percentage. The shorter the choke the less is required. Likewise big heavy shot usually require less constriction than small shot. A choke that is just right for one size of shot will seldom shoot another size quite as well, although as a general rule a gun that handles sixes well will also handle fours and twos very well and one that handles fives well will also handle threes and sevens well. Shot diameters vary with different makers and this must also be considered and is the reason at times a gun that shoots a given load of fours well will not do as well with a different make of the same powder load but shot made by another company. This chapter is written mainly for the man with a double gun or a single or repeating gun with a regular barrel. For the man with the repeater or single fitted with any of the compen-sator chokes, he usually has three degrees of choke tubes that can be attached at will and can obtain about any desired degree of constriction. Even more versatile is the Poly Choke with its many degrees of constriction. This device enables the gunner to really study choke in any degree he wishes. Though it may be possible, to date we have never obtained quite as high a pattern count from any variable choke as with fixed choke barrels bored and hand tuned for a given size shot, a given powder load and a certain make. On the other hand the variable choke will enable the shooter to get about any desired pattern in an instant. This would require days of shooting to find the right load for the fixed choke gun. The variable choke is also far more adaptable to different shot sizes from buck to No. 7½ than any fixed choke gun can ever be.

On the final analysis, the choke should give us that even spread 30 inch pattern at the range which we must take our game. While it can seldom, if ever be made to give a 30 inch spread at 15 to 25 yards, nor an even 30 inch spread out at long range, the various degrees of choke do go a long way toward that ultimate goal. Chokes are somewhat like the nozzle on a garden hose. The right amount of constriction will direct the stream of water in one single column, but choke it down too much and it will be a cartwheel spray all over the landscape. Too much choke will do about the same thing in a shotgun. What we want and need is an even 30 inch spread of pattern at the given range where we are most apt to kill our game. At very close range the pattern will be too small and we must wait out our birds or else shatter them. At extreme long range the pattern will be too big and too thinly spread to make uniform kills certain. There is however a definite range where we can be reasonably certain of clean kills. With any gauge or shot load and we must confine our shots within the brackets of those ranges from the point where the charge will kill without too much mutilation of the game, to the extreme range where it will still throw certain killing pattern. Beyond that range all is guess work and more wounded birds will be lost than those secured. One should never shoot beyond the certain range of his pattern. Some one once said "to hit is history, to miss is mystery," but we learn from our misses and mistakes.

CHAPTER SEVEN

Chokes and Their Uses

MOST BEGINNERS in the shotgun game order and use too much choke for their ability. They will learn faster and kill more game if they do not use a full choked gun to start.

The degree of choke, however, must be governed by the ranges at which you must take your birds or fowl. What you want is as near an even 30 inch spread of pattern at the range at which you kill your game as possible. This will give you some leeway in accurate gun pointing and the aim can be off the mark a few inches on either side or high or low a few inches and still kill, providing the bird is well within that 30 inch circle. Thus instead of a single small rifle bullet, you have in effect a killing circle of 30 inches to throw at the bird and with which you should make connections as soon as you master swing and proper lead for the speed of the bird, the velocity of your load and your own mental reactions. Some folks have very fast mental reactions, others are slower in their mental processes and their impulse from the brain to the trigger finger. This in turn affects the amount of apparent lead necessary, but with that big 30 inch circle you are throwing at your bird, you have a very good chance of connecting.

At really close range, say 15 yards, the true cylinder bore, no choke at all, can be used; but true cylinders are seldom bored, if at all, in this day and age due to the fact that a full cylinder with bore running exactly true to the thousandth of an inch from cone to muzzle, with no constriction, seldom throws a pattern that is worth a Continental. True cylinder patterns are seldom round, are very patchy and most of the time, have great holes in the pattern. For these reasons they are also very uncertain on game and you may make a clean miss with a perfect hold. For this reason practically all gun makers of note, who want their guns to shoot well of course, usually add a small amount of choke. It may be only .002 or .003", but it will be there to round up the patterns and to give them a more uniform even spread without a lot of big holes or bunched shot.

Many gun makers make no chokes more open than an improved cylinder and we firmly believe no one should ever order cylinder bore, but even for the close range work order either improved cylinder or Skeet No. 1 or No. 2 boring, which is not far from the

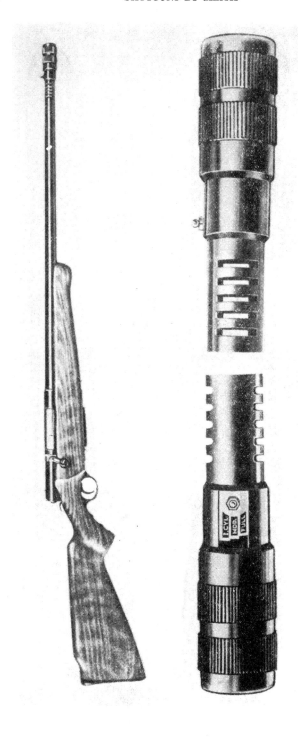

Top: New Mossberg Model 185K, 20-gauge and Model 190, 16-gauge, 3-shot Shotgun With Mossberg C-Lect-Choke. Bottom: Right, Top View of New Mossberg C-Lect-Choke and Ventilated Barrel on Models 185K and 190. Left Side View of the Same Choke.

same thing. If a woodcock, ruffed grouse or quail or pheasant breaks cover at a few feet to say 10 yards from the gun, then these boring are the best to be had and these degrees of choke will take them with certainty to 35 yards from 12 and 16 bore guns. Smaller gauges should have a trifle more choke even for short ranges than is permissible with the larger bores and heavier shot charges and the 20 bore, even for close range work should be bored about 50%. With the little 28 bore or the Magnum .410 we believe the full choke is best to be certain of a killing pattern, even though very much smaller with these small bores, hence we consider the small bore gun the arm for the expert, not the novice. The improved cylinder bore or choke should throw 45% patterns in a 30 inch circle at 40 yards and is usually very deadly from 12 and 16 bore guns up to 35 yards. Such a choke when used with small shot like No. 7½ or 8 for small birds and giving 45% patterns will usually shoot a bit higher percentages when used with big shot, but this boring must be considered the short range choke. It can also be secured from full choke guns by the use of Brush or Scatter loads as currently produced but both Remington-Peters and also by Western-Winchester and we presume as well by Federal Cartridge Co.

Shot, as they travel up the bore of a gun, are compressed between the over-powder wads and formerly the top wad, but now are compressed only between the over powder wads and the built up air pressure in front of the pellets. This pressure is not unlike the pressure in a hose and when the choke is reached, the shot must be further compressed. The elimination of the hard crimp and top wad saved at least 5% in patterns, as most shot were deformed in the forcing of the crimp and the chamber cone, not by the choke. We believe very few shot are deformed in the choke of a gun, as pressures have fallen off to such an extent by the time the shot have reached the muzzle, there is not enough remaining pressure to blow a small soldered patch out of a hole in the side of the gun barrel. If pressures four inches back of the muzzle when shooting 1¼ ounce ten bore loads would not blow out the soldered patch of about .22 caliber in diameter we had in an old hammer L. C. Smith, then we fail to see how the pressures at that point in the barrel can deform very many shot.

The true cylinder bored gun will throw about a 26 inch diameter pattern at 20 yards and will usually count about 40% at 40 yards in a 30 inch circle, but some of them will only throw 35% patterns. It is the most useless of all borings, having no choke at all. Most so called cylinders have .002″ choke.

The 45% choke known commonly as improved cylinder is the useful choke for close range shooting and will cover about 24 inches at 20 yards. We have never seen a breech loading shotgun that would throw patterns covering a 30 inch circle at 20 yards but that ancient musket we used to shoot would come pretty close to scattering them that wide. Also I have seen a gun or two that was badly overchoked and threw cart wheel patterns that big but with a great hole in the center of the pattern.

Skeet boring, so called, is usually very close to the improved cylinder or 45% choke. It may vary slightly one way or the other from the true improved cylinder, but is designed to give the best even spread of pattern at 20 yards range. Improved cylinder patterns usually cover about 24 inches at 20 yards and spread across a 30 inch circle at 25 yards. Such a pattern is usually effective out to 35 yards with certainty and slightly farther on large birds.

It is the proper choke for short range, quail, grouse and woodcock shooting as well as Skeet shooting. The man hunting quail in the west should usually have more choke in his gun and around 50% first barrel to 55% second barrel for doubles is about right. For average all around quail shooting by an experienced shot this 50 to 55% choke is about the deadliest quail gun to be had. The 50% choke is often known as the quarter choke. It is a good short range boring, not quite as wide as to spread as the improved cylinder but a better and more uniform killer out at 35 to 40 yards. It will usually kill fairly well even on small birds to 40 yards. The quarter choke should throw just about a 30 inch pattern at 30 yards and at that range is the ideal degree of choke.

Many Eastern and Southern grouse and quail shooters using double guns like an improved cylinder first barrel and a 50% quarter choke for the second barrel or at most 55% second barrel and with very good reason. The quarter choke will also make about 25 inch patterns at 25 yards and about 20 inch at 20 yards, in other words it spreads just about an inch to the yard of range and is a very useful quail gun.

Pump and auto loaders usually come with improved cylinder modified or 60% or full choke 70 percent. The man with a patent choke such as the Poly or similiar devices can get about any degree of choke he wishes on the repeater or single loader, so is not necessarily handicapped over the double gun man.

The next degree of choke is the so called modified, or usually 60% boring. This is a very useful all around choke, good on most anything that ranges from 30 to 45 yards. It usually gives one of the most evenly spread of all patterns.

Modified choke is a very good choice for the beginner for a duck and pheasant gun. It will not shoot as close or as centered a pattern as will the full choke gun but will give the shooter a much more even spread of pattern and a larger pattern as well, permitting clean killing, where he might likely miss with a full choke gun.

Modified is a good choke for decoy duck shooting, for jumped ducks and pheasants that do not rise to far out and for general all around shooting. It is probably the best choke for the novice for general duck shooting. Usually if the gun throws modified 60% patterns with low base light loads it will throw about 70% patterns with larger shot in the heavy duck loads. Then it becomes a ¾ choke or by present standards a 70% gun. This is probably the most favored degree of choke for the trap shot and works very well on average clay birds shooting. Some also call this 65% to 70% boring an improved modified. It differs from full choke more in the even spread of the pattern and with less centering of the shot charge than it does in actual diameter of pattern. For the average man, who is not an expert shot, it is a good second barrel choke for double guns, or for first barrel for any man using a double for a duck gun. The ¾ choke will put most of its killing spread in a 30 inch circle at 40 yards with of course some stray pellets outside, but anything in that 30 inch circle is very apt to be plastered at 40 yards if the shot size is right for the bird shot. The ¾ choke will usually count about 5 to 8% higher than the true modified, and with modern ammunition will usually throw full 70% patterns.

This 70% used to be the old standard full choke boring, but except in small bores the modern full choked gun in 12 and 16 gauge will usually go at least 75% in a 30 inch circle at 40 yards.

For average shooting of anything up to about 50 yards the ¾ choke is hard to beat and probably the best for the average shot.

Lastly we come to the full choke. As before stated it used to be considered standard at 70% and that was all the companies then claimed for it, but even then a little judicial testing of different size shot and different make loads would nearly always produce 75% patterns and very often 80% as well. Since the advent of the improved cup seal and lubricated expanding over-powder wads and the folded no-top wad crimp, the old 70% standard is now obsolete and most any full choke gun will go 75% or better. Some few will even do 85% to 90%, but rarely.

This is the choke for all long range difficult shooting and good full choked guns with loads that really fit the choke as to size of shot and powder charge balance will usually put most of the killing spread of the pattern, that is, the really deadly portion, say 65 to 70% of the charge, into about a 24 inch circle at 40 yards. Even this does not equal that first full choked 6 bore muzzle loader that Fred Kimble bored to throw the entire charge into a 30 inch circle at 40 yards and most of the time when he was careful of his loading into a 24 inch circle at 40 yards. This is the choke for all pass shooting, for long range duck, sage hen, and pheasant shooting where you need that dense centered pattern to carry a killing pattern to extreme long range. It can be told at a glance at the pattern from the ¾ choke as the shot will be so much more densely centered in the middle of the pattern. This is our own favorite pattern for most shooting here in Idaho where the ranges average long. The shooter however must be able to do better than average gun pointing to take advantage of its long range killing qualities, otherwise he would be like the dub rifle shot with a long range scope sighted rifle. It is the choke for goose shooting and we prefer it for all difficult shooting. True it's easier to hit with a more open boring, but if you center that full choke pattern the bird is dead and crumpled in the air and if Keith can't hit them, Keith can miss them with a clean conscience. I would always prefer a clean miss to a cripple, and on any game, either feathered or furred, prefer to kill clean or miss clean. If we miss then that is our fault and we can still have a lot of fun trying.

The formation of chokes in the gun bore vary a great deal. Some makers prefer a very short choke, only the last inch of two of the muzzle taking the total constriction, while others prefer to build their guns with a long gradual choke extending some five to six inches. Still others will have from one to three or four inches of gradual choke and then the last half to one inch of the muzzle ground out a perfectly true cylinder.

The object in this they claim is to choke the shot charge together and then give it a chance to unscramble itself and form in even layers before it finally exits from the muzzle. They also believe the gas flare is more uniform on the over-powder wads at the muzzle when this system is used. We have seen many Winchesters and Ithacas with that last half inch ground parallel and no doubt a lot of this was done in relieving an overchoked gun to give the best patterns with a given shot size and powder load. Of this we do not know but are very sure they were exceptionally good shooting guns.

Guns that have not enough choke have often been rechoked by the recess choke method, often called the jug choke. With this choke the bore is relieved or enlarged back of the choke for several inches, making the gun really over-bored at this section of the barrel, then when the shot charge expands to fill this enlarged portion of the bore, it must again be squeezed or funnelled through the choke which owing to the enlargement of the rear of the choke, gives the choke proper considerably more constriction, to the full amount of the relieving or enlargement. In this way, if the barrels are thick enough, an improved cylinder can be changed to a ¾, and if still thicker, even to a full choked gun, by such over boring or jug choking back of the choke proper.

Small shot and light powder loads such as the 3½ dram 1⅛ ounce No. 7½ trap load require considerably more choke than do heavy duck loads of 3¾ drams equivalent, progressive powder and 1¼ ounces of large shot, say No. 4. Very often a ¾ choke with the trap load will throw full choked 75 to 80 percent patterns with the heavy duck load. There is no cut and dried rule for choke boring and no two barrels as a rule are exactly alike, though we have a ten bore Ithaca and a 16 bore Ithaca that come as close to being exact as any I have ever seen, or ever expect to see. Both these guns average exactly the same for both barrels but that is a very exceptional performance and both guns had considerable work by the best barrel men Ithaca had at the factory years ago when they were built. We have owned many more doubles and still have others but their pair of barrels always differ some at least in percentages.

When pattern tested at the factory it is seldom that two barrels give exactly the same percentage even though they have tried their hardest to bore both exactly alike and many that will measure exactly the same inside from chamber to muzzle will for some reason unknown to man not shoot the same. A fine barrel man can tinker with them and usually relieve one or recess choke the other until they do give very close to the same patterns but this requires a lot of work and a change of make of ammunition may reverse the percentages of the two barrels.

The boring machines must work to some tolerance and in choking some tolerance must be allowed. The final testing and grinding out of the choke at the muzzle usually regulates the two bores for the desired degree of choke. I have seen many fine shooting doubles, one barrel of which was larger at the muzzle than the other and yet they threw the same percentages or very close to the same. By the same token I have seen some doubles, one barrel of which showed that considerable relieving had been done while the other looked as though it had never been relieved at all and yet they both shot near the same percentages. The human element must be considered, for it is ever present, and different machines will also vary slightly in their boring and different steels will cut and polish differently and one barrel may show a slight scar from the reaming and have to be polished more than the other to remove this. All these things in turn affect the exact amount of constriction at the muzzle to produce an exact pattern percentage.

As the tables will show the larger the bore the more constriction the gun will stand for a given degree of choke and the smaller the bore the less choke the gun will require in thousandths of an inch for a given degree of choke. While a 20 bore in full choke may do nicely with from .029" to .033" constriction, a Magnum ten bore may need from .040" to .048" or even .050" constriction at the muzzle.

Many full choked guns made thirty years ago are now a bit overchoked for modern heavy duck loads with heavy shot charges, large shot sizes and progressive burning powders. These guns can be relieved slightly in the choke and often greatly improve the count of the patterns as well as to give a more uniform spread of pattern. Too much choke and the shot will spread all over the side of a small building at 40 yards but usually with a thin center or a big hole in the center. An over choked gun is worthless for any type of shooting until the fault is remedied. So much for choke boring. We will get around to that chapter on patterns soon and attempt to show just what can be expected from some degrees of choke.

Variable Chokes and Compensators

Owners of all single barrel guns, either single loaders or repeaters, can now have variable chokes fitted to give them any desired degree of choke. Further, many of these devices will give almost instant change from one degree of choke to another. Many of these patented attachable chokes also incorporate a muzzle brake, or compensator, that greatly reduces recoil, some as much as 35 to 40 percent.

We are not going to make any attempt to list them all or to describe them all but will name and describe the better known ones. This does not imply any inferiority of others not listed, but will give the reader a working knowledge of them and what can be expected from them as a whole. Nearly every month sees the addition of a new muzzle brake or adjustable choke to the market, and like the many makes of fine English guns, we cannot take the space to list them all so cover some of the better known ones only.

All variable chokes and all compensators as well add nothing to the appearance or clean lines of a fine gun, in fact they greatly detract from its appearance and give it much the same appearance as a German 88-mm gun, a deadly effective device, but no thing of beauty.

First let us look into the patent chokes alone. These devices enable the shooter to change from one degree of choke to another, so as to make his gun a more versatile weapon for any type of shooting he is likely to encounter. Some of them, like the little Poly Choke and the very similar Mossberg choke enable the shooter to change from one degree of choke to another by simply turning a small sleeve near the muzzle a fraction of a turn. These devices have the choke separated at one end into segments and the sleeve is simply a collar, like that on a split-collar wrench. To attain a heavier degree of choke you merely turn the graduated sleeve, thus compressing the segments of the bore into a smaller circle or smaller choke with a resultant smaller pattern from the shot charge. These two devices are perhaps the fastest to change of all makes and only a couple seconds is required to change them from full cylinder to full choke. Like all the rest of these chokes they are unsightly on the gun, but do also have the advantage of offering more of an eye catcher in fast shooting, so that in spite of their inherent ugliness they are very effective in actual shooting.

They also enable the shooter to fit his choke to any load he is likely to encounter. A few strings at the pattern board will enable him or her to set that variable choke for any degree of spread of pattern desired within the limits of the gauge and shot charge. Over the years we have fired many cases of shell through them and have tested nearly all the current makes. They are almost indispensable on the gun intended for varied shooting. Such a device will give you a Skeet gun or upland gun for close range work on snipe, woodcock, ruffed grouse, or quail and yet with a twist of the sleeve you can instantly set the gun to full choke for a long range duck gun. Over the years we have found that with heavy duck loads the best full choke patterns were usually obtained at a modified or improved modified setting rather than at full choke as the full choke was usually too much constriction for the heavy loads for best and closest patterns.

Thus a man may go out for quail and carry his gun set improved cylinder and run onto a flight of ducks out at longer ranges and be all set for them in a couple of seconds. We see no need for them whatever on the long range duck and goose gun or on pass guns which should always be full choked, but even here they will enable the shooter to set his choke to give best patterns with any individual lot of shells if he will run a few patterns. However, for the all around gun or the upland gun they are a valuable addition to the weapon and almost indispensable for the man whose shooting ranges and game varies a great deal. Also for the man who must make one gun do for all his shooting, in other words the all-around shotgun.

With the double we can have one barrel bored full and the other modified or even improved cylinder and have instant selection of boring but with the single barrel weapon we must use whatever degree of choke is bored in that one barrel or else fit a variable choke.

Light field loads usually require more choke for a full choke pattern than do heavy progressive powder duck loads and the variable choke enables the shooter to adjust his choke for about any spread of pattern at a given range with a few shots at the pattern board or some old worthless building. While they may upset your esthetic sense of beauty, they are very efficient devices and very much worthwhile on any gun intended for all around shooting. The plain Poly Choke without compensator is our choice of them all. But please bear in mind this is just one man's opinion and the writer is not infallible.

Next let us look into the compensators or recoil reducing devices that come along with the patent chokes in many instances. The first one we saw and used was the old Cutts, invented and patented by Col. Cutts and still sold by the Lyman Gunsight Corp.

We first tried this device on a .30-06 Springfield rifle with of course no choke device. It was the most effective recoil reducer we have ever seen as the rifle simply pulled away from our shoulder at each shot. However the muzzle blast and report was thrown back in our ears in the prone position to such an extent that a couple of clips almost deafened us for a couple days. That was around 20 years ago. Since then we have tried most of the shotgun compensators on the market. They all reduce recoil greatly, some as much as 30 to 40%. But we have not found any that completely eliminated shoulder recoil to the extent on shotguns that that early Cutts Comp. did on the Service rifle. Likewise all we have tested, Weaver Choke, Power-Pac, Cutts and many others have all thrown the muzzle blast back in our ears to such an extent that we much prerfer the recoil of any shotgun to that deafening ear-splitting muzzle blast. On the Skeet or trap ranges where one can pad his ears with cotton or slip ear protectors in them, then the compensators will greatly reduce fatigue that normally comes from firing long strings and we are not at all sure but what one is often better off deaf in a big match anyway. Under the strain of hot competition what one doesn't hear won't hurt his shooting.

Both the Cutts and the Weaver chokes employ separate tubes for each degree of choke and this fact in turn necessitates the packing along of extra tubes and a wrench to change them. These two chokes will give a change of choke and pattern but only at the expense of some time involved in the change as well as the extra tubes and wrench which must be carried. The Pachmayr Power-Pac is in the same category and comes with three tubes and a wrench for their removal and installation.

The latest Poly Choke with compensator as well as some others that incorporated the Poly Choke all have that same instant choice and selection of choke degree through the turning of a sleeve. We believe the improved Poly Choke with compensator or some of the other compensators incorporating the Poly to be the simplest and best of the lot. The new Mossberg compensator and patent choke is very similar to the Poly in action and has a series of vertical slots cut in each side right through the outer portion of the barrel on each side back of the variable choke which closely resembles the Poly in operation. When the shooter requires a compensator to reduce recoil in addition to a variable choke we believe he would do well to select one of these devices with instant change of choke by the sleeve method, rather than lug around extra tubes and a wrench for their installation.

Reduction of recoil is accomplished by these compensators by slots or vents cut through that portion of the compensator allowing the gases to flare out through these vents, thus acting on them in such a way as to pull the gun forward at the same time the shot charge is leaving the muzzle. They thus utilize that last of the gas in the barrel to reduce recoil. At the same time they reduce the actual muzzle blast on the shot charge and tend more to prevent the over-powder wads from being driven through the shot charge and on very short barrels at least they must thus be responsible for an improvement in patterns over convention shotgun barrels. We believe their use in the field, however, offers some chance for pellets to be sheared from the charge and fly out to the side and with some possible attendant danger to a brother shooter standing alongside of the muzzle. We have learned of several persons being thus stung with stray fragments of pellets at times from their use when standing well to the side of the shooter. This is a very rare occurrence but not an impossibility and should be remembered.

We well remember one time Bob Shook of Durkee, Oregon, and the writer were hunting blue grouse on Lookout Mountain. The birds had climbed high on the mountain and we had dropped our reins and left our horses stand in a clump of timber while we worked the highest slopes and ridges. Bob was working up a ridge just across a small gulch or coulee from me when a big cock bird raised above us and came down that gulch with wings set and going as if the devil was after him. We waited until he passed between us then raised the old 16 bore Ithaca, picked up the fast disappearing grouse and swung ahead for lead and let her go. Down came the big heavy blue grouse in a cloud of feathers from the 1⅛ ounce of No. 5 shot, but at the same time we heard Bob say "—damn your old shotgun." Looking around we saw him holding his face with both hands and could not understand what had happened to him as the bird was going right down the gulch and directly away from the two of us. Blood was running down his face, and he finally picked up his gun and came across to me. There was one of my No. 5 shot imbedded against his skull in the middle of the forehead. Taking my jack knife I soon had it extracted and found it badly battered, evidently before it struck Bob in the forehead. That shot had to hit the bird and turn almost straight back to ever come back up the mountain and strike Bob as it did, which only goes to show what can happen even with every precaution taken. That grouse was at least 45 yards below us and going like all possessed when hit and Bob was only some 15 yards from me and at exactly the same angle from the bird as my own position. The grouse was too high in the air for the pellet to have hit a rock or tree and return so we assumed it must have hit the bird on a wing or other bone and returned to take Bob square in the forehead.. It would have destroyed an eye if it had hit as it cut right through to his skull. That is the only time we have accidentally shot anyone, but it was a lesson we will always remember. Since then we have taken many birds when out with companions and had them do the same at exactly the same apparently safe angle, in fact shooting away from the two of us and such a thing has never again occurred but shows the possibility of a stray pellet being deflected out some of those events on the various compensators.

We believe the vents should be on top and bottom of the barrel rather than on each side as they would then tend to throw the blast away from the shooters ears to a greater extent. Also should ever a pellet or fragment be driven out a vent it would then go either up or down and be harmless to a fellow shooter. Shot are deformed in the forcing cone, and at times fragments are thus sheared off the pellet, such deformed shot are the ones most likely to short cut to get out of the gun and emerge through a vent and fly off at some crazy angle. Had we been shooting a compensated gun that time with Bob Shook instead of a bull choked double barrel we would no doubt have blamed that stray pellet onto the compensator and maybe wrongly at that.

There can be little question but that on short barrelled guns, compensators, through their reduction of the muzzle blast, also further good patterns but on long barrelled guns, this is not so apparent as on 24 inch to 26 inch barrelled guns. We do not believe any gun with compensator attached should have less than an overall barrel length of 26 inches. However we did test a Magnum 12 bore model 12 Winchester with only 24 inches of barrel and a compensator attached in back of a Poly Choke. It was a surprisingly good shooting gun and we killed many crows to a full 70 yards with it and the 1⅞ ounce load of No. 4s. The Muzzle blast, however, was terrific and gave us a headache though the recoil was quite light.

Poly Chokes or other variable chokes are very useful in fitting the gun for a given buckshot load. Most guns won't throw buck worth a whoop, but with a variable choke you can soon adjust the choke to the load and obtain very fine buckshot patterns.

We once owned a fine No. 4 New Model Ithaca single trap with Poly Choke on its 30 inch barrel, tube being about 28″ without the choke. The elevated ventilated rib also matched up well with the enlarged choke. We liked that gun very much and used it for some time in ammunition testing. It could be adjusted to give any desired pattern with any make of good shotshell and we also found that when set at modified it threw exceptional patterns with nine pellets of No. 00 buck.

That gun would throw an excellent improved cylinder pattern or an equally good full choke pattern with about every desired degree of spread in between those two and we consider it a much more versatile gun that if it had not been equipped with that Poly Choke. We also tried it with rifled slugs and found the best setting to be modified choke for them. It would make 4 inch to 5 inch 50 yard groups of five shots each consistently. Of course the flat elevated rib and the double sights helped a lot in such group shooting. We believe variable chokes invaluable for those single barrel shooters who must hunt their deer with buckshot, as they can then fit their choke to the load and obtain a really dense killing pattern to 40 yards at least.

Shooters who have not used a compensator or variable choke should always borrow a gun and try them out before having their own gun so equipped as many will not like the blast of a compensator, while others will simply be delighted with its recoil reduction. You can figure on a reduction in recoil of from 25 to 40% in the main.

The enlarged patent chokes also usually raise the front sight on a gun and for many these compensated guns or guns with Poly or other chokes shoot slightly low. It is well for all to try them out first before they have one fitted to their own gun. With many of the older pump and auto loaders the compensator and patent choke made a very effective eye catcher on the end of the barrel and lined up about right for elevation with the matted strip down the top of the receiver. With other guns we have tested the increased height of the front bead seemed to make the guns shoot low for us, while when guns with elevated ventilated or high ribs were used the top of the patent choke and front sight came to just the right elevation over the rib. We have even seen some guns with a strip of metal sweated to the top of the receiver or rear end of barrel to raise the line of sight to compensate for the high front sight, and this worked out very well indeed. The bevel block of ivory or other white material as designed by Bob Nichols also works out very well with a poly or other patent choke. At any rate give the devices a careful test before having them fitted as we have known shooters to have them fitted to their guns, then to turn around and order new replacement barrels when they found they did not like the devices.

Since writing this chapter we have tested a Mossberg bolt action shot gun with their compensator on it consisting of some transverse slots milled in each side of the barrel. It does not deflect the muzzle blast back in our ears at all, neither can we see that it decreases recoil much if any from standard 20 bore recoil. However the gun has a very small 22 rifle size butt plate which may make the recoil feel normal when in reality it is lighter than normal.

CHAPTER EIGHT

Stocks and Stocking.

MUCH OF THE BEAUTY of a shotgun lies in its stocking. The beauty of outline as well as the color and figure of the wood and the patterns of the checkering all contribute to a beautiful and practical gun. With plain finished guns, the beauty of outline still must be considered as well as the perfection of fit to the individual, for a perfect shooting gun. The strength of the gun is also dependent on proper stocking and proper fit of wood and steel at grip and fore-end and at the junction of the butt stock and frame. The shape and drop of the stock and the thickness and elevation of its comb have a very vital bearing on how any individual will shoot with that particular weapon.

Trap shots in particular, are as fussy about stock fit as an old hen with a single chick, and with good reason. They well know everything in their business depends on a proper fitting stock. The comb of the stock must be of the exact height to give them perfect elevations with the spread of their pattern. The length must be just right to allow a perfect grip on the gun and perfect comfortable position of the head and cheek on the comb and the length must be just right for the position of the two hands and to keep the thumb away from the nose in recoil.

With too short a stock the thumb will strike the schnozzle in recoil; with too long a stock the gun will be unwieldy and slow as well, and also seems to kick one more than with a stock of proper length. To some extent stock length can be governed by the position of the forward hand, but it must never be too short or the thumb as it crosses the grip of the stock will strike the nose, and tears and good shooting do not go together. If the stock is a mite long one can grasp the forestock farther to the rear and the gun will then mount and handle very well, but there is a limit even here. Trap stock are usually much straighter and longer than either Skeet or game stocks and for the reason that the shooting is all at rapidly rising birds. The gun is mounted and the head dropped forward hard on the stock before the bird is ever called for, so such stocks are then an asset but would be detrimental to fast mounting and fast shooting under either field or Skeet conditions. One will usually do better shooting with a bit shorter stock than he thinks fits him best in the field, especially if he has on heavy clothing.

The comb of the stock guides and holds the eye in proper position over the breech of the gun and it must be just right for each individual to do his best work. Shotguns are pointed by the two hands and the head should be bedded tight and solid yet with comfort on the stock comb, then as we swing with the bird the whole top of our body swings as a unit and we depend on foot work and the twist of our lower body to follow the game or target. If the stock comb be too high the gunner will overshoot and if too low there will be a steady tendency to under shooting. Shooters vary much in facial conformation; some have high cheek bones and some have

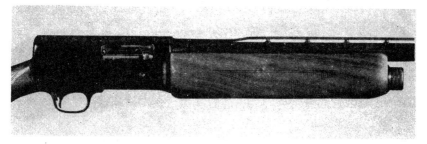

E. C. Bishop Standard Fore-end for the Remington Auto Loader.

low cheek bones and a stock that fits one perfectly will seldom fit the other type.

Some shooters are hollow chested and narrow shouldered while others have wide, deep chests and wide shoulders. Some have short arms and short fingers and some abnormally long arms and fingers. Homo Sapiens is an adaptable cuss, but there is a limit to his adaptability, and beyond that his shooting will suffer. He will always do his best work with a gun that fits him perfectly down to the last minute detail. Women also differ from men in the shape of their shoulders and arms and usually require different stocks. The very wide shouldered person with short neck will usually want cast-off in this stock, while the more resilient person of more normal build will not want any cast-off and some very narrow chested individuals may even like a bit of cast-on. The toe of the stock for most women should be cast-off slightly on account of their breasts, but it is seldom they need any cast-off to the comb or heel of stock. The English almost universally like a cast-off stock. Americans seldom do. The English as a rule shoot a straighter stock than do we and almost always a straight grip as well. On the Continent the Germans in particular went even more to thin knife edge combs than the English and nearly always too high a comb as well. Just what there is about their shooting habits or facial contours that should demand such abnormally high combs, and thin ones as well, is beyond me. We have seen many of them with not over 1¼″ drop at the Comb and not over 2″, and often less, at the heel. One was forced to shoot those guns by feel alone and with the level of the eyes well above that of the gun barrels; in fact, snap-shooting.

Time was when about all American guns were stocked with far too much drop at both comb and heel and too much down-pitch as well, and they then defeated the purpose of a shotgun stock and forced one to consciously aim the darn things, to hit at all. We have never seen such faults as a rule with English guns and owing to the influence of the trap and Skeet shooters, the standard American stock is now around 14″ in length with a drop of around 1⅝ at comb by 2¼ to 2½″ at heel. This is a far cry from the stocks of the eighties, nineties and even into this century when they often went

New E. C. Bishop and Son Custom Extension Fore-end on Model 12 Winchester.

for 3″ drop at heel and 1¾ to 2″ at comb and a down-pitch of about three inches as well.

Such gruesome stocks were also hard kickers as they tended to make the barrels of the gun recoil upwards to a much greater extent than with straighter stocks. Even as a boy when we ordered our first good double gun, a No. 3 Ithaca, the standard stock was 14″ in length with a drop of 1¾″ x 2¾″. Though we learned to shoot it, we finally learned also that it was much more bend than necessary. Early stock combs were also too thin; but of late years American stocks have much improved in dimensions until today, we believe the standard American shotgun stock will come nearer fitting the greater percentage of shooters than any other stock design in the world.

The English stock is almost standard with straight grip and there can be no question but the straight grip gives the gun the cleanest lines of any. American standard stocks are almost universally with a long pistol grip. It adds nothing to their lines or beauty and little to utility as usually made, as the grip is so long it merely flares slightly at the rear of the shooting hand. There can be no question, however, that a well designed and made pistol grip does afford a better control of the gun with the shooting hand, than a straight grip can ever afford. This is especially true with heavy, hard kicking duck and goose guns, and the well shaped pistol grip allows the shooter to pull them in snug to his shoulder and also hold them so in shooting. The pistol grip also allows slightly more wood and weight in the butt stock to balance the barrels and action. The nearer we can get the greatest concentration of weight, namely, the action of the gun between the two hands, the better will the piece balance and the faster we can swing the gun. Too long a stock throws the balance too far forward, yet the stock must always be long enough that you can grip it firmly at the small of the stock with the thumb over the top of the grip and still maintain that hand position with no chance of busting your nose with the knuckle of your thumb. This relation of thumb knuckle and the nose, is a very good guide to stock length. Have it just long enough to adequately protect your nose in all positions and no more.

Any additional length beyond what is needed, makes the gun slower to mount, slower to get on your bird, and slower in your swing when following and leading. It also places the left or forward hand farther back on the forestock, which in turn gives the weapon more weight forward and is detrimental to fast, even swing of the piece.

The stock is the unit, which with the two hands unites the body and the gun into a whole, and when mounted the gun should become a part of the upper body. The head should be down firmly but comfortably on the comb, with the eye in exactly the right position and relation to the shotgun rib. A perfect fitting stock permits just that, and anything that is not a perfect stock fit, will not in turn permit you to do your best work, either in the field or at the targets. If you like the clean lines of a straight grip, then get one, and if you prefer the feel and excellent grip of the pistol grip then get that style.

Next the stock comb. This is your rear sight so to speak, and it simply has got to fit your individual facial contour and throw your shooting eye the correct distance above the rib. Also when cheeked firmly but comfortably it must throw your eye in exact line over the top of the rib. Folks with full, fleshy faces may require thinner combs than folks with thin angular faces. The main thing is to have a stock comb thick enough to adequately support your cheek and cheek bone and throw your eye automatically in perfect alignment both laterally and for elevation as well. Here is where the cheek rest comes in. It is almost universal on German guns but seldom seen on English guns, while many Americans have tried it and found its advantages. We figure the more your face comes in even contact with the cheek piece or comb the better and the cheek piece allows far more facial contact than can any ordinary stock comb. Usually trap combs are much thicker than hunting gun stock combs, for the reason that trap guns are mounted and the head firmly bedded on the comb before ever the bird is called for. In field shooting the gun must be mounted in the twinkling of an eye the while the eye follows the bird and figures lead. For this reason Skeet or field combs usually are thinner than trap combs but they should be thick enough to force the eye to find that correct position automatically and even in the fastest of snap shooting. The position or relation to the point or forward portion of the stock comb to the thumb knuckle is also of utmost importance. It should be far enough forward to adequately support the knuckle of the thumb and to allow the pulling of the piece in solid to the shoulder, especially so on straight grip guns. Even with pistol grip guns it is still important to have that stock comb just the right distance back of the thumb in normal shooting position to support the thumb and back of that portion of the hand. It also helps keep the thumb knuckle forward of your sneezer in recoil. If the comb is too far to the rear it will not support the shooting hand and thumb as it should and if too far forward, then it does not leave adequate room for the thumb to come over the grip and properly control the gun.

Next is the top of the comb itself. With standard stocks the swing to the left for right handed persons and vice versa for south paws will in turn carry your cheek bone well forward on the stock, and if that elevation of the eye over the rib is then correct, you will find that when you swing to the right and the face is farther to the rear, then your eye will be lower on the stock and you are apt to shoot low. The more bend in the stock or more drop at the heel of stock the more difference you will find in elevations of your pattern in these two extremes of position. That is the reason for the Monte Carlo Comb. We like it on all shotguns, as it is the same height at both ends with relation to the rib and thus keeps the eye at the same elevation over the rib regardless of which way you may swing in following a fast flying bird. It gives you more uniform elevation in either trap or field shooting and is very much worthwhile, though it does add nothing to the lines or beauty of the gun, in fact detracts from the clean lines of the stock. However we figure this is one extra that is very much worth while. It also permits the long-necked man who shoots with head erect and likes a lot of drop to his stock, to still maintain even uniform elevations for his pattern regardless of which way he may swing.

The cheekpiece should flare out well from the body of the stock and be long enough to accommodate the cheek in any position, whether you are swinging far to the left or far to the right. It makes for uniformity of facial position on the stock hence also for uniformity of the eye over the rib of the gun. We prefer cheek pieces on all guns both rifles and shotguns even for fastest work. A too thin cheek piece is but little better than an ordinary stock comb and gives not much more support to the cheek. Shotgun cheek pieces should be much longer than rifle cheek pieces for the reason that when a right hand person swings to the left in following a bird his face naturally comes far forward on the stock comb, but when he swings to the right if he is right handed then his face is apt to come much farther back on the stock comb. The cheek rest must be long enough to accommodate both extremes of position.

The cheekpiece, we must remember, is an integrated part of the stock comb, really a prolongation of it down toward the belly of the stock. Given a good perfect-fitting thickness of stock comb, the cheek rest adds materially to the amount of the cheek the stock supports.

E. C. Bishop and Son Custom Stock on Model 12 Winchester Showing Superb Carving, Wood, and Checkering with Fred Etchen Type Short Pistol Grip

The more of the cheek that comes in contact with the comb and cheek rest, the less likely is that stock to bruise the shooter's face or cause a gun headache.

The cheek rest should be perfectly flat, not convex, nor yet concave, for best results, so it can slide under the cheek in recoil. This is also just what the Monte Carlo comb will do if the stock does not have excessive heel drop; that is, slide back from beneath the cheek bone in recoil. With conventional stock design and a high comb and low heel, the gun has a sharp up-chuck and the barrels raise considerably on firing, with the net result that the comb of the stock hits you a sharp rap under the cheek bone. If the stock has a very thin sharp comb this can become very painful after a few shots. Comfort makes for confidence and both are needed in the shooting game.

One should never aim a shotgun like a rifle. The face must be bedded solidly on the stock, so that gun, arms, hands, shoulders and the shooter's head become a wedded integral whole, then the shooting eye should be looking at the bird or target, and only dimly seeing the gun at all, but the subconscious will dimly see the rib in line or the two ivory sights in line but with the line of sight at the breech well above the rear end of the rib or breech, usually around ⅜″ above it. Some of the barrel or rib should show up between the front and ivory bead on guns with such sights and the same elevation of the eye over the breech holds true with gun with only a front bead or no bead at all. When a gun has proper rib pitch and proper stocking to thus hold the shooter's head in correct position over the tube or tubes, he sees his whole target clearly and is in a position to see and judge any quick turn it may make in any direction, thus greatly simplifying his rapid mental calculations for lead in any conceivable direction. To be right, the gun should then throw the center of the pattern just over that front bead and should center it right where you look.

Some trap shots of course prefer more elevation of their patterns to automatically take care of fast rising targets, but we prefer the pattern centered just over the front bead with the eye seeing over the rib about ⅜″ above the breech end of the gun. We can then take care of birds much better that have passed over us or birds that are actually going down, as in blue grouse shooting on steep mountain ridges, where the game takes off and sails out and down the mountain. A high shooting gun is hopeless for average blue grouse shooting, just as it is for pass duck shooting, where you take the birds after they have passed over the blind or stand.

In Britain the prospective gun buyer goes to his gunmaker. There he will be correctly fitted with a proper gun stock just as a tailor will measure you and fit you with a suit of clothes.

This is accomplished by the use of a try-gun. A regular shotgun, having adjustments for all degrees of bend, cast off or cast on, as well as any amount of comb drop. Their expert gun fitter will take the customer to the target range and while he shoots clay targets carefully adjust that try-gun until the shooter is perfectly fitted. Then and then only will they take down all stock dimensions and the gun he orders will be stocked to those exact specifications.

This is a far different procedure from the usual one in America, where an individual may suddenly decide he wants to go duck or grouse shooting on the week end, and then rushes to the nearest gun store and grabs the first gun that appeals to him from the rack, purchases it and some ammunition, and departs the place. This usual American rush is also the reason that many people who would have become fine wing shots, never become more than very mediocre performers. Their guns do not fit them in the first place and may be totally wrong for the type of shooting they want to do.

In selecting a gun, a bit of intelligent study of your body conformation, as well as what use to which you will put the gun, is in order if best results are to be achieved. Lacking the adjustable try-gun in most American gun stores, we can at least try for fit and feel as many different guns as possible. The Skeet and trap ranges are also excellent places to see and try for fit many different types of gunstocks, remembering that the average Skeet gun will usually be stocked more to field specifications than will the usual straight trap stock, intended for those rising birds. At the trap range you will have an excellent chance to observe the different types of guns in action, particularly in doubles trap shooting and this will in turn help you no end in deciding what type of gun you want, whether pump, auto, side-by-side, or over-under double. Remember also, that the average Skeet gun usually makes a top flight gun for quail, ruffed grouse or woodcock, both in stocking and also in boring.

We believe all shotgun stocks should have a big, deep wide, soft recoil pad. This pad clings to the shoulder when the gun is mounted, also helps to maintain the position of the butt on the shoulder in fast repeat shots, and is vital to success. Many guns made in this country come equipped with a slick hard rubber plate that slips around on the shoulder more or less each time the gun is mounted. Such butt plates have no place on a good shotgun, and should never be accepted. The recoil pad, of soft rubber, not only absorbs a lot of the recoil of the piece, but also aids materially in maintaining perfect position of the gun butt on the shoulder. It is a must. In this respect the British are prone to simply checker the butt of the stock with no plate or pad at all. Some will add heel and toe plates only leaving the center of the butt just the checkered wood. Formerly Parker finished many of their guns in this way, however we believe better work will usually be done if the gun is equipped with a soft recoil pad.

If the gun comes with only a hard slick rubber plate or a steel plate or the British checkered wood butt and if it is a bit short for the individual shooter then he can add one of the many slip-on rubber recoil pads that are most satisfactory in every way and not only take up a lot of recoil, but also protect the butt of the stock to no small extent. If the stock comes too long then it must be cut off anyway so one might as well have the recoil pad added at the same time. Remember again, comfort makes for confidence and good shooting.

Next let us look at the fore-end. On all automatics the forestock comes back to the front end of the receiver, being long enough for the longest armed individual and yet coming back to the frame far enough to permit a perfect grasp by the shortest armed individual. The grasp of the forward hand on the forestock or around the barrels on side-by-side doubles helps materially in absorbing and dampening out the effects of recoil. Fine trap single guns are almost all stocked with a wide beavertail fore-end that is narrow at the front of the frame but, as it extends out along the barrel, becomes ever wider. This feature in turn prevents the forestock from kicking back through the grasp of the forward hand in actual shooting, thus forces the forward hand and arm to absorb a major portion of the gun's recoil

Thus we see, that both the auto-loader and the single trap gun are well equipped, not only to help the forward hand absorb recoil but, with both guns, the forestock is long enough for the longest arms yet comes clear back to the frame; thus accommodating the lad with short arms. Women usually have shorter arms than men and usually grasp the forestock farther to the rear or nearer the frame. With the over-under we have the same long, deep fore-end as with the auto-loader, but with the pump gun, the standard fore-end is just right for the long armed person and usually the slide is too far out for the short armed person. Here is where the extension fore-end or slide handle comes in, and for all short armed persons the pump gun should have the extension fore-end, thus permitting them a good, firm, com-

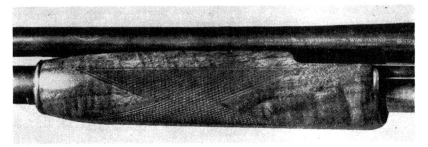

E. C. Bishop and Son Custom Standard Extension Fore-end for Model 12 Winchester.

fortable grasp of the slide handle at any point from the frame for-ward. Many custom stockers specialize in fitting these extension slide handles or fore-ends for the pump gun. Among the better-known out-fits furnishing them is E. C. Bishop & Sons of Warsaw, Mo. They are a necessity for the short armed pump gun shooter, and their lack in former years was one very good reason why we never liked a pump gun.

Next and lastly we have the side-by-side double fore-end. On the usual game gun it is very small very shallow and simply provides a home for the ejector locks and fills out the gap from the angle of the frame to the barrels, as well as holding the gun together. Little more is really needed on the game gun where lightness is wanted. The forward hand usually grasps around the two barrels out in front of the forestock anyway unless the shooter has very short arms. In al-most all field shooting, one seldom fires enough at one time to heat the barrels to where they would be uncomfortable, but in England and on the Continent and in Scotland they do have grouse and pheasant drives that require almost continuous shooting. Here, also, they usually employ a second gun and a loader to keep them loaded. Even then at times their shooting is so hot and continuous as to heat the barrels past the point where they are comfortable to hold in the hand. The answer to this problem then and also for double trap guns, used in long strings of doubles at the trap, is the beavertail fore-end.

The English also have a leather covered metal shield clipping around the barrels that will form a grasp for the forward hand and a protection for it from the heat of the barrels in continuous firing. The Beavertail fore-end, however, is the answer and should be fitted to all side-by-side doubles that are to be used in very long strings of continuous shooting. We do not like some of the short paddles formerly furnished by some companies, such as the first beavertails by Ithaca, which were far too short and fat. Neither do we like the square-ended beavertail furnished on some doubles and the abrupt rear end of some found on L. C. Smith guns. The beavertail should be long and graceful and should gradually raise up from the front of the frame until it covers half of the barrel. It should be just wide enough to properly cover the lower half of the barrels with no extra thickness or weight that would in turn run the balance of the piece too far forward. We particularly like the beavertail fore-end as formerly furnished on some of the old Parker double traps. They are beauties and carry the same graceful lines as the rest of the gun yet are amply long for any arm length, providing a perfect grasp for the forward hand. The single and double trap guns are the only place we have found where the beavertail fore-end is a real necessity and while many are fitted to rifles, we never could see the logic of such fore-ends on rifles. Only persons with very large hands and very long fingers might find them advantageous.

Cast-Off or Cast-On

The English almost universally use cast-off in their stocks, just why we do not know; also, they usually favor thin combs. Cast-off is a great boon to the gun stocker who has a fine blank and wants to make a cheek-piece stock. Most shotgun blanks and most rifle blanks for that matter, are too thin to afford a proper cheek rest, thus the man who has a blank only two inches thick, and yet has an order for a cast-off stock, can, by giving considerable cast-off to the heel and comb, get out a fair cheek rest from the narrow blank.

Cast-off stocks permit the shooter to place the butt of the gun solid against his shoulder and yet keep his head and neck more in a straight line with the body. We never could see the cast-off stock ourselves as one has merely to turn the body at more of an angle to the point of aim to bring the straight stock in proper line with the cheek. However the cast-off stock does permit the shooter to face his target more squarely and this must be the reason why the British prefer such stocks. We can see no difference in shooting whether one faces his target more squarely or whether he places the left foot more ahead and the left shoulder forward for right handed shooters; and we firmly believe that the only real necessity for a cast-off stock is for the use of the very wide shouldered individual with a short, thick neck. It may then prove very advantageous. Most any person of

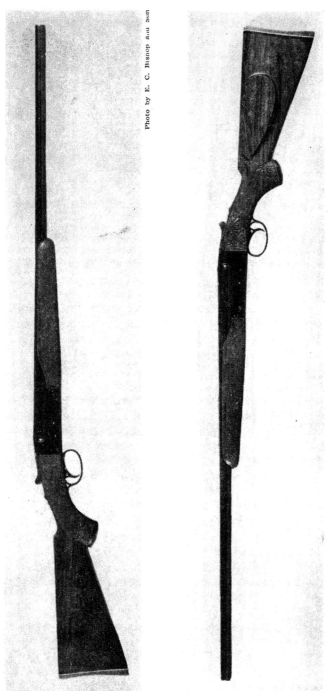

Photo by E. C. Bishop and Son

Winchester Model 21 Double Gun Custom Restocked by E. C. Bishop and Son.

normal build can, however, learn to shoot a cast-off stock with little difficulty, but on the whole it never seemed to permit firm, hard cheeking of the gun comb as does a stock with no cast-off.

A cast-in stock is seldom seen unless it was made for a southpaw. Most all cast-in stocks are originally made for southpaws and for the same reason the cast-off stock is for the right handed shooter. With right handed shooters about the only individual who would want or could use a cast-in stock would be a person with abnormally narrow shoulders and a thin, hollow chest. The cast-in stock for a right handed person would be a cast-off stock for the left hander. We still believe that facial contours have as much or more to do with fitting a man with a cast-off stock than bodily conformation and the man with a very wide face usually likes a cast-off stock while the individual with a thin face usually likes a straight stock and might even prefer some cast-in. German guns are usually stocked straight but many Belgian guns have cast-off. We believe it more of a fad than a utility. One thing you can bet, if you order an English gun it will have cast-off unless you specify it be straight.

Wood for Stock

Next let us look at the material for fine gun stocks. We have seen nothing quite the equal of fine figured Circassian or French Walnut. It is very dense, is hard almost as ivory, yet usually light in weight and tough as well so makes the most perfect of all gun stocks. As a general rule only the finest guns will be stocked in fine French or Circassian, but many of the plainer, less expensive, good double guns will use a straighter grain French or Circassian. In the finer blanks the cost will often run from $50 to $75 just for a shotgun stock blank with matching fore-end piece. These are things of beauty, and nothing in nature is more beautiful than a well-figured piece of French or Circassian walnut, with contrasting streaks and whorls or cloudy effects of light orange and black. When made up into a well shaped and designed gun stock, they, like a beautiful woman, need little further embellishment. Their natural beauty greatly enhances the general beauty and value of any fine gun. American crotch walnut often runs to very fancy wavy effect and general beauty but it is usually a heavier wood and likewise most crotch walnut of American variety shows flaws and is prone to season check after a few years.

This best wood should be slowly seasoned at least five years before it is ever made into a stock. In America, at least, we kiln dry the wood and bring it down to the proper moisture content in a very short time, then it is prone to warp and twist and also check, and such rapid curing is deterimental to the wood. English gunsmiths usually keep their fine woods in their lofts for five years before they touch them. Formerly some outfits cured their wood by

Photo by E. C. Bishop and Son

Winchester Model 12 Custom Restocked by E. C. Bishop and Son. Note Extension Slide Handle and Fred Etchen Type Pistol Grip.

cutting the green logs and placing them in ponds for about three years before they were ever sawn into planks.

Most all low-priced standard-grade guns in this country are stocked with plain American walnut and over the years it has well served its purpose and when properly seasoned makes a good strong and lasting stock. The grain should run perfectly straight in the grip or small of stock for strength and the forestock should also be fairly straight grain. The toe of a gun stock should also carry the grain nearly straight, right up the belly of the stock and one should never select a blank where the grain runs out at an angle in the belly of the stock from the toe. Such a stock is very apt to split the toe off the first time it comes in contact with hard ground or is accidentally dropped on the butt. If the grain does not run out to the belly at the toe and is straight in the grip, then the more figure we can have in the rest of the stock the better and the more beautiful it will be.

Some American firms have recently gone to plastic stocks. These are finished to look like most beautiful walnut, but they have their faults. They are thin hollow shells and will break right through if they get a hard knock and are also prone to warp when exposed to strong sunlight or placed too near a camp fire. We do not approve of plastic stocks in any form. They are no doubt cheap to manufacture and when new are nice to look at but we would never trust one as we saw far too many failures of the continuity with them. We also do not like laminated stocks in any form but if you want to see them in plentitude you have only to examine the rack of guns at any big trap shoot. Trap shooters are very particular about their stock fit and as they use the guns they are constantly having the combs or drops changed. Also, as the guns are swapped or sold back and forth the new owner often has different ideas about stock fit and hies himself to his gunsmith and has a new comb glued and pinned on and shaped to suit him, so you may well find stocks that have been changed so many times that only the main center of them from grip to butt is original. Fitting a new comb thus or a new pistol grip is usually much cheaper than making a new stock and many trap shots are constantly changing their stocks. We have seen them buy a fine trap gun with a stock that to us appeared and felt perfect, yet in a few days, especially after a bad run at the traps, they would hop on the comb with a horse rasp and cut it down, then in a week or two they would have some gunsmith glue on a new comb and start over again. We believe such men would do well to study their bodily conformation, stance, etc., and fit themselves out in the first place and then learn that gun and stick to it unless some glaring faults in the stock develop.

We have noticed most of the top notch shots get a gun that fits and then money won't buy it nor will they allow any changes in it. Some are fitted with an adjustable pad which is a good thing, as it

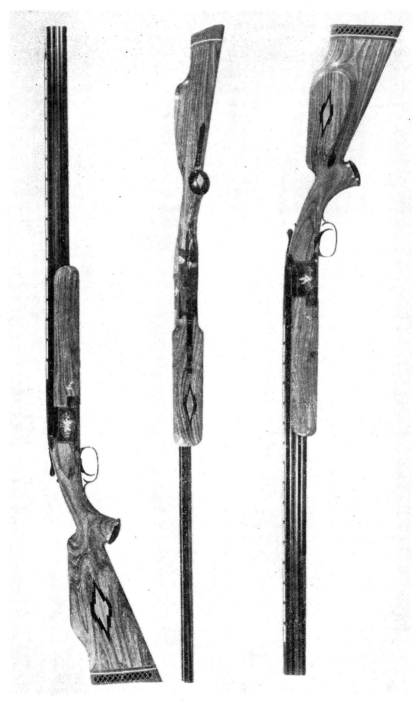

Browning Over-Under Gun Stocked by Weatherby in Mesquite Wood for Herb Klein of Dallas, Texas

permits adjustment for more or less drop without a lot of carpenter work on a fine stock.

For stock finish we believe the best to be the so called London dull oil finish. It will not scratch, and gives a depth of finish not equalled by any other method. It is also the most lasting gunstock finish we know of. Its surface is easily renewed by rubbing a tiny bit of boiled linseed oil into the stock after being out in wet weather and rubbing until the stock is perfectly dry, when the beauty of the finish is completely renewed. Most low grade guns and many rather fine guns made in this country are varnished and we never did like varnish in any form on a gunstock. It is prone to scratch, also flake and chip off, leaving the bare wood; and if at all possible one should always specify an oil finished stock. Oil finished stocks will usually run at least $25 more in cost but are worth it on a gun you are going to use a lifetime.

Next we come to checkering of the gunstock and fore-end. Checkering does not add to the beauty of fine woods, but it does afford a firmer grasp for both hands on the gun and gives one a confident feel that it is not going to slip. Checkering in itself can be beautiful if not over-done. Too much is about as bad as not enough. With the large beavertail fore-ends found on the single and double trap gun, a large checkering pattern is in order, but the grip checkering pattern should be just enough to cover where the hand normally grasps the gun. Coarse checkering with no attempt to properly file up and raise the diamonds is an abomination on any gun and we would much prefer the cheaper grades left plain unless a proper checking job is done. A fine checkering job cannot be done on cheap porous walnut, so unless the grade of the wood warrants checkering the stock should just as well be left plain. The checkering of course does add something to the grips on the gun but unless done properly looks like the devil. We would confine checkering to the better grade guns and would also use a grade of walnut sufficiently good to warrant a nice job, rather than trying to doll up a poor and porous grade of wood with coarse checkering that looks like it had been done with a jackknife.

Square types of checkering never look well and one should use only the long graceful diamonds well filed up to a point, then it adds a finished look to a fine gun as well as adding materially to its handling qualities. As a rule carving should be left to the furniture maker, but a carved border to the checkering, properly executed in base relief, with the leaves, etc., small and in keeping with the lines of the gun and engraving, is nice and enhances the beauty of the checkering job. It can easily be overdone and usually is overdone on most German guns. The finer British and American guns, however, usually carry just about the right amount of fine delicate carving as a border for the fine checkering, and when carving is soused it is beautiful and all to the good. Such a well-carved border combined with long, well shaped and pointed diamonds running in even rows adds a finish to an otherwise fine gunstock not obtainable by any other method. However, too much carving, or too coarse a checkering pattern or square diamonds or an inartistic job in general is much the same on a gun as too much paint on a woman. It detracts rather than enhances her natural beauty. You want beauty, not gaudiness. Flat checkering or flat carving never looks well and neither has any place on a fine weapon.

A finely finished gun stock of good figure will present a beauty never approached by poor woods or gaudy carving. With the fine oil-finished stock you can simply look right down into the wood, the checkering will have a delicately carved border in base relief, with each scroll or leaf raised in detail and the diamonds of the checkering will be long, slender, and graceful. Such a stock will be a joy to handle as long as you use it.

In the stocking of a good shotgun, there should be no cracks or gaps at the junction of wood and steel at any place and the fore-end should contact the fore-end iron as though it grew there. The same is true of the stock at its junction with the frame; there should be no suspicion of a gap at any point. The wood should contact the frame at all points in a hair pinching fit and the top strap and lower tang and trigger plate should also be inletted perfectly tight in the wood at all points. This makes for a sound strong, gun as well as a lasting fit and a total absence of looseness over many years of continuous usage. If the gun is not so stocked then it was never properly finished and you may look for other troubles in the locks and action as well.

Cheap machine inletted stocks can seldom compare with fine hand-made stocks for the above reasons. They are permissible on low-priced machine production weapons, but never to be tolerated on fine guns. When looking over a lot of guns in the selection of a stock that fits the individual best is also a fine time for him or her to also take stock of the different types of shotgun and decide at the same time which they prefer, auto-loader, pump, or double and side-by-side, or over-under in the double, as well.

As you study stock fit, you can also study the guns themselves and their actions and which type of shotgun would suit you best. You will have a general idea of what use to which you will put the gun, whether for upland work, duck shooting, trap shooting, Skeet or a general purpose all-around gun. Remember the Skeet gun is usually ideal for ruffed grouse, woodcock and quail in dense cover and you can get all the dope on that gun on the Skeet range. Gauges, various borings, shot sizes for different game, etc., will be covered in separate chapters.

One more thing. In picking a gun or gunstock, make sure that the grain of the wood runs straight in the grip or small of the stock. If you do this, all well and good, but if you don't, then sooner or later you may have a broken stock while out in the field. We once had a very fancy grained stock on a 16 bore Ithaca. Don't think we have ever seen a prettier piece of wood. It was one of those very rare pieces of nature's handiwork, like an exceptionally beautiful woman. However, that beautiful burly wood ran cross grained in the grip of the stock. One day Bill Casper and the writer had been out for sharp-tail grouse. We had had a very good day and my old hunting coat was simply loaded with the big birds. They had been feeding on the grain of a stubble field for over a month before the season opened and we were then allowed a huge limit. We stopped to eat a sandwich. Standing the gun in front of me I grasped it with my knees as I attempted to take off the heavy coat and get the weight off my shoulders while eating. In my struggles with the heavy coat the gun slipped from the grasp of my knees and fell forward into a tall clump of rye grass. It did not hit hard at all as the grass cushioned its fall, but that beautiful stock said "chuck" and broke short off in the middle of the grip. Maybe it was a good thing for me, as I then started using other guns, finding I could shoot none of them as well as the old 16 bore Ithaca until I got hold of a No. 4 Ithaca 12 bore and had Frank Pachmayr restock it to my order. Then business picked up, but when I did get the Ithaca restocked at the factory I then found I could no longer shoot its standard stock dimensions so sold it. Otherwise I might never have been prompted to use the many shotguns I have over the years and thus make this treatise possible.

CHAPTER NINE

Shotgun Rib and Stock Pitch

MANY SHOTGUN SHOOTERS do not realize the effect of rib pitch on their elevations any more than they do the effect of stock pitch. Briefly, rib pitch means the amount the front end of the rib varies in actual height in comparison with the height at the breech end of the barrel or barrels. Rib pitch controls elevation to no small extent. Many ribbed barrel trap and upland guns have the rib considerably lower at the muzzle end than at the rear end of the barrel, thus to give the sighting plane a lower angle than that of the shot charge and thus cause the bulk of the charge to go above the point of aim for rising birds. Many trap shots want their pattern to center about seven and one half to eight inches above the point of aim at 35 yards, their usual distance to take care of rising birds. Also, many experienced field shots prefer about the same amount of rib pitch for general upland work. For such shooting the birds are usually raising and this amount of rib pitch helps in the necessary elevations for such shots.

For pass shooting, such a height of the rear end of rib may well be too much as you may then wish to take birds after they have passed overhead. In this case aim must be low or you will over-shoot. Generally speaking it is safe and best to have rib pitch correspond at least with the trajectory of the shot charge over a given and usual shotgun range. Likewise it is usually best to have the bulk of the charge print just over the point of aim, so that we can "float" our birds, in other words see them clearly above the barrel or barrels or rib. Much rib pitch means a very high shooting gun and it can easily be too much. I have used some guns that had an excessive amount of rib pitch and I habitually overshot everything that jumped until I changed the point of aim definitely by fitting a Weaver Shotgun Scope and sighting the center dot for exactly 50 yards. Then and then only could I hit with those extremely high rib pitched guns.

By the same token we have owned and used many shotguns that shot low—not enough rib pitch and any time one held in the usual way, with the eye seeing about ⅜ of an inch over the top of the rib at the rear and the bird floating right on top of the front sight in straightaways, the charge would go low; and if we hit at all it was with the extreme top edge of the pattern. This also is bound to ruin any man's confidence but can be cured very easily by adding a Rowley cheek pad to the top of the comb, thus forcing the aim to be higher over the rear end of the rib and giving the same ultimate effect as if one had more rib pitch, when the patterns would be placed at correct elevation.

While stock fit can well control elevations, rib pitch also gets in its share of the dirty work and should be right for best results. Usually if we place the tip of the forefinger over the top of the rear end of the rib and then see the front sight clearly over said forefinger tip we have the eye in about the right relation to the barrels for usual shotgun work, but if the gun has excessive rib pitch, it will then shoot too high. Likewise if there is not enough rig pitch it will shoot too low. Either way you will not score the clean kills that are entirely possible with the same gun when the rib pitch is correct for your method of aim.

When the aim is thus taken and the bird seen clearly above the front sight, you are then in a position to note any turn or twist

The use of a straight-edge for determining stock drop. "A" is drop at heel; "B" is drop at comb; "C-D" is length of "pull," that is, length from butt plate to trigger.

in its flight and to lead correctly. Lead or forward allowance is simply aiming where said birdie will be when the shot charge arrives. Except on straight-aways one never aims at the bird if he would connect and correct rib pitch helps him greatly in seeing the bird high enough over the gun to estimate its direction and speed and thus throw his shot charge where it will be when the bird arrives. Remember also that slightly too much forward allowance or lead is better than not enough as your shot string out and do not all arrive at the same instant. Experience alone will teach correct lead for a given bird, and when we switch to a faster or slower bird over the same ranges, we will likely miss until the lead is corrected. Many experienced shooters specify the rib pitch desired in ordering a new gun, either single or double, with a rib, and it is well to do so. Also you should always pattern the gun at a pattern paper or old barn and determine

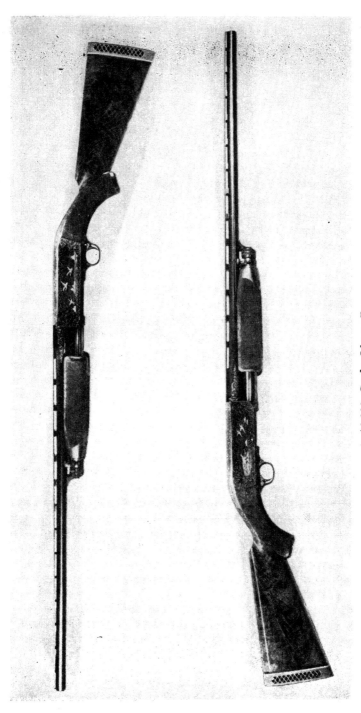

A $2,000 Grade Ithaca Repeater.

the exact elevation of the center of your shot charge when you cheek your gun in normal stance. This will tell you whether you need more or less rib pitch, or for the gun in hand, more or less comb height to counteract any deficiency, one way or the other in rib pitch.

Most ribbed shotgun barrels have this feature well taken care of but we have seen some that had too much rib pitch and shot much too high for us and also some that did not have enough and shot much too low. The man with a standard single barrel without a rib, often finds this true when he fits a Poly Choke or other variable-choke device. His front bead is then raised higher and his shot charge goes lower. The only answer to this is to fit a flat bar over the top of the action or rear end of the rib to compensate for the extra height of the front sight or else raise the stock comb through the addition of a Rowley cheek pad or a laminated stock comb to compensate for the extra height. Most trap grade ribbed barrels have plenty of rib pitch and usually work out about right with any of the variable chokes on account of their high ribs, but the plain barrels very often shoot much too low with such devices. When slug loads are used for deer shooting the deficiency is even more apparent and one should always check his gun and know before he takes the field.

Usually one can get an idea of how a given shotgun will shoot for elevations by examining the rib, if it be a ribbed barrel gun, either elevated ventilated or solid rib. If the gun has excessive rib pitch-down at the muzzle it will shoot high regardless of the stocking. We have a fine Westley Richards double with such excessive rib down-pitch at the muzzle. It is the sunken rib type and the rib at the muzzles is actually well below the top of the barrels. This is the highest shooting gun we own and something will have to be done about it, probably have a gunsmith make and fit a short ramp with either the big Lyman ivory bead on the front or one of Bob Nichols excellent monoblocks of ivory on top of the short ramp. Last fall we had just finished a run of five mallard and twelve straight cock pheasants with the old Askins No. 5 16-bore full choked double, then one day we took the delightful little 12 bore 6¼ pound Westley out. That evening but one pheasant jumped in range but he was a big cock bird and got up within 15 yards of us. We proceeded to miss him clean with one barrel after the other, then remembered this was a high shooting gun and we had not used it for a year. Passing an old log cabin we stepped off 35 yards and shot at a knot. The charge landed a full foot to 18″ above our point of aim with the eye seeing some ⅜″ above the rear end of the rib and floating the knot over the big ivory front bead. Again we tried the other barrel and again the same thing happened, clearly showing were our two 1⅛-ounce charges of No. 6 had gone, when shooting at that cock pheasant.

This little 26″ barrelled gun has a stock drop of 1¾″ at comb by 2¾″ at heel, the old standard stock, and with all other guns we have such a stock drop would be much too excessive for us and would cause us to undershoot everything. However, with this, the finest shotgun we own as to grade and price, we consistently over-shoot everything, except a steeply rising bird and even then we often catch him with the bottom of the pattern. We will have the above mentioned ramp fitted and then expect business to pick up the next time we use this handy little gun.

Another illustration of excessive rib pitch, is a fine Ithaca Skeet grade 28″-barrel, full-choked, 16-bore Model 37 with elevated ventilated rib. That gun is stocked very well indeed and fits us perfectly yet the rib pitch is excessive and the little gun throws its patterns almost as high as the Westley Richards. One day we were right in the midst of a fine rise of cock pheasants the big birds getting up at about 25 yards, one after another, and going off at easy quartering angles. We missed them, one after another, clean as a whistle. Disgusted with our shooting we headed for what was left of an old barn in a nearby field and proceeded to shoot patterns, finding the gun threw the whole closely centered pattern above our point of aim. This gun shot beautiful, tight, evenly spread full choke patterns with sixes, but threw them so high we could do nothing with it on fast shots and had to consciously hold down under the game to hit; which procedure is all wrong for any shotgun shooting as it utterly destroys swing and timing. Finally we had a Weaver 1-X shotgun scope fitted and sighted it for 50 yards so the charge centered under that big center dot reticule. Then business picked up and we killed the next six cock pheasants we jumped clean and some of them at a good 55 yards. That Weaver 1-power scope was the only cure for that gun.

Generally speaking, if the rib is lower than the muzzles of double guns at the muzzle, then the gun will shoot high and it should be at least level with the tops of the twin tubes even with sunken rib types. When the rib is high at the rear and the standing breech is well up over the barrels at the chambers then the rib should also be well above the muzzles to throw the charge at right elevations.

As before stated many trap shots like their guns to shoot a good seven to eight inches high at 30 to 35 yards, but this is usually too much for us and such guns very often shoot too high for us for this reason. This is due usually to rib pitch alone as most good trap stocks fit us very well. We have never done Trap or Skeet shooting but game shooting in all its angles is an old number with us and if the gun shoots too high, due either to excessive rib pitch or an up-pitch of stock then we will miss a great many birds. This is especially true of ducks that have passed overhead, or pheasants or grouse that rise and then tip over a low ridge or blue grouse or ruffed grouse that sail off down a steep mountain. If the pattern centers right over the top of the front bead in our usual shooting stance all is well and we can go right to work with such a gun on any game, but if it throws the pattern a foot to 18″ high at 35 to 40 yards then we are sunk as far as consistent hitting is concerned.

One lad we used to hunt with had an old 97 Winchester, and a very good shooting gun at that, in 16 bore. The gun had the low comb type stock and shot very low for both of us unless we consciously held our heads well up and with line of sight well over the breech. One day he stuck the barrel through the spokes of a wagon and gave it a slight bend upwards for about a foot of the front end of the barrel. I told him he had probably ruined the gun, but when we patterned it, we found the gun then shot just right. The center of every pattern was just over the bead when the head was held normally and the stock cheeked firmly as it should be. From then on he shot like a house afire with that gun as long as I knew him. You could take the gun apart and easily see the upward bend in the last foot of the barrel, but it was just what that particular gun needed. No doubt a straighter stock would have cured the fault without bending the barrel, but at that time stocks were hard to come by, and dollars as well, so he did the next best thing.

Stock Pitch

Stock pitch is the amount the barrels tip down from the vertical when the gun is stood square on its butt plate. This can be seen at a glance if the gun in question is stood up with the top of barrel along a perfectly square wall. Let the full butt plate rest solidly on the floor then slide the gun back to the wall until the breech touches and the amount the muzzles are away from the wall is the amount of down pitch to the stock. We have seen some guns that were actually pitched upward and many with zero or no pitch at all. Stocks that are pitched upwards usually shoot much too high and have the habit of kicking off the shoulder in recoil. Our personal preference runs from about one to not over two inches of down-pitch. This gives the heel of the stock some chance of clinging to the shoulder in recoil, yet is not enough down-pitch to make the gun shoot low. Guns would recoil straight backwards if the stock were a straight prolongation of the barrels, which it is not, hence the raise in recoil. Thus down-pitch also affects elevations to a great extent and the greater the down-pitch the lower the gun will shoot and vice versa. Many old time guns had a four-inch heel drop and about that much down-pitch. They usually shot low as well and one had to consciously hold his aiming eye up over the ribs to avoid shooting low with them. A gunstock should fit and all one should have to do to obtain perfect facial contact is to drop the head forward on the comb after the gun is mounted and the bird on the wing. He should then cheek the gun firmly and if stock comb height and rib pitch and down-pitch are correct his pattern will then go just over the point of aim for about two thirds of the charge and should center the pattern a few inches over the front bead. When one uses such a well-fitting gun long enough the subconscious takes over and he can then do fast snap shooting without being conscious of aiming at all. However he must know his gun from long practice before this is true. If you have a gun with insufficient rib pitch and it shoots low, you can correct it to some extent changing the stock down-pitch to less and if the gun shoots too high, then a little more down-pitch will often correct the fault.

Shoot plenty of patterns and study your gun and the relative placing of the patterns with relation to point of aim when the gun cracks and you can thus often improve your shooting by a little judicial adjustments to stock or rear end of rib. The British employ a try-gun that allows any amount of drop at either comb or heel, cast off, cast in or any amount of pitch either up or down and when they fit you with a gun during actual shooting, these measurements can then be given the new gun so that it will fit and shoot equally well. It will continue to shoot well also unless you change your style of shooting or stance or head position. We should employ these try-guns in this country but do not. Lacking them the best we can do is to fire at paper squares or the sides of old buildings and learn by actual shooting just where our pattern centers with relation to point of aim and thus correct either our hold or the gun to bring the pattern centers to the desired point above the actual aim.

Factory made standard grade guns usually are about correct for both rib and stock pitch, but beware the custom made gun or the older ones until you have tried them at paper targets to make sure of their elevations. Usually, if the stock pitch is not over two inches down to zero pitch, the gun will handle about right, but if it has more pitch it is very liable to shoot too low, especially on all rising birds. Also the plain single-barrel gun that has been fitted with a patent choke must be tried to prove that it does not shoot low. If it does do so when we must raise the comb of the stock or else fit a block on the rear end of the barrel to force us to take a higher aim over the rear end of barrel, to compensate for the higher front sight.

With the plodding, slow, one-eye shooter, who aims a shotgun much as though he were using a rifle, the Weaver one-power shotgun scope is often a great help, for with it he can sight the gun to place the charge anywhere desired for elevation.

Long range pass shooting often calls for more elevation than usual shooting under 50 yards and one should shoot his gun enough at the usual ranges employed on passing fowl to know absolutely how high to aim over the breech of the gun to compensate for the drop of his shot charge. Strong side winds must also be considered as they will drift a shot charge clean off the point of aim at 50 yards and beyond. Small shot will be drifted much more than larger pellets and it is well to shoot enough in strong cross winds at a big paper square to know the winds effect at such ranges on your shotgun pattern.

One fall a friend loaned us a high grade Fox ejector 12-bore. That gun had up- instead of down-pitch to the stock and was pitched upwards almost two inches. It was a freak, straight grip stock, a beautiful thing as to the fine circassian wood but that up-pitch was all wrong for us. We never could get in the second barrel as it always kicked off our shoulder in recoil, even when gripped and held rather tightly. It shot fairly high but not excessively so as it had an elevated ventilated rib that was abnormally high at the front end. Maybe that was the reason for the up-pitch of the stock, someone had tried to make it shoot high by cutting off some stock and fitting the pad with such an ungodly up-pitch. That gun butt would simply slip down off my shoulder at each shot so that we had to again mount the shot for the second barrel and by then the game was usually getting out of range.

We used to borrow Jack Rowan's old lifter-action Parker 10-bore when still a small kid in knee pants, living in Helena. It had 32" barrels and about a 3" drop at heel and the same in down-pitch.

It was very heavy, over ten pounds, for a skinny kid, and altogether too slow for jump shooting, but when the fall flight of northern ducks was on at Helena Lake, we would get a good blind picked out and on the pass shooting, where plenty of time was to be had in mounting the gun and aiming we did very well, as that old hammer Parker would really shoot. The excessive drop and down-pitch only enhanced the recoil and how those big tubes would lift in our skinny hands in recoil. We shot full loads of either Remington Arrow or Winchester Leader with No. 4 shot and when plenty of time was to be had for mounting the gun and aiming it did fine. Its weight also made it carry through beautifully once we started the swing. However we usually went home with a gun headache along with a mess of fowl when using that big gun. One day Chuck Rowan and the writer were in a blind, and some distance across an arm of the lake two more men were parked. The ducks seemed to fly up and down that long narrow arm and the two parked across from us would wait until the birds were between their blind and ours and then let it fly. Their shot peppered us liberally, and were No. 4s as we found on picking some out of the skin on back of our necks and from our clothes. We yelled at and cussed them out soundly to stop shooting toward but they persisted. Finally Chuck took the old Parker ten-bore and dug a couple long shells out of his pocket loaded with B Bs. He yelled at them to duck their heads and holding high enough over them to drop the big shot on them he gave them one barrel after the other. We saw some of the heavy shot strike the water from each barrel short of their blind, but results were instantaneous. Both men jumped out of their blind with wild yells and started running away. Chuck calmly reloaded the old gun with two more of the heavy loads and holding still higher, gave them both barrels again. We never saw the pair again when shooting on the lake, but later I heard a doctor was called in to extract heavy shot from a pair of Austrians from the East Helena smelter. Some of that smelter crew were a hard lot, and three were killed in one knifing spree there at the time.

At that time we aimed a shotgun much as a rifle, and shot with our head well up above that ancient Parker. Such aiming was absolutely necessary with the old gun and its excessive drop and down-pitch. By all standards it was a very low shooting gun.

The standard in shotgun stocks has changed greatly over the years and most all shotguns are now stocked straighter than formerly and with less down-pitch and many factory standard stocks carry zero pitch. Down pitch also emphasizes recoil and makes the up-chuck of the gun greater in recoil. While we do not advise it, many shooters with single barrel guns without a rib can change their guns elevations by bending the barrel up or down and we heard of one gunsmith who employed this method with all single barrel guns without ribs to correct their elevations for any given shooter and he was very successful at it.

When ordering a new gun from any custom maker or factory, one should always specify the amount of down-pitch desired and should also tell them exactly where he wants his pattern to center over the front bead and give them the elevation of his line of sight also over the rear end of rib or breech. With this data, they can then build you a gun that will shoot exactly where you look and to the right elevation. Such little things are vital to becoming a good wing shot.

CHAPTER TEN

Shotgun Sights

GENERALLY SPEAKING, shotguns are pointed, not aimed, but there are many shooters who do not use a shotgun enough to learn snap shooting, and if the gun does not fit them perfectly, they must aim to some extent. Some folks are handicapped by having their master eye on the left side for right handed shooters and vice versa for left hand shooters. This condition further complicates matters for them and they must have some fixed relation of the eye to the gun barrel to hit. Shotgun shooters should keep both eyes open at all times.

Most good shots prefer a level flat rib on trap and skeet guns and many like them on game guns as well and want only a couple of ivory sights on that rib; a big bead on the front and a small bead placed some 12″ to 14″ to the rear and about at the front end of the forestock. We belong to this class and we prefer such a rib and such ivory sights. Many shooters want nothing at all in the way of sights and shoot by the feel of the gun alone, pointing it with their two hands as they would a broom stick or the index finger of one hand. They do good snap shooting, but are usually sunk when a long shot comes along. We believe the good shooter should know and be able to use either system; either snap shooting or the swing-and-lead system which entails some degree of aim. When one is used to a gun with a level, flat rib and a couple of ivory sights, the subconscious takes over the aiming part of the deal. The master eye looks over that rib and without conscious thought lines up those ivory sights and sees that there is the right amount of rib showing between the two sights, thus giving the shooter perfect elevation. From there on out the cheek is glued to the stock and the gun held firmly to the shoulder and pointed and the shooter is conscious of looking on at his fast-flying target and figuring lead as he does so, but just the same the subconscious has taken over and is really aiming the piece. At times it is difficult even for the most expert shots to say definitely just where the snap shooting form and the swing and lead methods are used as at times both systems are blended into making the shot.

On most all long range difficult pass shooting the gun must be very accurately pointed and this can be done only with the aid of some sort of sights, or a gun that has been used so long that one knows instinctively where it is pointing with relation to the eyes.

Many shooters always close one eye when shooting and are usually the slow, plodding type of shotgun shot, yet many of them are very deadly game shots and they do aim the gun. They have never learned proper shotgun form or snap shooting and for them, at least, sights are necessary.

Shotguns as they come from most makers, except trap and Skeet guns, usually have just a simple, cheap, little brass bead on the muzzle of the barrel or the rib of the gun. For many shooters this is all that is wanted or needed, but we notice most of the fine long range shots prefer the two sights on a level rib. Some shooters

Weaver Model K-1 Scope Sight, One Power for Shotgun Wing Shooting and for Rifles on Dangerous Game in Brush. Shown with Weaver Shotgun Mount.

will complain that they cannot shoot a double gun because of the wide barrels. We believe they are simply kidding themselves as we can see no difference between shooting a single or double barrel at game, in fact believe the broader muzzle of the double materially helps in fast shooting. The eye sees or should see over the rib anyway and it makes no difference to us if a big barrel is on either side of that rib or if it is a single barrel gun. We automatically check the alignment of that sighting rib or front sight with relation to the breech end of the gun anyway and when shooting at game are conscious only of following the game for lead, but if we miss we do have a record in our brain of just where those sights pointed when the gun cracked. This in turn helps materially in correcting for the next shot.

Bob Nichols once developed and wrote up a front shotgun sight that was a dandy, being a small block of ivory the width of the rib at the muzzle. This was an instant eye catcher and gave you the position of that rib and its elevation instantly and we believe is a very good front sight for all shotguns. We would still prefer that the gun also had a rear sight of ivory placed some 12 to 14″ to the rear of that front Bevel-block as Bob called it. Such an arrangement is very useful in dim lights or for shooters with poor eyes, as it enables them to see their sights without looking at them, so to speak; in other words automatically, by the subconscious. Aim should always be well above the gun, enabling the shooter to clearly see and float his birds, and also to note any twist or turn in the direction of flight.

All shooters should pattern their guns to see where they shoot in relation to the sights or rib, and all will find the two ivory shotgun sights of the Nichols Bevel-block a distinct aid when patterning a gun to keep that pattern centered on the 40″ square of paper.

Another form of shotgun shooting definitely demands sights and that is deer shooting with slug loads, which are mandatory in some states. Buckshot are short ranged and sights are not needed much with them but with the slug load one should always have some sort of sights to enable him to accurately AIM the shotgun for certain placing of his slug and clean killing of the deer. A big aperture peep sight like the Williams combined with any type of bead front is excellent for this work. One learns many things when testing double barrel guns with slug loads and a great many of them have never been properly regulated in the first place and their two barrels do not shoot into the same group. Such guns are about hopeless for slug use unless one uses buck in one barrel and slugs in the other. Good guns however will group both barrels together with either buck or ball or slugs. A few slug loads will tell you much about the regulating of your double barrel gun, when fired at a target.

When the Nydar optical sight came out, some folks thought this was the answer to their prayers. We never could see that contraption perched on the top of a fine gun nor could we see how it could possibly work under the varied conditions of light and weather. Many trap shots had them installed only to get out to the traps some rainy morn and find they had nothing except the foundation for a bird nest on top of their guns. When the light was good this sight projected a circle of light around the target with a big bead to center it with. In practice in the gun store it looked good but in stormy weather and a cloudy, poorly lighted sky the circle and dot were often conspicuous by their absence. We noted they soon pulled the pesky things off their guns and went back to a bead front or double ivory shotgun sights.

Years ago Bill Weaver brought out a shotgun scope with no magnification, just a plain clear large field with fine cross wires and a big bead imposed at their intersection; this is the most accurate of all shotgun sights. His first model had a 75-foot field at 100 yards and his latest model carries a full 95-foot field at 100 yards, ample for all shotgun aiming even on fast crossing birds. For the man who just must aim his shotgun, this is the answer, also is the answer for slug loads on deer and also for the man with very poor vision. The man with poor vision can adjust that Weaver shotgun scope to fit his eyes and can then see his birds very clearly and if he can see them at all as they raise, he can place them in the field of that big scope and catch them clearly for the shot. It also allows him to perfectly judge his lead for any angle shot.

Bill brought out his last shotgun scope with no adjustment of the ocular lens and we immediately wrote in and kicked and urged that he bring it out with a proper focusing ocular lens so the individual could fit it to his eye. Bill did just that and his present shotgun scope is all it should be. No scope or rear peep sight adds a thing to the lines or beauty of a gun but they are efficient aiming devices for use of slugs or for the person handicapped with very poor vision. With Weaver's top mounts they can be removed or replaced at will and the bases do not interfere with ordinary shooting as they are low enough that the eye sees over them anyway. Thus for the person who consciously aims his gun at all times, for the deer shooter using slugs or for the person with poor vision who needs to be able to see his bird clearly, the Weaver 1-X shotgun scope is the best sight he can install on his gun. Incidentally that 1-X Weaver scope is also excellent for all close-range, fast rifle shooting in the brush as well.

This scope sight will also enable the gunner with poor eyes to instantly determine whether he is shooting a hen or a cock pheasant, something that many with poor eyes have a hard time determining until after they kill the illegal hen.

We have seen many types and colors of front shotgun sight. Some are red, some gold and some a combination of ivory and gold. We prefer the plain white ivory to all colors, though the gold front sight is also excellent but for our eyes at least in dim lights the red beads appear black and are no help at all. You want something the eye can catch instantly without looking at it as the eyes should be on the game. Nothing has proven superior for us to the ivory sights, though the scope is better for us with slug loads and other such deliberate work as in patterning a gun for long strings, in either ammunition testing or gun testing for percentages.

Most good shotgun shooters depend more on the fit of the gun than on any kind or type of sights and that is the way to shoot a shotgun, but the simple, low ivory sights will not in the least interfere with such shooting and may at times be of inestimable value if you get a streak of missing from your fast snap or semi-snap shooting and they will enable you to have a mental picture of where the gun was pointing when you shot and thus help you correct your lead for succeeding shots. If these ivory shotgun sights are used in connection with the British tracer pellet load, one will soon know exactly why he misses and where the pattern goes as well as how the sight picture appeared when he shot.

Very fast aerial sixgun and rifle shooters all use their sights but they have done so over a long period of time until the subconscious takes over the actual act of aiming and we strongly suspicion that many fine shotgunners do the same thing.

George Turner had a run of bad shooting after knocking the big front bead, off of the Browning over-under he used for doubles. We put on another bead for him when he was here and business picked up as he was soon back in stride in that toughest of all shotgun competition the traps. So much for shotgun sights.

CHAPTER ELEVEN

Shotgun Extras

FIRST we will take up ejectors. All single and double barrel guns have extractors, but far from all of them are fitted with ejectors. A small portion of the bottom of the chamber at the rim of the case is cut out and into this fits the extractors and holes are bored for the legs, so they will accomplish primary extraction when the gun is opened and are operated by the fore-end.

With all plain extractors, when you open the single or double barrel gun, the empty case or cases will be pulled back out of the chambers a half-inch or more so they can be easily grasped with the thumb and forefinger and removed from the gun. You must pull them out with the fingers or turn the gun upside down and shake them out, either a very slow method if you happen to be in a hot corner with birds raising all around you.

With ejectors, the extractor accomplishes primary extraction and pulls the case back out of the chamber enough to loosen its grip on the chamber walls, then the ejector lock fires and that case is kicked clear of the gun automatically. All guns should have ejectors, as they greatly speed up the operation of reloading the gun.

With double guns the ejector kicks out the empty regardless of which barrel is fired or if both are fired both are kicked clear of the gun when it is opened. In other words they have automatic selection. Thus if you fire but the one barrel and open the gun only that fired case will be ejected and the loaded case in the other barrel will merely be extracted back a half inch from the chamber and fall back into place as the gun is again closed.

Some cheap single barrel guns have ejectors that are really automatic but not selective, in other words when you open the cheap single, the ejector kicks out the case either empty or loaded and when unloading these guns you simply hold the palm of the hand over the breech as you open the gun if you have not fired to keep the loaded shell from being ejected onto the ground. If allowed to be ejected behind you it may strike a rock corner or other sharp pointed surface with the cap and be fired as the weight of the loaded cartridge is ample to set off the cap if it comes in contact with a sharp rock as it is kicked out of the gun by the ejector. We once opened a single barrel long tom 12-bore with 40-inch barrel and the loaded shell hit in a patch of gravel behind us and exploded, blowing the paper case to bits but doing no harm otherwise.

It's a pleasure to use a fine double with ejectors. When you shoot and open the gun, the fired cases are ejected clear to the rear and you hear the soft punk of the ejector locks. One should carefully check the ejectors of a gun and see if they fire together. The two empty cases should be thrown an equal distance from the gun and right together and the ejector locks should fire at the exact same instant if properly adjusted.

When birds are raising one after the other, ejectors are a necessity if you would get in the utmost in shooting pleasure, for you simply open the gun and drop more loads into the chambers and close it and are again ready for the next bird or birds.

Of course all repeating shotguns extract and eject their fired cases, so what we have written applies only to single and double guns. A man who used to live here named Casey Morris had an ancient ejector single barrel gun with the most ingenious loading device we have ever seen on the left side of the frame.

When you fired and opened the gun, the ejector kicked the empty clear behind you, then this loading device that was clamped to the left side of the frame automatically dropped another load into the chamber. You could fire that and again open the gun and that case would be kicked clear and the third loaded shell dropped into the gun. He was very fast with that ancient gun and also very deadly on game with it, seemingly opening and closing that gun almost as rapidly as some shooters would work a bolt action gun. The arrangement held but two extra shells, which with one in the gun, gave him three shots as fast as he could push over the top lever and open and again close the gun, the loader and the ejector taking care of all other manual operation.

When we were young very few guns carried ejectors, as at that time a great many shooters used the long brass shells and reloaded and they did not want these expensive brass cases thrown out on the ground or rocks. Game was then so plentiful they did not need to hurry in reloading the gun as they were safe in the knowledge that plenty more game would show up in a short distance. But, as paper case production increased and the paper shot shell loading developed, ejectors became more numerous, especially on the better grades of guns, until today, few people will buy a double or single shotgun without ejectors in the higher grades and many want them on the lowest priced guns. We believe all single and double guns should carry ejectors. Ejector locks very seldom get out of order as they are simple and rugged in construction and though they must stand cocked at all times except when the gun is opened and they have fired out the empty cases, they seem to take it in stride and one rarely sees anything more wrong with the ejectors than to get out of timing or have a push rod bind a bit so that the two do not function simultaneously when both barrels are fired.

Sometimes the split stems of the auto ejectors may become dirty and gummed up and require cleaning, but that is about all the attention they need. Most British guns employ flat springs while American guns and some British as well use coil springs.

Elevated, ventilated ribs are another very worthwhile extra on about any shotgun. They cost good money, usually $30 to $50

Best Quality Westley Richards Box Lock with Single Trigger Ejectors and Hand Detachable Locks.

or more extra, but do give you a perfectly level, flat sighting plane. While the snap shot would never know they were there, they are a distinct aid to the shooter who shoots by swing and lead and who also subconsciously sees his rib and sights. Such ribs give the side-by-side double the same narrow sighting plane as found on the over-under or on any repeating or single-loader trap gun. They can be applied to any shotgun and greatly add to its appearance as well as to its efficiency in the field. The elevated ventilated rib also tends to break up and disperse heat waves over the barrel and for this reason is very popular with Skeet and Trap shots who must fire such long, continuous strings at targets. The new L. C. Smith, even in the cheapest field grade has a solid rib but placed so high that it practically duplicates the elevated ventilated rib in efficiency. The barrels are also low enough that you see only that flat level rib as you look over the gun to pick up the bird. We believe either this high flat, solid rib or the elevated ventilated rib add much to the ease of accurate aim on long range game. They also leave little reason for the shooter to claim he can not shoot a double gun. Our opinion is that if he cannot shoot a double gun with such an elevated ventilated rib or the L. C. Smith high, solid rib, then he cannot shoot any shotgun at all.

The ventilated ribs do require more care in drying and oiling after being out in the rain but also give the gun a finished look and to our notion are far superior to any sunken or low rib. They require a higher stock comb however and if fitted after the gun was stocked by some custom smith, then you may find your stock a bit low on the comb for perfect fit. However if your gun shoots too high, then an elevated ventilated rib added with the right amount of rib pitch will cure that high shooting tendency. We prefer an elevated ventilated rib on all guns.

On the over-under they give the gun a very deep appearance when added to the superimposed barrels, yet this is more than offset by their efficiency in breaking up heat waves and giving the shooter

A Boxed Set of Duplicate Pair Westley Richards Patent Detachable Locks.

that flat, level sighting plane not possible on a plain single barrel whether the top tube of an over-under or the barrel of a repeater or single-loader.

The next extra is the Monte Carlo Comb. We have already told how it greatly furthers even elevations, whether you are swinging to right or left as the cheek bone is held at the same elevation in either position with the result the shooting eyes maintain that same even elevation over the rib of the gun and the patterns go to the same elevation. It's a very worthwhile extra, but really detracts from the clean lines of a fine gun. Monte Carlo combs also add weight to the stock, thus aids in balancing a long heavy pair of barrels or the long action and barrel of a repeater. When a Monte Carlo comb stock is made with a good wide shotgun cheek piece it gives the very best contact between the shooter's face and the gun and helps to make uniform cheeking of the gun possible.

The cheek piece also adds weight and is especially nice in conjunction with the Monte Carlo comb feature on heavy pass guns or heavy duck guns for all around duck shooting. Such stocks will, however, necessitate hand stocking; and hand stocking while by far the best is also much more expensive so the shooter that orders a Monte Carlo comb and cheek rest can expect to pay at least fifty dollars more for his stock. If he can afford it, he will find the addition very much worthwhile. The more of your cheek that comes in contact with the stock, the more comfortable that stock will be and the less will be the tendency to bruise the face in recoil. Shotgun Monte Carlo combs are straight on top and the same drop at both point of comb as at the bump or rear end of comb, hence the gun drives back more in a straight line in recoil, and is much more comfortable on a hard kicking gun than any conventional stock design. Many years ago, in fact almost 18 or 20 to be exact, we had Frank Pachmayr stock a fine old No. 4 Ithaca 12-bore ejector in fine Circassian with our idea of what a proper shotgun stock should be. It incorporated both the Monte Carlo Comb and the cheek piece well flared out from the belly of the stock. We wrote it up and published pictures of it in *Outdoor Life* at the time. Many shooters soon saw the efficacy of the design and went to it for their own gun stocks. We had Pachmayr also make and fit a fine beavertail fore-end of the same figured Circassian and this gun is today one of the finest stocked shotguns it has been our pleasure to use.

Next we have the beavertail fore-end. On single barrel trap guns it has served for a great many years. Being long, it gives the trap shot choice of forward hand position and on such guns it tapers from the width of the frame forward into an ever increasing width. Thus when firing it allows them to take up a considerable amount of the recoil with that forward hand. It also keeps the fingers away from the line of sight and a hot gun barrel when used in long strings. All single traps are usually built with such beavertail fore-ends and they need them. With double guns, the beavertail is unnecessary on game guns but when properly made and thin and long enough, it does cover the sides of the barrels nicely and gives the shooter a chance to absorb considerable recoil with that forward hand. In addition it helps keep the fingers from curling up over the barrels too far when they would interfere to some extent with aim for the long fingered gent. We do not like the short, fat paddle that Ithaca first put out on their double trap guns, but their later version is ideal. Also all the beavertails we have seen on the Parker gun were about perfect. Some other makes had crudely designed and clumsily shaped beavertail fore-ends that actually detracted from the appearance of the gun. Fox usually fitted a very neat beavertail. The beavertail should never be too wide on double guns, just wide enough for the wood to come up around the barrels and be quite thin at that point also. Likewise the rear end of the beavertail should be a gradual slope upwards from the frame and fore-end iron to the level along the barrels, never a square end at this point as some guns are made. This square rear end of the forestock then gives the gun a clubby unfinished appearance. Such fore-ends add weight forward of the balance of the piece and really need the addition of a cheek piece and Monte Carlo comb to balance the piece unless the barrels are very short. To us the beavertail looks out of place on light upland guns or on any gun that does not have the more massive cheek rest Monte Carlo comb. They are a very worthwhile addition to any trap or Skeet gun and all such guns should be so fitted.

Shotgun Grips

The English prefer the straight grip stock and it is the cleanest, most streamlined looking stock of all and also probably the most efficient for two-triggered double guns. We like its clean, racy lines even in pump guns. It also makes up into the lightest of all stocks. If the point of the comb comes at the right point over the rear end of the grip to offer adequate support to the base of the thumb, then there is really not much difference in ease of handling of the straight grip or the pistol-grip gun. The British will have nothing but a straight grip or a half pistol-grip at most. Likewise the straight grip allows the hand to move freely and easily when shifting from one trigger to the other on double guns and is one reason it is preferred by many on double guns.

The average American pistol-grip is so long that there is really not a great deal of difference between the feel of it and the straight grip gun. However the pistol-grip does give one a firmer grasp with the shooting hand and on heavy guns aids in pulling the gun back firmly in the hollow of the shoulder. Many of our finest trap shots including the Etchens will have nothing else but a close full pistol-grip on all their guns. The pistol-grip also adds more weight to the butt stock and is for that reason useful in balancing long barrel guns. The shooter should select whichever type he likes best and stick to it. We shoot all types and can see little or no difference in our shooting whether the grip is straight for full pistol but do believe in guns with very heavy recoil like the Magnum ten-bore, that the pistol-grip has something in its favor. We believe however the grip should be either a clean lined straight grip, or else it should be a full

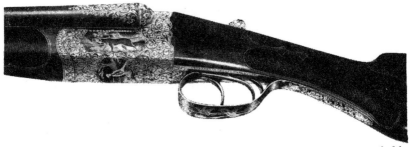

Westley Richards Model de Luxe Best Box Lock Shotgun with Detachable Locks and Ejectors.

and well curved pistol-grip and not the average American pistol-grip abortion with the grip cap so far below the little finger as to afford only a slight swelling of the grip at the rear portion. The half pistol-grip comes in the same category and is the poorest shaped grip of all for appearance sake. The short, well curved pistol-grip on double guns however necessitates the single trigger for best work.

Recoil Pads

While we are on stocks is a good time to cover recoil pads. We believe all shotguns should have soft rubber recoil pads. Though they will not last as long as a well-shaped checkered or engraved steel heel plate, they do offer considerable reduction of recoil, also make the gun stick to your shoulder when mounted with no trace of slipping or sliding and gives one a confidence in the fit and feel of his gun, not possible with the cheap slick hard rubber butt plates fitted to so many American guns. The English usually just checker the butt of the stock and let it go at that and it gives them the lightest possible stock, but a good soft rubber recoil pad of the solid type like the Noshock offers not only a great deal of protection to the toe of the stock, but also to the gun as well. Even when the gun is standing in a corner of a room, that soft recoil pad will not slip and let it clatter to the floor. If the gun has only a checkered butt and is a trifle short then it is well to add one of the light slip on rubber pads as it is just as efficient in absorbing recoil and protecting the stock and in clinging to the shoulder as a fitted pad, This is also the easiest way to lengthen a short stock to fit,

Many trap guns have pads adjustable for drop and this is a fine thing on such guns as the shooter can thus adjust the pad up or down to give him the exact drop of butt plate he wishes.

On guns of heavy recoil such as the Magnum 12-bore, the Super and Magnum tens, soft rubber recoil pads should be mandatory as they help greatly in absorbing recoil. We never did like the many pads put out in this country with a lot of trestle work between stock and the outer rear surface of the pad. Such pads soon deteriorate and crack out and in addition are prone to become filled with mud or snow as well. Likewise we have no use for the Jostam sponge rubber recoil pad, for while it is a great recoil reducer it also deteriorates very fast and a little gun oil or solvent will simply perish the thing in short order.

On small bore guns up to and including 12-bore standard, the engraved steel shotgun butt plate is very nice; or the engraved heel and toe plates as fitted on many English guns and the skeleton plate of the fine old Parker. These also last a lifetime and do not have to be replaced as do about all soft rubber recoil pads, but whenever the shooter is using heavy loads or hard kicking guns we

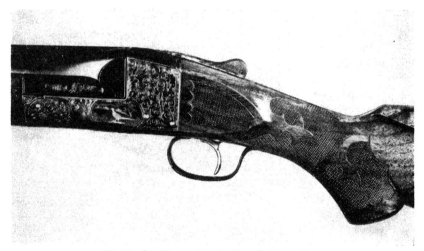

5E Grade Ithaca Single Barrel Trap Gun.

believe he is best off with the soft rubber recoil pad either of the fitted solid type or else the slips on pad when the stock is short.

Single Triggers

We believe all double barrel guns should be fitted with single triggers. For one thing the single trigger gives you the same length of pull for both barrels, for another it is faster than if you have to shift the hand or finger to fire the second barrel. A correctly positioned single trigger gives the double man two shots just as fast

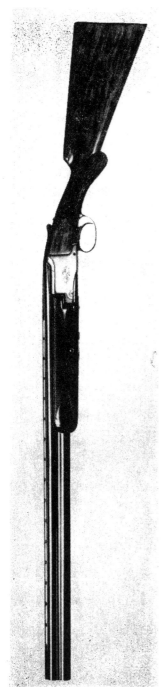

Browning Super-posed Shotgun. It is Made in 12 and 20-gauge.

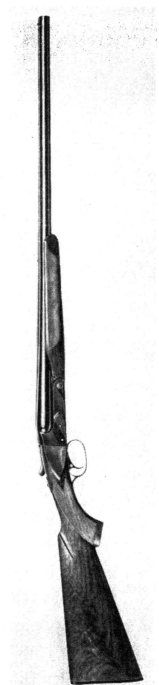

Winchester Model 21 Standard Grade with Beavertail Fore-arm.

as he can recover from recoil and pull the trigger. Thus it saves time and saves conscious thought in regard to shifting the trigger finger. However if you use single triggers then you must have them on all your guns or sooner or later you will do as we have, jump a nice mess of mallards, kill one and then pull until you go blind on that same trigger before you think to shift the finger, with the result that the second fowl you have picked is then either out of range or at long range and your timing is spoiled and you may well miss anyway. If you go to the single trigger, then get them on all your double guns. We have used them for a great many years and have them on about all our guns; even three double Westley Richards rifles also have the single trigger. Some may argue that the gun will double with you. This can and has happened with some single triggers we have seen, but most of them when properly made and adjusted are just about fool proof. We believe they are no more prone to double than is a two-triggered gun in many cases and we have seen many two-triggered guns with one sear worn that would double from the recoil of the first barrel. The late Bill Hall of Durkee, Oregon was out in a boat shooting geese down on the Klamath country. A high flying goose came right over as Bill sat in the stern of the boat using a big Magnum ten-bore Ithaca with two triggers. He killed the goose but the recoil threw him backwards off balance and in trying to regain his balance he pulled the other trigger of his two triggered gun. Recoil promptly upset him into the lake, but he came up and laid the gun in the boat, went down again, came up again, grasped the boat, when his companion slowly towed him to shore. We have shot a Magnum ten-bore Ithaca for a good many years, originally fitted with Ithaca's single trigger; it has never doubled on us at any time and we have absolute confidence in that trigger.

We remember one time a goshawk was after the chickens at the ranch and we slowly poked a 12-bore Ithaca No. 4 double around the corner of the house from the back porch and shooting left handed so as not to expose more than an arm and the gun muzzles to his view we blew him off the back fence. However the gun kicked off our shoulder and the left barrel went up through the roof of the porch, the charge at that few inches from the muzzle boring a hole through rafter and roof just like an auger. Whether our finger slipped to the second trigger when the gun kicked off our shoulder in that awkward left handed aimed position or whether the lock fired from the recoil and jar of the left barrel we will never know, but we got that killer hawk also bored a hole through the roof of the porch. It was a two-triggered gun. So we do not believe there is any more, if as much, danger of double discharge from a good, well-designed and fitted single trigger than there is from a two-triggered gun. All shotguns should have the sear bites amply deep enough to preclude any possibility of double discharge and trigger pulls should be heavy enough to prevent this.

The single trigger gives you smoother easier timing and you have only to think of pulling the gun down out of recoil, picking up your second bird and making a smooth, even swing onto and past him for that double, while with the two-triggered gun you must also shift the finger to the second trigger while you are making your second swing and kill.

Many times have we heard men tell of shooting at ducks or geese at long range with a double gun with two triggers. They have stated that range was so great they thought they could kill if they fired both barrels, so they pulled both triggers at once and killed the bird. Doubtless they would have done just as well had they

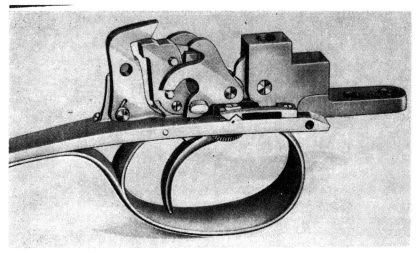

The Westley Richards Single Trigger

fired but one shot at a time as we have never been able to get two patterns on one sheet of paper when we consciously tried to pull both triggers at the same time. One lock always fires faster than the other and the second barrel even though it makes one report seems to go elsewhere. As a further test we took a double barrel 450/400 double elephant rifle and aimed it at a target in the field over clean white snow and pressed both triggers as near the same time as possible. One bullet went on the mark, the other way low, and the recoil was like both barrels of a 12-bore; rather heavy. We also tried it with a 375 Nitro Express double rifle and in every case the first barrel went to point of aim and the second one way low. Whether the second barrel of the shotgun also kicks down or not we do not know but strongly suspect this as it is true of several double rifles we have tried. We did own a fine 600-bore double rifle but never had any hankering to try both barrels of it at once as we had all the recoil we cared to handle at once from one barrel with its 900 grain slug and 110 grains of Cordite.

At any rate, we believe this thing of pulling two triggers at once to make a long range kill is simply wasting one barrel. Thus the single trigger gun is just as good in this respect as you cannot get both barrels to fire close enough together to keep the two patterns together anyway and double guns are regulated to take care of the side recoil of each barrel and when both are fired at once, never have thrown both patterns to the same point of impact for us. Against a dangerous beast at real close range, feet, not yards, it might be well to give him both barrels simultaneously, but unless he was almost on the muzzle of the gun one would be far better off to shoot and shoot again for that second barrel, so the single trigger is no handicap even for such a situation.

Gus Peret was grinding away on a movie camera taking pictures of a wounded and maddened lion, while his partner teased the lion into charging. Then when the lion made up its mind and really came for him, he jumped backwards for some reason, tripped and fell down after hitting the beast again with his 405 Winchester. The lion was on him instantly and started chewing his legs. Gus quit the camera, ran to a gun bearer in the rear and grabbed a double ten-bore Ithaca and rushing up placed the muzzles against the lions ribs back of the shoulder and pulled both triggers, However only one barrel of the gun was loaded and that heavy charge of shot went into the lion's heart. It dropped him on Gus's partner but he kept right on chewing, so Gus dropped the Ithaca and reaching under his partner pulled the 405 out from under him, then working the lever, he threw another cartridge into the chamber and shot the lion through the brain pan at the base of the ear. This killed him, but the man died anyway of septic poisoning in spite of their best efforts to save him. Had both barrels of that ten-bore been loaded it might in that case have proven efficacious in dispatching the big cat. Gus Peret is a big man, afraid of neither man nor devil, and did all he could have to save his partner.

My friend John Burger prefers his double 12-bore shotgun for close range work on either lion or leopard at close range to any rifle and he has sat up nights waiting for and killed man-eating lions with this gun and a charge of SSG Buck, but he does not shoot until the lion has singled him out and is almost on top the gun muzzles. Such a stunt requires plenty of cold nerve. It also proved what a charge of buckshot at a few feet to a few inches from the muzzle will do in the way of killing. If a wad of cotton is tied on top the gun muzzles, it helps materially in directing the load after night if there is any trace of a moon or after glow in the sky.

Some single triggers employ a mechanical shift, while others employ recoil for the shift from one barrel to the other. While most single triggers are of the mechanical shift variety, some employ the

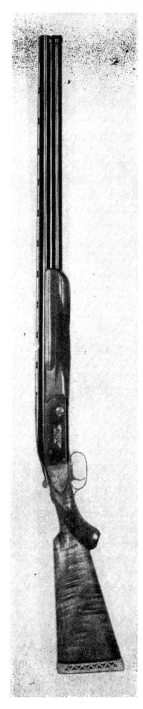

Trap Grade Remington Over-Under Model 32. This Gun is No Longer Made.

recoil for operation of the shift such as the new Browning over-under. Both systems seem to work well when properly made but we must admit a preference for the two-pull type as exemplified by the Parker in America and the Westley Richards in British makes, to take one each of the best known makes from each country. The recoil operated system is usually called the three-pull single trigger, recoil giving the second pull necessary to set the device for the second barrel. Again simplicity and a minimum of moving parts is to be preferred. Nearly all American and foreign makers will furnish single triggers, German, Belgian, British, French and Italian as well as American. Some are excellent, some prone to give trouble as they become worn. We prefer to select the simplest and best designed of the lot in two stage pull.

Any good single trigger will give you the same stock length for both barrels, it will also give you faster time on that second barrel. Further you will not bruise the second finger against the trigger guard when firing the right barrel and reaching forward for that front trigger. You can maintain the same firm steady grip on the small of the stock for both barrels and you do not loosen up the grip of the right hand nor stretch the trigger finger forward to reach the front trigger. When shooting two-trigger guns, the proper way, they say, is to fire the rear trigger first, then the recoil drives the gun back through your hand until the trigger finger is positioned just right for the right barrel and the front trigger. This seldom worked out that way for us. Likewise the left barrel was usually the full choke barrel on most guns. We also have short fingers, so long ago developed a fondness for the single trigger that required no shift of either finger or grip on the gun to change from one barrel to the other. We have also used several nonselective single triggers and they worked just as well for us as the selective type as we usually prefer both barrels bored the same. Three of our best and most used double shotguns are bored full choke in both barrels, so the selective feature is lost in their use. The other double is a Westley Richards bored about 50 and 60 percent and we keep the single trigger set for the right or more open barrel on this gun. It is used only as a grouse gun anyway or for the first days of the pheasant season when the birds raise close to the gun.

Of one thing we are sure, if you are used to a single trigger gun, then it is very hard to ever go back to a two-triggered weapon. We had a fine Wm. Cashmore double 12-bore 30" full and modified boring, an exceptionally well-made box-lock gun that shot superbly well. The left barrel, however, was the modified choke and we had to simply force ourselves to hold the trigger finger at the rear of the guard until a bird flushed so we would shoot the more open barrel first. At other times we lost the second bird of an easy double, both on pheasants and grouse as well as mallards, by killing one bird, then pulling that same trigger again for the second shot, and when the gun failed to fire and we realized the trouble, then our frantic shift to the other trigger usually spoiled our timing and we missed clean. That fine Cashmore was made and proved for our heaviest 1¼-ounce 12-bore 2¾″ loads and we liked it, but finally sold it on account of being used to single trigger guns. We should have had it fitted with a Miller single trigger and kept it as such guns are not easily found in fine English makes now days.

Another asset of the single trigger gun, is that it provides ample room in the trigger guard for the shooter who habitually wears gloves when shooting on cold days. The two triggered gun is then about hopeless for him but the single trigger gives him ample room. Personally we never could hit anything with a glove on the trigger hand so always shoot even in coldest weather with the shooting hand bare. We further believe that a single trigger contributes materially to perfect timing of the second barrel and thus aids materially in hitting with that second barrel as there is less likelihood of one hurrying to place his trigger finger for the second barrel. You know the trigger will stay right where it is and you forget all about any necessary shifting of the hand and finger and concentrate on your swing and lead for the second barrel as you pull the gun down out of recoil. Possibly shooters who have always used the two-trigger gun would find themselves handicapped with the single trigger until they used it enough to be thoroughly familiar with it, but for us at least, it has been a great boon to good shooting. As to its utter reliability when of good make one has only to consider the fact that Sutherland, who was probably the first man to kill 1000 elephants, used a pair of Westley Richards double barrel .577 caliber rifles originally fitted with the Westley Ricahrds single triggers. His life depended on those great guns and they never let him down.

CHAPTER TWELVE

Ornamentation

WHEN ONE GOES over about $250 to $300, for a gun, even a double gun, he is buying chiefly, ornamentation. Some fine double guns may run a bit higher even in plain finish, when real fine lock work or detachable locks are called for, or especially well figured French or Circassian walnut. In the main, however, the chief cost of the higher grades runs more in the amount and kind of engraving or inlay work and the amount and detail of checkering or carving of the wood.

When a man can afford the best, then engraving certainly adds to the beauty of the finished arm. It also makes it in a sense more durable as an highly engraved arm will not show scars nearly as badly as will a plain finished weapon. German arms were very often over-embellished, especially in the matter of checkering and wood carving. Except for a finely carved border to the checkering patterns we firmly believe that carving is more appropriate for furniture than fine guns. However a bit of carved border adds greatly to the depth and finish of the checkering design on a fine arm, but it should not be overdone as many German-made arms were. We have even seen the entire butt stock and fore-end completely covered with carving, game scenes and all. This made the arm look cheap and gaudy. Fine figured stock woods need no other embellishment than a good high-grade oil finish and a limited amount of checkering on the grip and forestock, surrounded by a small neatly carved border or fence, and in fancy patterns. Such a small carved border and pattern is also excellent on the stock ears of box-lock guns and the same is true of some pump and automatic stocks. Fine checkering adds something to the firmness of the grip on both fore-end and grip of stock, but is not as durable as plain well-finished wood. When the stock and fore-end are made from beautifully figured French or Circassian or native walnut, showing all the inherent beauty of nature's finest handiwork, we can see no need for checkering or carving patterns beyond the grip and forestock, as the checkering can never be as beautiful as the natural coloring and contrast of color and grain in the wood itself. An over-dose of checkering or carving on such a fine stock is like too much rouge and paint on a beautiful woman. It detracts rather than adds to the overall picture.

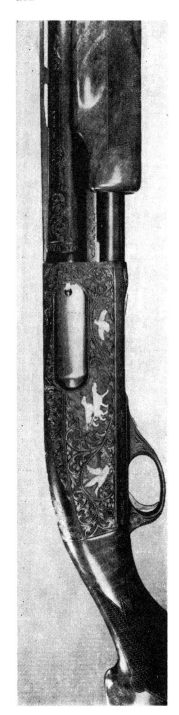

High Grade Model 870 Remington Repeating Shotgun.

The higher grade English guns usually have about the right contrast in the amount of checkering for a fine gun, any more is usually superfluous. Big beavertail fore-ends on trap guns usually look well with a fairly large checkering pattern, but even here the pattern should not be so large as to exclude the beauty of the wood. Fine guns are usually checkered with a very fine pattern running from 20 to 24 lines to the inch. Too fine a checkering does

Winchester Model 12 Magnum 12-bore.   Owned by Glenn L. Martin.

not stand up as well as a coarser pattern, but too coarse a pattern such as 16 lines to the inch is in turn out of place on any fine arm. Usually a pattern running from 18 to 24 lines to the inch is much nicer looking. The diamonds should be long and well pointed up, to look and feel right. This in turn means going over the pattern many times by hand to bring out the utmost in the diamonds. Only fine dense and hard wood is worthy of, or will hold fine checkering in all its detail, through years of usage. Such work is lost on cheap porus woods and the diamonds will soon chip off, leaving a stock that looks much worse than if left entirely plain.

While the checkering of a gunstock does not make it wear better as to finish, but rather makes it even more vulnerable to dents or scratches, the engraving of the steel of action and tangs actually adds to the durability of their finish. But no amount of engraving will make a fine gun out of a poorly made or constructed weapon. Engraving when properly and tastefully executed, enhances the natural beauty of outline and workmanship and imparts a finish that looks as well or better after years of wear. As the blueing wears away from the higher surfaces the patterns of the engraving stand out more in relief. An engraved gun does not show many scratches and dents that would show up instantly on a plain polished finish or surface. We like engraving on all fine arms, but do not like to see any engraving at all on cheap poorly made weapons. It is then totally out of place and simply an effort to hide poor fitting and materials. A finished gun does not necessarily have to be engraved to show its quality. We have a so-called plain finished, best quality Westley Richards, double 400-bore rifle and it plainly shows its quality. The only engraving on that fine rifle is on the top rib near the front and rear ramps. The frame is simply case hardened in colors and the maker's name inlaid in gold on each side. Yet that rifle stands out as a best quality job, through its very fine careful fitting of the hand detachable locks, its fine lines and balance and the fitting of bolts and barrels to action and the beauty of its finely figured French or Circassian walnut stock.

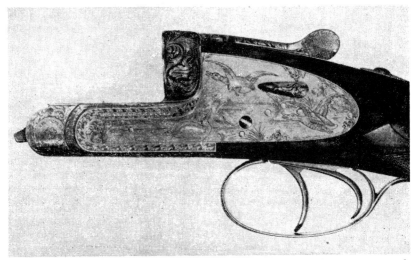

Holland & Holland "De Luxe" Grade Gun Showing Special Engraving with Hand Carved Fences, Hand Detachable Locks.

German guns are very often over-engraved for the quality of the weapon. English, American and to some extent Belgian made guns are usually engraved in keeping with the grade and quality of the weapon and this is as it should be. Engraving takes on many styles. We do not like flat topped relief engraving that is so common on German weapons. Beautifully executed, deeply cut fine scroll of English pattern is always in good taste. American engraving except on the very finest grade guns is apt to be coarse and crude as compared to the better English and German work. Such engraving does break up an otherwise plain surface but adds little to the beauty of the weapon unless properly executed. Fine bas-relief work cannot be beat, and is excellent for game scenes. When game scenes are added to the patterns of engraving they should be perfectly executed and portray well-shaped birds that can be instantly recognized as to species. If you cannot tell instantly what kind of bird or fowl is portrayed then the job has not been properly done and only an artist can get away with game scenes. The engraver must be an artist and have an eye for the over-all picture of the finished weapon and know where to engrave and where not to and what designs are most appropriate. We have always considered big game scenes

A $2,000 Grade Ithaca Repeater.

out of place on a shotgun and likewise consider birds or fowl totally out of place on a big game rifle, regardless of how well they may be executed, even to fine bas-relief in gold inlay.

For a flat surface, where relief work is not wanted, the fine English scroll, when deeply cut, is hard to beat. It wears well and hides very deep bad scars from rocks, etc., and always imparts a finished appearance to the weapon. When relief work is wanted it should be bas-relief, with the flowers or leaves or game birds from a darkened background. This is the most expensive of all engraving, but when properly done with the game birds inlaid in gold and then chiselled away until they stand out with perfect form in high relief, is also the most beautiful art of the engraved. Flat inlay work does not look nearly as well but is quicker and more easily done.

We have examined some best examples of both English and German relief engraving, high bas-relief that was simply beautiful, also some of the work of R. J. Kornbrath and some of his pupils that was equally outstanding. An engraver must be first an artist and be able to cut his design or game in the steel and to model the birds in gold before he is a finished engraver capable of the highest grade work. Poorly shaped or flat birds have no substance or form and do not stand out as do properly executed bas-relief game birds. One can enjoy looking at really fine work for hours and marvelling at the detail and depth of the picture portrayed.

Another beautiful form of engraving is fine scroll inlaid with

Fine Hand Work on a High Grade Model 870 Remington Repeating Shotgun.

Custom Built Winchester Model 21 Made for Spencer T. Olin of Western Cartridge Co.

gold. The contrast of yellow gold with a black blued steel surface is startling to say the least, and beautiful.

We believe all guns should be ornamented in keeping with the grade of the weapon. If the shotgun is a medium priced weapon, then we believe it should carry a moderate amount of fine, tastefully executed scroll. Enough here and there on the action and straps and fore end iron to break up the monotony of plain steel, but not overly engraved above the quality of the weapon.

Given a well made, good fitting gun with finely figured wood and it is surprising how much a little finely executed engraving adds to the finish of the piece. When the weapon is plainly a best gun, then it can well be engraved in keeping with its quality. Coarse engraving always appears gaudy and we do not like it on any weapon. On the best quality gun, the frame, locks, if a side-lock, tangs and fore-end irons and also the rear ends of the barrels can well carry fine engraving, either complete coverage in fine English scroll or a combination of fine scroll and game scenes or bas-relief work in flowers and leaves with game scenes and the birds raised in high bas-relief in gold. Usually such an engraved piece will prove a best weapon if of English or American make or even Belgian, but in German or other makes one will at times find such engraving covering a multitude of sins in the fitting and lock work of a poorly constructed weapon. Any gun maker of note will engrave his weapons in keeping with their quality and value and this is as it should be. Individual designs can also be carried out to suit the most exacting taste and if a man has the money and appreciates these finer things in life there is no reason why he should not have them. Our only plea is that the ornamentation be in keeping with the quality of the weapon.

In the past American guns have been engraved according to grade, and in most cases more by mechanics of the engravers trade, rather than by artists. Each gun of a certain grade will carry exactly the same engraving and one can tell the grade of the gun by the engraving. We cannot say that we believe in or adhere to this system. If your wife buys a new Easter outfit and walks down the street, only to meet several more women with the identically same outfit, she is not going to like it a bit. Men are not so different when it comes to fine guns and we firmly believe that the higher grade guns should be individually engraved, never exactly alike. The water table has ample room on which to stamp the number of the grade of gun and we do not necessarily have to engrave every single piece of that grade exactly alike.

Man's individual taste varies just as much in the style of engraving, checkering, carving or inlay work, that he wants on his gun as it does in his choice of a woman for a life partner, so why not give him some leeway in the matter of ornamentation of his favorite gun. The English seldom produce many fine best-quality guns ex-

Holland & Holland "De Luxe" Grade Gun Showing Special Engraving on Base of Action and on Trigger Guard.

actly alike as to ornamentation and with very good taste and reason. We would do well to emulate them on this score. In this respect the Germans, Italians and French are more artistic in their engraving and will give the customer just about anything he desires that can be cut into or inlaid in steel. Practically all of our finest engravers have been trained in Europe or by engravers trained there.

Most gun companies of note, have one or more fine engravers on their staff. These may in turn train a number of apprentices until they can cut a routine job on a low priced or average shotgun, such as a No. 4 Ithaca or Specialty grade L. C. Smith, but the finer,

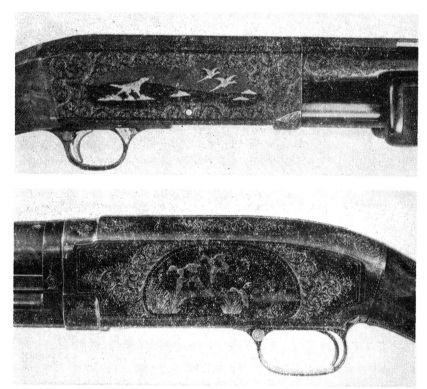

Highly Ornamented Model 12 Winchester Owned by Glenn L. Martin.

master engravers work only on the highest grade guns and it is there only that their full knowledge and skill is allowed to run free and untrammelled. Given an idea of what is wanted, they will do a most beautiful job of execution in keeping with the lines and quality of the weapon. It will also show individuality of taste as well.

Before about 1920, our finer engravers produced many beautiful examples of their art on our higher grade weapons, but from about that time on, there has been a distinct tendency toward very coarse flat-relief work with a coarse scroll and darkened background. It has never remotely compared with the finer more delicate and artistic work formerly produced on even the lower grade weapons. Take the Ithaca guns as an American example. We have owned two old No. 4 doubles that were beautifully engraved with birds and scroll, each different from the other, but since the advent of the new model rotary bolt Ithaca, No. 4 guns are as like as two peas in a pod as regards engraving and all with that coarse scroll. In their No. 5 model the gun carries a pheasant on one side and a woodcock on the other nicely inlaid in gold and engraved, but what a vast improvement there would be if they showed a little individuality in their birds and inlaid ducks and geese on heavy duck guns and upland birds of different species on such guns.

The old Parkers carried widely diversified engraving and inlay work and are still highly cherished weapons for this reason as well as their fine shooting and handling qualities. We have seen some very fine examples of game engraving on the old Winchesters of the '86 Model, also on some Marlin pump actions that is seldom equalled today. Generally speaking, the checkering design and border should bear some relation to the engraving on the gun or vice versa and they should be made to harmonize one with the other. The quality and coloring of the wood also affects the finished product.

While the English engravers are above reproach on their fine scroll work, we have seen some of the big game animals on topflight English guns that were very poorly done and did not compare with animal scenes of the better German engravers. On game birds, however, they were very good indeed. Nearly always, the English engraving is in keeping with the quality of the arm, something not always true with German and Continental arms, where a cheap gun may and often is covered with a very fine engraving job.

One of the most elaborate jobs of ornamentation we have ever examined is a fine early flintlock double shotgun in the N.R.A. collection at Washington. It must have been a presentation job for a king and certainly is a museum piece by any standard. The whole of the stock, locks, and much of the barrels are covered with finest engraving and gold filigree work as well as inlay work. This piece shows conclusively that the old masters of the flintlock era as well as some before them were artists in engraving and inlaying precious metals. Few men would want or could ever afford such an elaborate job on a hunting gun. There must be from six months to a year's work on it for a master engraver.

For the man who can afford it nothing adds as much of a finished touch to a fine gun as a bit of real gold inlay work, even though it be only a bird on the lock plate or trigger guard, or the owner's monogram or name. There is something about the contrast between yellow gold and blued steel, when applied to a fine gun that is not attainable by any other treatment in the way of metal ornamentation.

Acid etching is sometimes used to ornament guns but we believe it far inferior to engraving and would much prefer a very limited amount of fine scroll work to having the gun completely covered with the best in etching. Acid etching is, however, very useful and proper when used to darken the background in bas-relief work and to smooth it up in places and deepen the background to make the flowers, leaves or birds stand out in sharp high-relief. The modelling of the inlay work is also highly important if the job would

Westley Richards Best Quality Side Lock Ejector.

have the look of a master's job. Flat inlay work is never as beautiful, however, perfect the outline, but when inlay work is perfectly modelled to give it a form and substance and a roundness to fully portray the bird or animal and with a deep dark background in natural scenery, then the engraver's art reaches its very highest attainment. Finely finished and engraved guns are not for the lad who lays them over a barbed wire fence and uses the gun to pry the wire down, so he can step over, and though it is sacrilege to so use a gun we have often seen wealthy men so use them. Such abuse of a fine gun is like watching a man light his cigar with a ten dollar bill. He needs to have his head examined.

In conclusion, we believe a fine gun should be well engraved.

The owner is more apt to take care of the piece and he will enjoy a pride of ownership, not possible with a cheap gun. He will also be apt to study the game more and become a better shot. Wing shooting is an art, just as fine gun finishing is an art and the two should go together. We enjoy watching a fine wing shot with a fine gun in action. He has confidence in his own ability and in his gun and usually gets the most out of his shooting days.

CHAPTER THIRTEEN

Modern Shotgun Shells

MODERN SHOTGUN AMMUNITION is made almost entirely by machine methods, but well over 200 different operations are required to produce the finished cartridge. Paper cases are made in the form of long tubes and then cut to make several paper tubes the correct length for the given shot shell. The brass case head is formed from a brass blank by seven different drawing operations, from the flat blank, through the various stages of the cup to the heading operation and finally the fitting to the paper case itself. These operations are all performed by very powerful machines that can and do make the finest shotgun cases ever produced. After the case head is punched for the primer, it must be seated and the primer alone involves a considerable number of operations, such as forming the cup, forming the anvil, and the sleeve or outside cup, the loading of the cup itself, and finally seating the completed assembly in the head of the shotshell proper.

Pigs of lead are melted in the shot tower and alloyed to the proper hardness, then the molten metal is poured through screens of different size to produce the different size shot and dropped around 160 feet into a water tank to form the perfect spherical shot. These in turn are passed over screens that remove any imperfect or deformed pellets, any over- or under-size shot, and leave the final product only perfect, uniform and round. If the shot are to be copper coated, the plating process must also be accomplished before they are ready to load.

Base wads must be punched and over-powder wads of card and felt or the cup seal variety, before the components are ready for loading. The Ballistic Department will already have determined the correct charge of a given lot of powder for a certain load and shot charge. They will have ascertained the correct amount of pressure that must be applied on the over-powder wads before the shot are loaded and the folded crimp formed. Then the machines will load the ammunition. From the forming of the anvil, the battery cup, primer cup, fulminate and paper disc cover, of the tiny primer to the finished loaded shell, each operation is carefully gauged and inspected in each step, so that the final loaded shotshell represents the very highest degree of skill and science in its final perfected form. This is one very good reason why the hand-loader can seldom equal the work of the great loading companies. The careful handloader can usually load more accurate rifle or pistol ammunition than is possible by factory machine methods, but he can seldom hope to equal the loading machine performance of the great companies when it comes to shotgun ammunition.

Modern machine methods of shotshell manufacture and loading are thus far ahead of the best in hand methods. The powder will be loaded in correct charge, the over-powder wads seated with exactly the right amount of pressure, pre-determined for best combustion of the charge, the shot will be uniform and in correct amount and the folded crimp will seal the shell case as only a fine machine can do it. All these carefully inspected and checked operations add to a finished shell of uniform even velocity.

The good wing shot must have uniform velocity, if the load be a couple hundred feet slower than standard he may well shoot behind his bird, or if it be loaded to faster than normal velocity he may well shoot ahead of his bird. Absolute uniformity in velocity is a necessity for good shooting. No hand tools that we have used will give as uniform a pressure on the over-powder wads as is possible with machine methods. Black powder shot shell loading is one thing and smokeless powder loading something entirely different. The pressure placed on the over-powder wads, their exact fit in the finished shell case and the amount of crimp in the seal over the shot all have a vital bearing on the combustion and ultimate velocity of the loaded smokeless shotgun shell. Again, hand loaders must use the over-shot wad, and this does not help patterns in the least and it is very hard for them to get as uniform a crimp from a case that has once been fired.

The fired paper case, even the best high base variety must be full length resized and this operation after once being fired does in no way help the strength of the case. Once the crimp has been straightened out by firing the strength and stiffness of the paper has been greatly reduced and subsequent reloading and recrimping does not further a good, hard, stiff crimp, so necessary to proper combustion of smokeless powders. For this reason we believe reloading by hand with smokeless powders can never equal the performance of the factory shot shell. Velocities will seldom be as uniform and pressures will vary just as greatly. Patterns will likewise suffer.

We well remember, many years ago, doing considerable shotshell loading and could, by taking enough time, produce a very good load in most cases for some individual barrel and certain choke but the load would seldom shoot as well in another gun. Today the shooter is far better off, from every standpoint, to stick to factory loaded shotgun ammunition. Likewise very little, if any, saving occurs in hand-loading shotgun shells if the maximum performance is desired, and if your time is worth anything at all.

Photo by Western Cartridge Co.

Spark Photo of Shot Charge Leaving Muzzle. Improved Super-seal Wad Over Powder has Prevented Blowing-by of Gas—Hence Produces Better Patterns.

Photo by Western Cartridge Co.

Shot Charge in Flight. Note Super-Seal Wad Following Shot Charge.

Photo by Western Cartridge Co.

Spark Photo Showing Shot Charge Leaving Muzzle of Gun. Note Gas Blowing Through and Past the Shot Charge Tending to Spread the Pattern and to Blow Holes in it.

The companies have made great strides in recent years in the improvement of shotgun ammunition. Base wads have been improved, and a very great improvement has been made in overpowder wads. Some loading companies now employ lubricated wads that expand greatly when the pressure of the burning powder charge compresses them between the gas and the heavy shot load. This in turn absolutely seals the bore between the powder gas and the shot charge eliminating fusion and shot balling. These wads also impregnate the bore with lubricant when expanded. Other companies use an inverted cup in the over-powder wad system that expands equally well to seal off all pushing gas from the shot column. They in turn use a wax lubricant on the end of the folded crimp, that under pressure squashes out to form an even film of lubricant over the entire bore as the shot and wad columns move forward. These systems of lubricating the bore at each shot just about eliminate all traces of leading in a highly polished bore and make for perfect patterns.

Remington and Peters employ a small sticker over the folded crimp. We have heard many kicks from old trap shooters on this sticker as in dry climates they claim it tends to stick to the bore and fouls the forcing cone and first foot of the barrel, but it causes no trouble at all in damp climates.

Western and Winchester employ a slightly different form of folded crimp. The end of the shell being slightly indented around a form of edge crimp before the folded closure. This in turn leaves a slight depression that is sealed with a stiff wax lubricant. We believe this the finest of all shell closures we have seen and have put as many as 100 rounds through a barrel in continuous pattern tests without the least trace of leading occurring.

Formerly in pattern work we used to foul the gun with the first shot, then run a string of ten patterns and then give the bore a good scrubbing with a brass bristle brush or brass washers to remove all traces of leading before running another string. With these latest lubricated loads no trace of leading occurs in a smooth highly polished bore. The last Federal Cartridge Co. shells we tested had a frangible, easily destroyed and broken up, top wad. These simply disintegrate on firing and are a great improvement over the older solid card top wad which often rode on the front end of the shot column and caused it to spread from the air pressure. The frangible Federal Cartridge top wads are no doubt a great improvement over the older card top or over-shot wad, but do not compare with the folded crimp closure. Of the folded closures we prefer the Western-Winchester type with wax lubricant to the square fold of the Remington-Peters type with a glued sticker.

On the other hand, long pattern strings will show anyone, even the most skeptical, that he will have to get up very early and work very late to ever produce a hand-loaded shell that will equal any modern factory loads in performance.

We believe two of the most important advancements in modern shot shell loading to be the expanding type of over-powder wads and the folded crimp closure of the paper case. These two factors have contributed more to higher, more uniform patterns, than any others of recent development.

Folded crimp ammunition, is shorter for a given load, less bulky to carry and also lighter to the extent of the top wad. The day is now long past when one had to experiment with hand-loading to obtain the ultimate in patterns from his favorite gun. He can now soon find the best load with a few strings at the pattern board from each of the different makes of ammunition. Shot sizes as made by different companies may vary slightly, also variations in the case and wadding may also make one make of shell shoot better in one gun than in another and the reverse will often be true when a different gun is tested.

Modern shot shell loading has now reached such a stage of perfection that we believe further improvement in shotgun performance will be up to the gun makers rather than the loading companies.

The reason behind such very high shot shell performance are multitudinous. The companies employ large and highly skilled laboratory technicians and also ballisticians. These in turn are aided

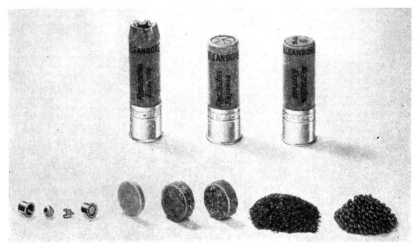

Photo by Remington Arms Co.

New Crimp Shotgun Shell and Components. Top row: (left to right) Loaded Shell Showing New Closure Open; Loaded Shell Closed; Loaded Shell Closed and Sealed.

Bottom row: Battery Cup; Primer Cup; Anvil; Primer Assembly; Over-powder Wad; Filler Wads; Powder; Shot.

by the most modern developments in pressure guns and chronographs and modern photography that can photograph the shot charge at any stage from the gun barrel to the target. They can X-ray the load in the shell for tipping wads or any slight defect. They can control the moisture content and the rate of burning of their powders to that last degree. Annually they fire millions of rounds to determine the best loads of given powders for different shot shell velocities. Nothing is left to chance, all operations are carefully gauged and inspected, every part of the case is gauged and inspected and long strings of every loading are run and patterns taken to determine their uniformity.

If the company asks these technicians for a given load of shot at a given velocity and pressure, they set to work and when it has been achieved, it is then tested for hundreds or even thousands of rounds. Lots of this ammunition are set aside in storage over a period of months or years and again tested to determine its stability under storage conditions. Ammunition is dumped into vats and soaked for hours or days to determine its water resistance. It is also stored at high temperatures and then test fired to determine how much the storage under such extreme conditions may raise pressures. The companies spare no possible effort to make their product safe, and lasting as well. They may even store it in very cold freezers for long periods to determine the effect of extreme Arctic temperatures on the powder and primer and their stability under such conditions. In time they know just what to expect from any given powder and what it will do under either normal or abnormal conditions. The handloader cannot hope to learn a fraction of their knowledge, and while he may produce good ammunition, it can never equal the product of the big loading companies.

Good shotgun shooting depends almost altogether on uniformity of velocity and pattern of the shot charge and only by such highly technical and intricate devices and equipment can this be determined. We shoot where the bird is going to be when the charge arrives, but if velocity falls off we go behind the bird and if it is spooked higher than the normal we are used to we may well shoot ahead of the bird. At close shotgun ranges a difference in velocity is not so apparent but get out on a pass and try long range duck shooting with a load that varies in velocity a few hundred feet and you are absolutely sunk. We have seen expert shots completely thrown off their usual stride when they were forced to shoot a light or moderate load, after using heavy duck loads, in pass shooting. Any change in velocity means a change in lead, and while we can get used to using a moderate low base load for average close range shooting and a heavy duck load for pass shooting, we usually wind up by missing clean when we try to shoot the light load at long range. This is one reason many fine game shots stick to one load for all their shooting in any certain gun and it is a very good idea. The late Capt. Curtiss claimed he always shot full choke guns and only heavy duck loads for his field trial shooting. He was a good performer, knew the spread of his pattern at any given range and knew the correct lead for those heavy loads for almost any range. Had he used different velocity loads his shooting would have suffered.

The loading companies have long photographed the shot charges in motion. This was started years ago by my friend the late Phillip P. Quale and later perfected to an astonishing degree. Spark photography and its later improvements enable the companies to greatly reduce shot stringing. They can see instantly what any given load is doing as to stringing, also the effect of the muzzle flare of gas on the charge and the effect of top wads, etc.

They can and do measure the time of flight for any given charge or size shot, measure its penetration in wood at various ranges and really know if their particular loading is up to standard or not. Modern scientific developments have in turn aided research until the modern factory loaded shot shell is the end result—the finest shotgun ammunition man has ever used.

The companies must load within a safe pressure limit, and pressures are held religiously within those certain safe limits. American shot shells are also loaded to higher pressures as a rule than are English cartridges. American gun builders subject their guns to

Photo by Western Cartridge Co.

10-gauge, 2½-inch Magnum Shell.

very heavy proof loads, while in Britain, the guns are submitted to the proof house, where they undergo the accepted proof load and are then stamped on the bottom flats of the barrels for that load. Usually the British proof loads are of much lower pressure than the American so-called blue pill or proof load, hence the reason American companies load to higher pressures.

The loading companies, if they dared, could give us superb loads for individual guns that would run to higher pressures than standard loads, but they must turn out loads that will reach standard performance in all guns tested and not in one individual gun and choke. Pressures must be held to within safe limits for the poorest gun tested and not just be safe in the finest gun. The ballisticians also know that the higher the velocity the harder it is to get uniform patterns in all guns, so must hold velocities down to where their finished loads will pattern well in about any gun they can be fired in. One notable exception to this general rule has been the development of the Magnum ten-bore. The Western people knew exactly what the bore and choke of the gun was to a ten-thousandth of an inch and could load only the long 3½" case, two-ounce load, to properly fit that individual boring and choking, thus in this highly specialized weapon they produced a very high degree of performance. If the gun makers could build a gun for just one given load and the companies could load but one shell for that same gun, then they could easily give us guns that would pattern 80 to 90 percent, because they would have only the individual variation in bore and choke diameter from gun to gun to contend with, and within those limits could produce very high patterning loads.

Pressure limits may be held to 9000 or even as high as 10,000 pounds but the loading companies know that a small bore with the same pressure actually develops a great deal more bursting strain than does a larger bore gun, so must load accordingly. They must load ammunition that will perform well in every make of gun on the market, thus they cannot hope to bring out the last degree in patterns in an individual gun, for when they succeeded, such a load

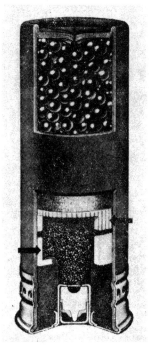

Courtesy Western Cartridge Co.

Section of Shotgun Shell showing cup seal wad over and under the powder to prevent gas from blowing past the shot charge.

might not shoot at all well in some other gun. Considerable variation in chambering, boring and choking occurs with different make guns and the ammunition must be held to a happy medium that will perform well in all of them. So we see the loading companies have a real headache.

One make of shells will perform best in John's gun and he will have nothing else while his partner Joe may find a different make shoots best in his gun and he is equally right in choosing that brand alone. When you get a gun or load that shoots well, that is a gun that handles all loads well, or a load that shoots well in all guns tried then you have something to stick with. The companies may load a batch of shell for test and find some guns are under-choked for the load while others are in fact over-choked for that same given load. Then they must scale that load down until it performs well in all guns. Velocities must be kept up to normal or penetration will fall off, and patterns must be maintained at any cost. It's a simple matter to work out a good rifle load that will perform well in several rifles of the same caliber but a real task to do the same thing with a shotshell.

Large shot can safely be given higher muzzle velocity than smaller shot, up to 1400 feet or a trifle over for the large pellets. They can also be made to pattern well at such high muzzle velocities, but smaller shot under No. 6 doesn't do so well at high veloci-

Typical Shotgun Shell Construction.

ties and are usually loaded to give around or slightly under 900 feet velocity. Heavy duck loads, being intended for shooting at and beyond 50 yards, require as much more velocity as is compatible with good patterns, while smaller shot intended only for shooting under 50 yards require far less velocity and produce better patterns at lower velocities. The big shot will stand the drive of high velocity while the small shot will not. While present-run modern shotgun shells are almost beyond reproach, they are not the last word or the very ultimate the companies are capable of were they limited to loading for one gun or cartridge.

Cheap loads mean a low base, cheap case, low cost wadding and light powder loads as a rule, and yet they can make them to give very high performance with small shot at reasonable ranges. On the other hand long range loads demand progressive burning powders, expensive high brass cases and the finest in wadding and shot obtainable. They necessarily cost more than the cheaper loads. Factory ballisticians can produce about any load ordered, but they will experiment with wadding, pressure, the over-powder wads and velocities as well as crimp closure until they get a uniform even load with a minimum variation in velocities and pressures, that will throw uniform good patterns. Then they will load and market that load and it will perform very well in about all guns and may do exceptionally well in some.

Even when the ballisticians have perfected a hand load that meets all requirements of the specification sent into them, the loading foremen may have trouble getting their machines adjusted to exactly duplicate the hand loads of the ballistician and must work for hours or days until their finished loads are coming off the machines, capable of delivering the exact average pressure, velocities and patterns set up for the load. Careful inspection covers the entire range of the loading machines and even the ballistician himself and his pressure gun, pendulum gun and chronograph, also powders, shot, wads and cartridge case components, so is it any wonder that modern shotshells have reached their present state of high efficiency.

When users of full choke guns wish to do short range upland shooting, they can simply buy some factory loaded so-called brush loads and go merrily on their way knowing they have a load that will give about an improved cylinder pattern from their full choke guns. Nearly all companies load these scatter or brush loads and by means of separating wads within the shot charge or dividing separators they do a very good job of opening up the pattern of full choked guns when it is desired to use such guns for close range upland work. Just another instance of the ingenuity of our loading companies in their endless endeavor to give the shooter the best in modern ammunition.

NOMINAL MEAN INSTRUMENTAL VELOCITY OVER 40 YARDS (410 BORE OVER 25 YARDS)
FULL CHOKE BARRELS

Gage	*Dram*	*Shot Wt.*	*BB*	*2*	*4*	*5*	*6*	*7*	*7½*	*8*
10	4¼	1¼	....	....	1025	1005	985	...	...	...
	4¾	1⅝	1065	1035	1005	985	965	...	...	...
	5	2	1065	1035	1005	985	965	...	...	...
12	2¾	1⅛	....	....	....	...	...	...	840	825
	3	1	....	....	965	945	925	...	...	875
	3	1⅛	....	....	945	925	905	...	870	855
	3¼	1⅛	....	....	975	955	935	...	...	885
	3¼	1¼	....	....	...	...	...	890	880	...
	3¾	1¼	1075	1045	1015	995	975	...	940	...
	4	1⅜	1065	1035	1005	985	965	...	...	...
	4¼	1⅝	1065	1035	1005	985	965	...	...	...
16	2½	1	....	....	925	905	885	...	...	835
	2¾	1⅛	....	....	935	...	895	...	...	845
	3	1⅛	....	995	965	945	925	...	890	...
	3¼	1⅛	....	1025	995	975	955	...	920	...
20	2¼	⅞	....	....	925	905	885	...	...	835
	2½	1	....	....	930	...	890	...	...	840
	2¾	1	....	970	940	920	900	...	865	...
28	2¼	¾	....	....	990	...	950	...	915	...
410-2½″	..	½	....	....	1020	1000	980	...	950	...
410-3″	..	¾	....	....	1020	1000	980	...	950	...

STANDARD SHOTGUN SHOT SIZES

Size	Diam. In Inches	Pellets per Ounce—Nominal
BB	0.18	50
2	0.15	90
4	0.13	135
5	0.12	170
6	0.11	225
7	0.10	300
7½	0.095	350
8	0.09	410
9	0.08	585
10	0.07	870
11	0.06	1380
12	0.05	2385
		Pellets per Pound
00 Buck	0.33	130
0 Buck	0.32	145
1 Buck	0.30	175
3 Buck	0.25	300
4 Buck	0.24	340

CHAPTER FOURTEEN

Shot Sizes and Their Use

FORMERLY the shot towers poured about any size shot that could be desired, many of them with little or no actual value or use to the gunner. More recently they have stopped manufacture of a good many sizes or at least stopped loading them. In many cases this has been an advantage as with so many sizes of shot no dealer could hope to keep stocked with everything. At the close of the muzzleloading days we have seen all sizes stocked in bins in the hardware stores, everything from buck to so-called mustard seed shot. Just what the latter were used for we never did learn as the smallest shot we have personally used in a shotgun, other than some of the little rim fire 22 shot cartridges, was No. 10 shot and we got them by mistake for a duck hunt. We ordered two boxes of fives and when we unwrapped them down at the lake for the mornings shoot we found we had two boxes of 12-bore shells for Joe Bogard's old Spencer loaded with No. 10 shot. Though we tried many times, we killed nothing that day beyond about 40 yards, but did smother three little teal that came within that range; not much game to show for over a box of shells used, so we went snipe hunting with the balance of the remaining box and managed to do fairly well on the jack snipe. One bunch of yellow leg plover also swung by within 30 yards and we did very well on them. Mother served us with snipe pie the next day.

In the target game, No. 7½ seem to be the accepted size for standard clay bird shooting and in Skeet the size is usually No. 9. For game shooting we personally have no use for anything smaller than 7½. No doubt a 20- or 28-bore will make a better pattern with No. 8 shot, but if the gun is a good one No. 7½ will usually offer a killing pattern to the limit of effective range of the small bore even on quail and snipe. Shot smaller than No. 7½ lose pellet energy very fast and drift very badly in any cross wind, so the only legitimate use we can see for them is the No. 9 shot Skeet load and we would much prefer 7½ for any type of small bird. If one were shooting English sparrows then there would no doubt be a legitimate use for No. 9 and No. 10 shot.

At the other extreme, buck shot loads are usually loaded with 00 buck counting nine pellets to the load in 12-bore, and very very few guns will throw a killing pattern with them over 40 yards and many won't do it at 35 yards. A smaller pellet buck load counting

15 pellets to the 1¼ ounce standard 12-bore load would be much more effective on anything from man to deer. In the Super ten-bore when buck are needed we much prefer a 15 pellet load and a 20 pellet load in the Magnum 10-bore to No. 00 buck. The English have a buck shot called SSG that is about right for 12-bore guns and useful also in the 10-bore. Under buckshot, the next size usually loaded is BB and we have never found much use for BB shot other than in the kid's air rifle. We have never owned a gun that would make really fine patterns with these coarse shot. If it did shoot them fairly well, it would always shoot No. 2 or No. 3 a lot better for percentages. Even in the two-ounce Magnum ten-bore load, patterns never counted very high and did not look good to me even for geese at 70 yards, while No. 2 would go regularly 85 percent and would have taken geese to 80 yards most all the time. No. 3 shot are big enough to carry pellet energy out to 80 yards and they went 93 percent from the big gun and to our way of thinking offered an even better goose load than No. 2 shot in the big ten bore.

Most 12-bore and Super Ten-bore loads for geese are loaded with No. 2 shot and just why, we have never been able to determine. No. 2s usually pattern fairly well from the Super Ten and Magnum 12-bore guns, but the pattern is usually very thin in all standard 12-bores at over 60 yards. The shot are simply too big for the 1¼ ounce load and No. 3 shot will do a better job of killing on the big fowl. When one is lucky enough to get within effective range of a golden eagle, as he hunts ducks along the swamps and creeks, then twos are a very good shot as the big birds are hard to kill and you simply must have heavy pellets to drive through to their vitals; even then several shots are usually necessary to bring one down. Small shot rattle off them like hail on a tin roof with little or no effect.

Many years ago when the 10-bore was considered the standard shotgun gauge, No. 3 shot were by far the most popular even for ducks, but the then standard 10-bore load of 1¼ ounces was not enough pellets to give a good pattern for ducks but did do better for geese than No. 2 shot. We still consider No. 3 shot the best size of all for the Magnum ten bores with two ounce loads and also consider No. 3 the best size for geese in both Super Ten bores, Magnum 12s and standard 1½ ounce 12-bore loads. Anything smaller than 3s lack pellet energy for the big birds at anything beyond 65 yards. Smaller shot do not have the weight necessary to break heavy wing bones or to penetrate to the vitals on frontal shots. It is questionable, to say the least, if No. 2 shot are better than No. 3, even in the Magnum ten-bore for goose shooting. You get so much better patterns with No. 3 that we believe this size will give more clean kills on geese than will No. 2 shot in anything from the 1¼ ounce standard 12-bore up to and probably including the two ounce

Magnum ten. No. 3 shot will drive through a mallard at 40 yards and will drive to the center of the big duck at 80 yards. They are heavy enough to break wing bones on geese as well, so with their much better pattern one is far more apt to register killing pellets on the big bird out at long range; and most geese are shot at long range. They are so big they often appear close when in reality they are at long range.

Major Askins used to make up a long range load, by slipping a cut 28-bore case down into the center of a ten-bore shell and filling all around the 28-bore case with any size of very small shot. This was to take the wear and tear of the forcing cone and choke. Into the 28-bore shell he loaded heavy shot, No. 2 or No. 3 and then pulled out the cut 28-bore case, leaving the big shot completely surrounded with a layer of fine shot. On the pattern board the small shot did the usual but those big pellets clustered together in the center of the pattern and such a load would kill geese out beyond the range of most factory goose loads. We tried it at his suggestion and it worked, and will still work to this day, as the small shot take up the usual deformation from the gun and leave those big pellets in perfect shape in the center of the pattern, just as the tracer pellet in the Eley English cartridge usually flies right in the center of the pattern.

Sweeley went even farther by making up shot containers that held the entire charge together out to fairly long range; but no company could ever be induced to go to so much trouble in shot shell loading. He once draw bored a long 34″ Ithaca single trap gun, removing most of the forcing cone and loaded up to 1½ ounces of shot in this standard 12 bore, which with his shot containers, produced long range patterns never obtainable before or since with factory loads. E. M. Sweeley and Maj. Chas. Askins probably did more individual shotgun experimenting than any other two men of our time.

Getting back to shot sizes, it's folly to use too small a pellet, as you will feather and wound a lot of birds that will carry on and get away, hit out too far for the pellet energy of the tiny shot. By the same token it is also folly to use too large a shot for the bird or fowl hunted as you will then have a pattern so thin that you can heave the family cat through it without being touched by a single pellet at times. That is the usual B B shot in all gauges under the ten bore and it is a pretty worthless size even in the big Magnum ten. For game shooting as far as we are concerned the companies can drop all shot smaller than No. 7½ from their list and also all shot larger than No. 2, except a small size of buck for specific uses.

No. 7½ will do us nicely for snipe, quail, doves, and all similar size birds including green wing teal. They will take all this game very nicely if we do our part.

The most useful shot sizes of all for most all guns from a 20 to a magnum ten for most wildfowl and large bird shooting, are sizes 3, 4, 5, and 6 shot, and we believe these should all be loaded in suitable gauges. No use in loading shot heavier than sixes in a 20-bore and no use loading fours in anything but a magnum 12 or super ten with 1⅝ ounces for the average duck or long range pheasant shooting. The 20-, 16- and standard 12-bore gun will do about as well on ducks with size as anything else, except at long range the 1¼ ounce 12-bore may kill a bit better with fives. Some rare standard 12 bores will also handle fours very well and are then useful on big ducks like mallards and canvas backs but as a general rule the gunner will be better off with fives or sixes than with fours in the standard 12-bore or any smaller gauge. We have run patterns for months, then taken our knowledge gained afield and tried it out on sage hens, grouse, mallards and pheasants and usually wound up by going back to sixes for the 16-bore and fives or sixes in the standard 12-bore; while in the magnum 12 and super ten we stuck to fours as the one best load for these big guns and by the same token threes proved the best for the two ounce magnum ten-bore when maximum effective range was desired for these various gauges.

Many shooters have good luck with a certain size shot and then use it to the exclusion of every other size, when they are often seriously handicapping themselves. Such a man once argued with me that No. 7½ shot were by all odds the best for geese. Another man claimed only No. 4 shot were worth a whoop as his gun threw them very well and he used them for quail and snipe and seemed to kill a lot of the time at that. Just the same he would have killed more of those small birds and killed them cleaner had he used No. 7½ or even No. 6 shot.

A few days work at the pattern board often takes a lot of conceit out of such folks and teaches them the error of their ways. It will also help them no end in determining just what sizes their gun handles best. Big shot will nearly always pattern higher than smaller shot in a given gauge gun and for this reason the loading companies like to load fours. We have even witnessed a lad hunting cottontails with No. 4 shot in a 2½″ .410-bore and also saw him wound and lose several bunnies that day as he had no pattern at all and when we finally persuaded him to shoot at an old barn, he immediately saw the reason. From then on he used 7½ shot and with good effect when the range was not over 15 yards.

No. 7½ shot are about the largest that will give good patterns in the .410- and 28-bore guns, and we never could see the reason behind the .410. It is now and always has been the poacher's gun, and is used more to pot game out of season at very close range on the ground than any other weapon. The 28-bore is the smallest gauge shotgun that should ever be manufactured and it will do all that the 3″ .410 will do and do it better, so why the .410?

The 20-bore will also pattern best with No. 7½ shot, but a bit longer killing range can be obtained when the 20 is used on ducks and pheasants by the use of No. 6 shot. Unless one was trying for geese then No. 6 is as large as should ever be used in the 20-bore and for all smaller birds No. 7½ is better.

In the 16-bore No. 7½ are again the best for the smaller birds, woodcock, doves, snipe and quail but for the larger fowl, mallards, canvas backs and pheasants, or the big sage hen the best size for this bore gun is No. 6. Some 16-bores handle No. 5 exceptionally well and when they prove this on the pattern board, then it is well to use fives for the larger fowl. We used to shoot Peters Ideal No. 5 shot, one and one-eighth ounces, and shot that load for a great many years with perfect success in a No. 3 Ithaca double, full-choked 16-bore. That gun threw fives better than sixes and was a better killer with them. We now have Major Askins' old No. 5 Ithaca 16-bore 30″, full choke both barrels, and they go a full 90 percent with 1¼ ounces of sixes in heavy duck loads, so that is the load for this gun; and last fall we killed 12 cock pheasants and five mallards with it before we missed a single shot, which goes to show what can be done with a gun that you have patterned and determined the best load for and have absolute confidence in both as to gun and load.

We have seen ducks killed just as far and just as cleanly as they should ever be shot at with a standard 12-bore with 1¼ ounces of No. 6 shot. For average duck and pheasant shooting it is problematical if a better shot size is to be had. However when the ranges are long such as pass shooting at Mallards or canvas backs or late season pheasants that are as wild as buck deer, then the gun that will handle fives or fours well will kill to longer ranges than will No. 6 shot. As a rule No. 5 shot will give the better pattern if the gun handles them well but for some reason not a great many guns handle fives well. As a rule the gun that handles fours well will also do well with sixes and the gun that handles fives well will also shoot well with threes, but the latter are too big in a standard 12-bore for anything but geese. Late season, heavily feathered fowl take a lot of penetration at times and the larger shot if they pattern well will kill to longer range than No. 6, but the fact remains that probably more ducks are killed today and more pheasants as well with No. 6 than any other shot size and with good reason.

When we turn to the 1⅝-ounce magnum 12 and super ten-bore guns there is no use in handicapping yourself with a shot that carries pellet energy to no greater range than 60 yards. These big guns do their best long range work on large ducks or pheasants with No. 4 shot and nothing smaller will carry pellet energy to a full 70 yards and nothing larger will give the best pattern for such birds out to that range. Fours are just right for the Super Ten and Magnum Twelve and they are the load that should be used whenever the ranges are such as to make their use necessary. For geese, with these guns, we would much prefer No. 3 shot to No. 2s, but the factories seem to have fallen into the habit of loading twos for geese and will load nothing else. Twos are a good goose shot but threes will give a killing pattern at 70 yards where twos will not from many guns. Threes also carry enough pellet energy for geese at 70 yards and we have seen threes driven right through the heads of mallards out at 127 yards by actual measurement which shows they carry plenty of weight for penetration on geese.

Shot Sizes For Different Gauges For Maximum Killing Range

Many times we are asked the best size shot to use for maximum ranges in the different bore guns for use on large birds like pheasants, blue grouse and sage hens as well as mallards and ducks of similar size. One must take into consideration that nearly all guns will throw one particular size shot better than it will another size if it is a fixed-choke gun. If with a Poly-Choke, Lyman Cutts Comp or Weaver Choke then you can often fit the choke to the load and size shot. However when you want average maximum range results for your particular gauge on such birds as pheasants and mallards, then here is a simple rule that will work more often than not and usually works very well indeed.

To obtain maximum killing pattern combined with pellet energy and penetration out to the limit of the gauge try the following:

.410-3″ and 28-bore guns use size 7½ shot.
20-bore guns with one ounce loads preferably No. 7 shot.
16-bore guns with 1⅛ ounces shot use No. 6 shot.
12-bore guns with 1¼ ounces shot use No. 5 shot.
12-bore Magnum 3″ use No. 4 shot. This with 1⅝ ounces.
10-bore Super ten with 1⅝ ounces shot use No. 4 shot.
10-bore Magnum 3½ inch with two ounces shot use No. 3 shot.

Again I am asked the effective ranges of such loads.

The .410 3″ and 28-bore should kill large birds with such loads to 30 to 35 yards.
20-bore to 40 to 50 yards.
16-bore 45 to 55 yards.
12-bore standard 50 to 60 yards.
12 Magnum and Super ten 60 to 70 yds.
10 Magnum two ounce 70 to 80 yds.
(Full choke guns in all gauges.)

For goose shooting one needs nothing less than the 1¼ ounce standard 12 and the Super ten and Magnum 12 and the big Magnum ten are much better.

Several times we have been caught duck shooting with the 16-bore loaded with No. 5 shot in 1⅛-ounce loads when geese came over. The big birds appeared to be at about 60 yards. We could hit them alright and get feathers on many occasions, but the shot simply rattled on their feathers without bringing down a single fowl. Had we been using the Magnum ten or Super ten-bore or a Magnum

12 we would have had goose dinners, that is providing the gun was loaded with threes or twos. For some reason we have not seen threes in many loaded shells lately and none except in the Magnum ten-bore, when it is a size best suited for geese in everything from the 1¼-ounce standard 12-bore upwards, through the Super ten-bore and Magnum 12 at least.

The companies are absolutely right in wishing to standardize the loads as much as possible, but they should retain our most useful shot sizes and we believe twos, threes, fours, fives, sixes and seven and a half shot should be made and loaded regularly in all hunting loads of proper gauge for the shot size. While we need only two powder loads, the low and high base variety of shells, one with the moderate load for usual ranges and the other the heavy duck load, we do need the above shot sizes.

In the deep south, soft shot were always the most popular and enabled quail shooters to use a size smaller shot that thickened up their patterns, as soft shot expand when they contact bones or any hard surface and this expansion makes them tear larger wounds and also stay in the bird. The Southerners firmly believe that soft shot are the best killers and with good sound reason. On the other hand the loading companies and all shotgun ballisticians well know hard shot give the best patterns and the least leading and that Lubaloy coated shot give even higher percentages and still less leading troubles. We have shot all types but prefer Lubaloy shot to even hard shot and hard shot to soft shot because of their cleaner shooting and better patterning qualities as well as better penetration on heavy birds. However, when you shoot quail, snipe, doves and woodcock, we are not at all so certain of our point and rather think the Southerner has something on the ball in his liking and claims for soft shot. The companies now load only hard shot or copper covered shot so the South will have to come to their use or else roll their own if they can still buy the soft shot. On large fowl, soft shot will flatten on a bone at times without breaking it at all where hard shot would drive on through and either break or greatly weaken the bone so it would break.

The smaller the shot used the higher the chamber pressures and the larger the shot the less will be the chamber pressures. Large shot also maintain much higher velocities over a given range than do small shot and large shot are drifted far less in a strong cross wind than are small shot. Try shooting patterns at 40 yards in a strong side wind and note how much you have to hold out, often 15 to 20" into the wind, to land a trap load in the center of the pattern paper, while a heavy duck load of fours will drift not over six inches in the same wind. This is something else to consider when on a duck pass in a strong wind as the big shot will then deliver their pattern with far less velocity loss and wind drift, but we must still maintain that killing pattern so there is no horse sense in using a size shot too large to deliver the desired pattern.

SKEET LOADS

Gauge	Load	Choke	Barrel Length	Shell Length	Chamber Length	Instrumental Velocity ±20 f.s.
12	1⅛ = 9	Improved Cylinder	26″	2⅝″	2¾″	920
16	1 = 9	"	26″	2⁹⁄₁₆″	2¾″	920
20	⅞ = 9	"	26″	2½″	2¾″	920
28	¾ = 9	"	26″	2¾″	2⅞″	920
.410 Bore	½ = 9	"	26″	2½″	3″	920
.410 Bore	¾ = 9	"	26″	3″	3″	880

BALLISTIC SPECIFICATIONS FOR SHOTGUN SHELLS—1947 SIMPLIFIED LIST (Revised 6-23-47)

Ga.	Length Shell Inches	Length Chamber Inches	Dram Equiv. To nearest ⅛ Dram	Shot Weight Ounces	Instrumental Velocities + 20 f. s. over 40 yards Full Choke Barrels — Size of Shot BB	2	4	5	6	7½	8	Length of Barrel In Inches
10	2⅞	2⅞	4¼	1¼			1025	1005	985			32
*10	2⅞	2⅞	4¾	1⅝	1065	1035	1005	985	965			32
10	3½	3½	5	2	1065	1035	1005	985	965			32
12	2¾	2¾	2¾	1⅛						840	825	30
12	2⅝&2¾	2¾	3	1			965	945	925		875	30
12	2⅝&2¾	2¾	3	1⅛			945	925	905	870	855	30
12	2⅝&2¾	2¾	3¼	1⅛			975	955	935		885	30
12	2¾	2¾	3¼	1¼						880		30
12	2¾	2¾	3¾	1¼	1075	1045	1015	995	975	940		30
12	3	3	3¾	1¼						940		30
*12	3	3	4	1⅜	1065	1035	1005	985	965			30
*12	3	3	4¼	1⅝	1065	1035	1005	985	965			30
16	$2\frac{9}{16}$ or 2¾	2¾	2½	1			925	905	885		835	28
16	$2\frac{9}{16}$ or 2¾	2¾	2¾	1⅛			935		895		845	28
16	$2\frac{9}{16}$ or 2¾	2¾	3	1⅛		995	965	945	925	890		28
16	$2\frac{9}{16}$ or 2¾	2¾	3¼	1⅛		1025	995	975	955	920		28
20	2½ or 2¾	2¾	2¼	⅞			925	905	885		835	26
20	2½ or 2¾	2¾	2½	1			930		890		840	26
*20	2½ or 2¾	2¾	2¾	1		970	940	920	900	865		26
28	2⅞	2⅞	2¼	¾			990		950	915		26
410	2½	3	—	½			1020	1000	980	950		26
410	3	3	—	¾			1020	1000	980	950		26

CHAPTER FIFTEEN

Buck, Ball and Slugs

EXCEPT FOR DEER HUNTING in the deep South, and some Eastern states whose laws make the use of a shotgun for deer mandatory, we do not have a great deal of use for buckshot for sporting purposes. They are usually worthless for all bird shooting. Very few guns will throw good killing buckshot patterns beyond 50 yards, even when a deer is the target and for anything smaller the big shot simply rattle around them with only a chance of a single pellet striking. We have watched hunters throw a lot of buckshot at geese and only once remember a goose being brought down with them and that by a broken wing. Of course if fired into a dense mass of geese as we once witnessed in a 40-acre field of new wheat in Missouri, then one should kill some geese, but that would simply be pot shooting. There is always the chance that if enough buck shot are thrown at geese at long range a stray pellet may register, but they are entirely too uncertain to be considered except for bigger game at close quarters.

At very close range, buckshot becomes a terrible weapon, and nothing is better for close range infighting either by the military or civilians. Many soldiers learned their efficiency in the jungles of the Pacific and many old Westerners have seen their devastating effect on man at close range. The killer of Jesse James met his end in Colorado from both barrels of a sawed off shotgun fired the length of his place of business. Even fine shot are a very lethal weapon at close range and we have known both bear and deer being killed with No. 6 shot at close range. Buck, however, with their greater weight and penetration, when concentrated together at close range are very effective on most anything and that is the way we believe they should be used, for defense work at close range.

Buckshot Deer Load

As previously stated some states prohibit the use of anything but buckshot on deer and in some southern states it is extremely doubtful of anything else, either rifled slugs or rifles would be as effective for the type of hunting necessary in those sections. Usually the deer are driven with dogs and shots beyond 50 yards are seldom obtained or taken. For such service a good patterning buckshot load is needed.

We have just finished a long string of patterns with Remington Super Ten Bore Nitro Express buckshot loads. These loads counted

16 pellets of No. 0 buck to the 1⅞-ounce load. The gun used was Major Askin's old Magnum ten-bore Ithaca No. 500,000. The range was 40 yards from the muzzle. It must be considered that this gun is over-bored for the two-ounce Magnum ten-bore load in 3½″ cases, so the above Remington load in its 2⅞″ cases necessitated a long jump by the load before it reached the forcing cone. Further the gun is over-bored for the big Magnum load. In spite of these handicaps of short shells in long chambers and over-boring, the poorest pattern counted 12 pellets in a 30″ circle at 40 yards and the best pattern counted the full 16 pellets or 100%. Some patterns put the whole load in 24″,

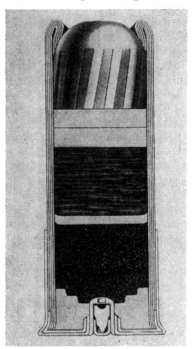

A Rifled Slug Shotgun Load.

while a few showed wider spread than the 30″ circle and some few showed poor pellet distribution. However the entire string averaged a full 90 percent, which is mighty good in any gun and especially so in a gun chambered and bored for the much longer 3½″ shell. For those who must by necessity or choice use buckshot on deer, we suggest a trial of these Remington 1⅞-ounce 16-pellet loads in their favorite Super ten-bore gun. The above loads put far more pellets in the 30″ circle at 40 yards from this gun than did some Western Super X two-ounce loads containing 15 pellets of No. 00 buck, which latter load evidently did not fit the gun at all as we could never keep all shot on the pattern paper. However, some years before his death

Major Askins wrote me that he had one lot of Western Super X magnum ten-bore two-ounce buckshot loads counting 20 pellets to the charge that put the entire load inside a 24″ circle at 40 yards from this gun. So far, though we tried handloading smaller buck that went 20 pellets to the charge, we have never had patterns to equal his or do much better than the above mentioned Western Super X 15-pellet two-ounce load. To date this Remington 1⅞-ounce 16-pellet load has shown the best patterns for us. We would like to find a two-ounce load that would put all shot in a 24″ circle at 40 yards as it would then be a killing deer load to 55 or 60 yards. Usually buckshot

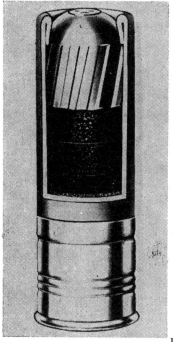

Photo by Western Cartridge Co.

A Rifled Shotgun Load.

are uncertain beyond 40 yards in 12-bore guns but this Remington load should kill regularly to 50 yards most of the time and the Majors' 20-pellet western load should have reached out to 60 yards with killing patterns. When hounds are used to trail up all cripples, few deer are lost wounded in the South.

Buckshot must chamber in the choke of the gun if they are to shoot well in it. If they don't chamber in the choke in even, smooth layers, then they will not pattern well. We remember one old Winchester Model '97 riot gun that put the entire nine 00 buck under the spread of my hand repeatedly at 40 yards. That was the best shooting buckshot gun we have ever used but it belonged to Uncle Sam. We

Photo by Western Cartridge Co.

Shotgun Load of No. 0 Buck.

would have given a lot for that ancient gun just to keep around as an alley cleaner.

Many times we have shot at eagles with buckshot with no pellets registering at all. They would make the big bird turn and swerve and get out of the vicinity in a hurry but they did not register on him at all and twos would have been much more effective. If buckshot are used as they should be, at 15 to 25 yards, they are very effective, but the range must be short enough to preclude the possibility of the big shot scattering very much. My friend, John Taylor, recommends the

12-bore shotgun with SSG buck shot for close range work in the brush on lion or leopard and with good reason, but he does not recommend them for taking anything at more than a few feet range. Our friend, John Burger, also uses buck a great deal and prefers them even to a heavy double rifle for close range work on lion and leopard and has sat up nights and killed marauding man-eating lion with the 12-bore double and SSG buckshot. However he waited until the big cat came in for him to just a few feet from the muzzle, then blew a big hole right into the brain pan and that was all there was to it.

Photo by Western Cartridge Co.

Shotgun Load of No. 00 Buck.

Down at the ranch we once had a timber wolf hanging around the ranch after night as we had a female cow dog he was very much interested in. The neighbors saw him kill deer during the winter on different occasions, but never could we get sight of him in daylight and use a rifle on him. As Mrs. Keith and the writer usually slept out of the house in a tent during the summer months, we tied the dog at the front of the tent. One evening son Ted slipped into the tent and told us he had seen the wolf across the meadow, so picking up the old Magnum ten loaded with two ounces of buck Western loads to the charge, we waited. Soon the wolf came past the tent in his swinging trot at about seven yards. We kicked open the screen door and gave him a load behind the shoulder. He let out one long howl but kept on going and we gave him the second barrel for the back of his head. It registered and he piled up. We examined him with a flashlight. That first charge had torn into him low behind the shoulders making a hole as big as a man's closed fist. The second load had struck the back of the head and bulged the eyes out of their sockets and simply shattered both neck and skull. The night was too dark to see the ivory sights on the gun but we were used to shooting it by feel anyway. Next morning we had a ninety pound timber wolf to drag off and the deer suffered less that coming winter.

Buckshot can be made to shoot together in a small pattern by stringing them on a fine copper wire. Then they are quite effective to 40 yards and this should be done for most deer shooting. Right now is a good time to say we would never hunt deer with a buckshot load unless forced to do so through lack of anything better to use, or where such use is mandatory. Where the jungle is so thick one cannot see over 20 yards, buck are more effective than anything else, and quicker on the fast targets. Many times we have jumped big mule deer bucks hiding in dense small lodgepole. Also old Whitetail bucks hiding in the second growth cedar of the Lochsa country. In those cases a ten-bore with buckshot would have been just the ticket as we were right on top of the big deer anyway but the brush and pine poles were too thick to shoot with a rifle. E. M. Sweeley used to put heavy shot in a sort of screen container and thus hold them together for long range; and the standard procedure when I was a boy in loading buck in long brass shells was to pour melted tallow over them before seating a thin top wad. This also was very effective and seemed to hold the big shot together much better than when simply loaded in layers in the case.

Several times we have tried to kill coyotes after night, at from 40 to 60 yards, with a shotgun and buck shot and though we hit and wounded some we never did get one that way. For best results one should push a wad down into the choke of his gun and then carefully fit shot in layers in the choke until he finds a size buck that will chamber smoothly and evenly in layers. We prefer a size that would chamber in layers of four or five to a larger size like 00 in a 12-bore that lays in layers of three. If the shot fit the choke evenly and smoothly in layers then that load will shoot very much better than a load that does not so fit and if tallow is melted and poured over them and the top wad replaced, it is even more effective.

If the shot be strung on a thin copper wire it will hold the load together, though they often describe some queer looking patterns on the pattern paper. If you have a Poly or other patent choke you can

A Cut-away View of a Buckshot Load.

regulate it to throw good buckshot patterns and for this reason the repeater is often the best buckshot gun if so fitted. We once played with a 12-bore trap gun with a Poly Choke and found we could get very good reliable killing patterns at a full 40 yards from it with 00 buck, and strangely enough we used a modified setting for the best patterns. Some guns seem to shoot buck better with improved cylinder choke. Nearly all guns in full choke that we have used, appear to be over choked for buckshot and simply scattered them wild. The Western load Major Askins had for our old Magnum ten was a honey and placed the entire 20-pellet load in just 24″ at 40 yards. We would like to have some buck loads for the big gun that would do that again, but some we ordered from Western carried 15/00 buck and would not stay on the 40″ square of paper and were simply worthless in this particular gun.

If you must use buck on deer, then by all means get busy and pattern the gun with different size buck until you find a certain killing load to 40 yards and then refrain from shooting at a longer distance. Where hounds are used in the South few if any deer are lost, as the dogs will trail them up, but we cannot imagine deer that have been wounded and chased by dogs as being good venison in any sense of the word.

The English have a couple of loads for most shotguns from 20- to 12-bore, loaded with patent ball, that are formed in segments and that break up on impact. They are the Lyon's Lethal bullets in the form of a sphere and the Kynoch Destructor bullets. The Lyon cartridge uses a ball that is in itself formed by many separate pieces of lead. They will give somewhat in the choke of a gun and can be used in full choke guns without damage to the weapon. This load naturally shoots a lot closer than any regular load of buckshot. It breaks up on impact into separate pellets. The Kynoch Destructor cartridge contains some 16 lead pellets in a lead case, that also breaks up on impact and flies quite accurately. These loads should be excellent for leopard or similar game at close range. We have no counterpart for them in this country. In the jungles of Central and South America shotguns are often used for big game, that is deer etc., up to the jaguar and when used at close range are very effective. In such jungles a shotgun is often far more useful than a rifle and when such is the case, one should have either buck, slugs or some of these English cartridges.

Round balls from shotgun have been used on the biggest game for over 100 years now, and while they do not compare with heavy rifles, are quite deadly if placed right. Gordon Cumming used a pair of 10-bore doubles with round ball even on elephant, and Sir Samuel Baker also used and often preferred a pair or three double ten-bores firing round ball of hardened lead with enormous charges of black powder for much of his early elephant shooting. In this country they have been used for deer shooting in some states that do not allow the use of a rifle. When placed in the chest cavity of a deer or along the line of the spine they are very effective but do not kill as well as rifle bullets when badly placed. They do bleed an animal well and leave a good blood trail. They should be fitted to the choke of the gun, as no ball that is too large for the choke should be fired through full choke guns. All factory ball loads are loaded with round ball of a size that fits the choke of the standard full choked gun, hence is a bit loose as to fit in improved cylinder and other borings. If round ball fit the choke perfectly or are patched with a greased linen patch to fit it perfectly like the old Kentucky rifles were loaded, then they will shoot into about 5 inches at 50 yards and are more certain and a better load for deer to that range than are buckshot from the average gun.

Accounts of the use of the round ball in muskets in the Revolution, prove their effectiveness, and anyone hit with one was usually out of the picture, either permanently or for a long time at least. Yet they were not very accurate and short ranged as well, and we often wonder if the troops had been trained archers and had a good supply of broadhead arrows if they would not have proven about ten times more effective against the trained British regulars as when armed with the old Colonial muskets. Certainly at 50 yards or under they could have delivered ten times as many shots with about equal accuracy and the broadhead would have been equally effective. They would have had less weight to carry and could have fired about five to ten well-aimed arrows to one musket ball.

Today the round ball load in shotguns is obsolete and totally outclassed by the modern slug load. We first tested the old imported Brennecke slugs and they were more accurate than any round ball loads we could buy and also cut a larger, cleaner hole in the target or game. Then with the advent of the American rifled slug we have a real lethal killer from the shotgun. Amply accurate in good guns for deer shooting to 50 or possibly 60 yards, it has been used for some years now with good results in states prohibiting the use of a rifle. We have targeted many slug loads in different guns and many guns will deliver 3″ to 5″ groups regularly at 50 yards. We believe the 12-bore the best of the lot for deer shooting and these will kill white tail in the brush nicely or any other deer if you can get within that certain range and do your part. Owing to their low velocity, they do not impart the terrific shock of a modern rifle bullet, yet they cut a far larger entrance hole and have a heavy sickening slap on them like hitting the animal with a hammer. If shotguns are fitted with double ivory sights or with a simple little rear peep sight or with a shotgun scope like Weaver's 1-X then very good shooting can be done with the rifled slug loads. We believe however it is a grave mistake to ever make these loads in smaller than 20-bore. They have been brought out even for the tiny .410-bore and weigh but 90 grains and in such small bore are not fit to shoot anything much larger than rabbits.

The rifling or lands placed on the sides of these slugs, impart a rotating motion to the slugs when they reach the air in flight and they may even start to spin in the bore. These lands on the slug also will not injure the choke of a gun and are easily swaged to a perfect fit in the choke. It is a revelation to shoot them in some double guns, as you may well find your two barrels do not shoot together at all, and we believe double gun makers would do well to target their guns with slug loads when regulating the barrels as it would eliminate many badly shooting double guns by instantly showing up the error in the divergence of the barrels. A short-barrelled auto-loading shotgun should be a very good tool in the brush for lion, leopard, or jaguar when loaded with rifled slugs and a full magazine capacity. They have penetration enough for brain shots on such beasts and cut a very large hole and we believe the 12-bore to be the most effective of the lot.

This brings us to the Paradox guns. These are a British invention, usually in either ten- or 12-bore. The last four to six inches of the muzzles are rifled with a broad shallow rifling and will spin the heavy British Paradox bullet with rifle accuracy to about 150 yards. The 12-bore Paradox slug is made in solid bullet form or in a hollow point form, the solid weighing 750 grains and the hollow point

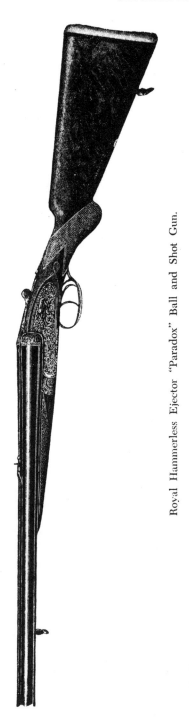

Royal Hammerless Ejector "Paradox" Ball and Shot Gun.

12-bore Cartridge with "Paradox" Bullet, Full Size.

Courtesy Holland and Holland, Ltd., London

SMOKELESS PARADOX

capped bullet weighing 735 grains. Both are very effective against big game and just about as accurate as a double rifle to 150 yards. These guns also deliver a good cylinder bore pattern, making them very effective on fowl or birds to the usual cylinder bore range with small shot. They are made by Westley Richards, Holland & Holland, and Jeffery and probably several other British firms as well. It is hard to find a more useful gun for close range brush hunting, where one must have both a shotgun and a defense rifle at the same time. The weapons are usually sighted the same as fine double rifles and yet stocked like your favorite shotgun and are very fast on the mark, be it feathered or animal game. They are however a good bit heavier than a shotgun of the same bore, as a rule.

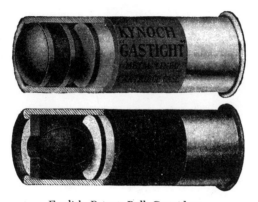

English Patent Ball Cartridges.

Courtesy W. J. Jeffery and Co., Ltd., London

A Fine Example of English Double-Trigger Shotguns.

BALLISTIC SPECIFICATIONS FOR BUCK SHOT, SINGLE BALL AND RIFLED SLUGS

Gauge	Length of Shell	Size of Buck	Numbers of Layers	Number of Pellets	Instrumental Velocities ± 20 Foot Seconds						
					0	00	1	3	4	Single Ball	Rifled Slug
10	2⅞"	0	4	16	1100						
12	3"	0	5	15	1100						
12	3"	00	4	12		1125					1400
12	2¾"	0	4	12	1125					1370	
12	2¾"	00	3	9		1125					
12	2¾"	1	4	16			1075				
12	2¾"	4	4	27					1125		1370
16	2⁹⁄₁₆"	1	4	12			1075			1340	1340
20	2½" and 2¾"	3	4	20				1075		1300	1360
410	2¾"									1360*	
Riot											
12	2¾"	0	4	12	1125						
12	2¾"	00	3	9		1125					

*Test Range 50 feet
Test Range Buck Shot—40 yards
Test Range Single Ball and Rifled Slugs—100 Feet

CHAPTER SIXTEEN

Patterns

WHEN YOU GET A NEW GUN, the first thing to do is to pattern it, not only to find out where it shoots for elevation, but also to determine the best shot size and the make of shell that shoots best in this particular gun. Put up a 40″ square of paper, preferably with thumb tacks, on a board background of some sort, at a measured 40 yards. You can build such a backboard in a few minutes with old boards or an old building that is no longer of any use can be used, provided of course it is empty and you know it to be so.

Stand with the muzzle of the gun on the line and throw the gun up quickly, shooting the instant the aim is centered on the target. You will soon learn just how the gun shoots for elevation. Its best to put one fouling shot through the gun before starting a string, then run five to ten patterns with that load. A ten-shot string is much the best to really tell what a gun or load is doing. Take a straight stick some 20″ long, split, and splice in a pencil at one end with tape or string, then measure carefully just 15″ from the pencil point and drive a small nail through the stick. Spread your patterns on an old table that you won't damage with the nail point, and by visual inspection determine the exact center of the pattern. Then set the nail point in the center and using the stick with pencil for a compass, scribe a 30″ circle. Count up all pellets inside the 30″ circle. The tables of pellets per load per size shot are given in this book, so they will give you a rough idea of how many shot of a given size are in your load. But different makes of shot vary slightly, so you should pull the shot for at least one shell and better two or three and count and average them. Then take that as a basis of your load.

Divide the number of shot inside the 30″ circle by the number in the load in decimals to get your pattern percentage. You may find that by judicious moving of the center nail about you can best encompass the greater number of shot and this is permissible, and correctly establishes the true center of the pattern. You will also find it advantageous to take a yardstick and pencil and scribe several lines across your 30″ pattern at even intervals, thus dividing the pattern into separate columns, then it is much easier to add up each column of shot holes and finally add the different columns. Running patterns is a lot of work, but is the way to determine just what any given gun or load will do. The gun will also kick, particularly if it is a heavy Magnum duck gun, when deliberately aimed and fired at a target, but that is also part of the work. Some advocate sitting down and aiming the gun like a rifle. We do not, and think anyone should stand up and shoot as if they were shooting traps or game. Check the alignment of the eye over the rib and shoot when it centers the 40″ paper.

To old hands at the game, who have run thousands of patterns, a few shots at 20 yards will tell them about all they need to know about any given load. Thus it is easier and quicker for them to determine the best load for a gun than it is for a novice, as they will simply shoot five patterns at 20 yards with each load and shot size and pick out the ones that look the most favorable, then go back to 40 yards and correctly pattern a ten shot string, count and average the loads and really know just what the gun and load is doing.

Only by thus patterning your gun can you ever know what shot size it does best with and what load of powder and shot for best results. The ultimate goal, remember, is an even spread of shot in a 30″ circle at the range you wish to kill your game, or take your clay targets. We may never get the perfect pattern with the whole charge evenly spread on such a 30″ circle but we can come fairly close to getting it at some ranges with most loads and borings. For close range work you will have trouble getting enough spread; and for long range duck and goose shooting you will have an even harder time getting a pattern that is centered enough to carry out to killing ranges and be effective. Use a shot size that will give you the pattern and if one shot is too large and leaves too many holes in the pattern then try a smaller size; but get that pattern first and then figure out the range to which it will be effective. Our chapter on shot sizes and their use will tell you what to look for in shot sizes. One gun may do best with twos, fours and sixes and the next gun may chamber threes, fives and sevens best, and the only way to know is to run enough patterns to prove which size is best.

Its a good thing to remember that you need at least four pellet hits on any given bird to kill and more are much better, but you must have four hits with a size shot large enough to carry their pellet energy to the range required, if you would make uniform, even kills. In this respect the size bird shot must be considered and the total weight of your shot charge as well as the effective range of individual pellet size. One could write a Bible on this subject alone, but a few illustrations should suffice to give the reader the idea of the requirements. Four hits of No. 7½ shot will kill quail, doves or snipe or woodcock at 50 yards nicely and four or more hits of No. 8 shot will do the same thing to 45 yards on any of these small birds. More hits are to be preferred but four hits or more of a shot size that is right for a given size bird will do the work, and as far out as you can get those required hits and the pellets are large enough to carry their energy and penetration, you will kill. We never did go much on paper energy figures in rifle loads and even less on paper energy figures per pellet in shotgun loads, but have thoroughly tested all shot sizes for penetration on most all sizes of feathered game at the different ranges and would much prefer to use the results of this practical experience to all paper energy figures for each pellet size at different ranges. The average gunner is interested in knowing what size shot to use and how far it will kill or can be expected to kill with a given load and that is about as far as he is likely to delve into the subject. More hits are required from small pellets per bird than from larger shot to effect a clean kill as a rule, but anything can happen, such as one pellet through the brain of a mallard at a measured range of 125 yards and it was a No. 5 shot at that. Purely accidental but did happen.

No. 8 shot usually carry pellet energy to 45 yards sufficient for snipe and quail; No. 7½ to 50 yards for such birds or teal and pigeons; No. 6 shot carry pellet energy to about 55 and even 60 yards if enough hits register (on larger birds of course, such a large grouse, pheasants mallards and similar ducks). No. 5 shot will carry pellet energy nicely to 60 yards, and sometimes in heavy loads to 65 yards, and are about all done for pellet energy at that range and of course on large fowl. They would not pattern well on small birds at all at such ranges. No. 4 shot will carry effective energy to 70 yards and seems about all done at that range and does not penetrate heavy ducks well beyond 70 yards as we have proven many times by actual experience. For ducks or pheasants or sage hens beyond 70 yards No. 3 shot are required and are the smallest size that can be depended on to carry a killing pellet energy with ample penetration, to 80 yards. They will go beyond 80 yards and we once saw a mallard dropped with three hits of No. 3 shot at 127 yards but that was more luck than good sense and a cluster of shot simply happened to strike the bird. Usually he would have flown right through the pattern at far less range unscathed. No. 2 shot will also carry pellet energy sufficient to penetrate a goose to the vitals at 80, 90 and even 100 yards, but the pattern is usually too thin to register enough hits for certain killing of a goose beyond 80 yards even with a Magnum 10 bore and 2 ounces of No. 2 shot. Even at 80 yards we wonder if two ounces of No. 3 shot is not a more effective goose load, if the gun handles them to a higher pattern percentage, than is 2 ounces of No. 2 shot from the same gun at a lesser percentage. Four hits of No. 2 shot is usually enough to up-end a goose in flight and five or six hits, or more, from No. 3 shot would be even better. At all ranges shot, the shot sizes must carry enough energy to surely break wing bones if struck fairly, and this means using a shot size in proportion to size of the fowl shot to insure such wing or other bone breakage and certain penetration on heavily feathered tough birds. Small shot like 7½ will kill geese nicely at close range, 35 yards we will say, by simply smothering the neck and head with the tiny pellets but it is like trying to make a brain shot on a big grizzly with a 25/35 rifle.

One should select a shot size in keeping with the size of the bird hunted and then shoot enough patterns to determine exactly how far he can reasonably expect those four or more hits per bird, and should refrain from shooting at greater ranges. You can sketch in a flying goose or duck in your pattern and see what chance you have at any range. Some pattern work should be done out to the maximum range of your gun. It will teach you a lot about how to hold for elevations and will also teach you what a strong side wind will do to your pattern and how much you must hold off into the wind to land the shot on the pattern at say 60 or 70 yards.

The smaller the shot the worse are they drifted by a cross wind and we have often had to hold over on the edge of the 40″ paper at 40 yards to center a light trap load pattern at that range. A heavy duck load required far less windage to center the pattern. Big shot like No. 4s were drifted much less than the smaller pellets, which is also another good reason for the employment of large shot for all long range shooting, so long as those four hits or more per bird can surely be secured.

If you use a variable choke device on a pump or auto-loading gun, you can secure about any desired pattern for any reasonable given range, by patterning the gun. If you are doing trap or skeet shooting, you can soon determine the proper setting on the Poly Choke or proper tube to use with the compensator to give you the best killing spread of pattern at the ranges you usually take your clay target. Pattern tests will also show up which make of shell best fits your gun.

Some experimenters have gone so far as to fit a wad in the choke of their gun, then find shot sizes that exactly fitted the choke in even layers, no loose shot or no piled up shot, just even smooth layers that filled the choke of the bore from side to side. They have even so handloaded these shot of a given size and charge in the cartridge and have run long tests with them, usually bringing up the percentage from 5 to 15 per cent at times. This proves that shot must chamber right in a choke of a given gun for highest performance. The average man will never take the time for such meticulous experimenting, but he can run a string of patterns with all available loads and shot sizes needed to determine which load and shot size best suits his needs.

You may want more of a spread of pattern than your gun throws at a given range if it be a fixed choke weapon. This also can be secured as a rule by experimenting with different makes of loads and different shot sizes. If you shoot a full choke gun most of the time and must have a more open boring for close range quail or ruffed grouse shooting, then you can always fall back on the scatter or brush loads put out by most companies and while they do seldom throw as uniform a pattern as regular loads they will greatly open up the spread of pattern and are very useful for close range brush shooting when a full choked gun is all you have to use.

Many hunters do not like their game badly shot up and if they take the game at close range and cannot open up their pattern or buy brush loads, then they can go to heavier shot with fewer pellets per charge and thus cut down on their game mutilation. Where the shooting is open they can wait out their birds to a suitable range, but if close cover is the rule then they must shoot or forego forever the chance at that bird. Then is when they must do something about their pattern spread and its density if they would have birds fit for the table. When shooting such vermin as crows, horned owls, hawks and magpies we do not care how badly they are torn up, but game birds should be treated as such and shot only for table use and then with a suitable size shot and pattern spread to insure clean kills with a minimum of mutilation. We much prefer birds killed with four or five large shot to birds that are simply plastered with fine shot. The size of the bird and the range shot, should govern your pellet size and degree of choke as much as possible.

We are killing our game with approximately 80 to 90 percent of the shot charge in most cases, as the shot deformed in the chamber when forcing the crimp and those deformed in the cone, are usually strays on the pattern sheet and if they strike within the 30″ circle, they are of course counted. In actual game or target shooting, however, they are the deformed shot that are either laggards in the shot charge or so badly deformed that they soon drop out of the shot column.

In recent years since Phillip P. Quale invented spark photography and showed conclusively just what a shot charge actually does in action, the loading companies have made great strides in cutting down shot stringing. Up to that time we were probably killing our game with only about 70 percent of the charge. Major Sir Gerald Burrard ran a considerable number of tests on a pattern board attached to a car traveling past the gunner at good speed for that time and the type of car used. These tests showed that those laggard shot in a shot column did string behind to some extent, though his target speed never approached the top speed of many of our game birds in flight, yet it showed that a part of the charge passed behind the bird anyway. All pass shooters have aimed ahead of a single duck and killed him only to occasionally see another bird to the rear of the one aimed at killed as well by stray pellets. Most of the time, these stray laggard pellets that trail along behind the main charge due to deformation in the cone or otherwise, do no damage, but they thus cut down the possible patterns we should be getting.

Large shot always pattern better as a rule than smaller shot when both sizes fit the gun equally well. This for the reason that large shot deform less in the cone and large shot can stand more deformation and still remain in the charge than can smaller shot.

A leaded or rough shotgun barrel will abrade and wear many shot out of round so that they become fliers when fired, and are not effective. The higher the polish of the gun bore and choke the less shot will be deformed and if that evil forcing cone was only lengthened considerably, still less shot would be deformed and more would reach the pattern paper to be counted inside that mystic 30″ circle.

New barrels as they come from the factories will never shoot as good patterns at the start as after they have had years of usage and become shot smoothed as we term it, which is nothing but further polishing as thousands of charges of hard shot are driven up the tube and also many cleanings with both patches and brass brushes. We have seen guns shooting exceptional patterns that had to be returned to the factories to have ribs resoldered or chokes changed slightly and as a rule they never shot as well when they came back until after again being used for long periods. The microscopic marks put in them from the reboring had to be again polished out before they were capable of top performance. A shotgun barrel may look highly polished and perfectly smooth from either end when you look through it, but if it were sawn lengthwise so you could make a close inspection of every inch of the bore and choke you would see many cross marks made by the reamer. These, though invisible to the naked eye when viewed from either end of the barrel are there, nevertheless, and are one cause of many defective shot that never go where they should.

Although 40 yards is the accepted standard range for gun and shotshell testing, used universally to determine the exact performance and percentage thrown by a given gun or load, the hunter need not necessarily test his gun or load at that range unless he is interested solely in the percentages it throws or in finding the best pattern for that or longer ranges.

If you are shooting quail at 20 to 30 yards, you might just as well, and in fact better, test your gun and load at the usual range at which you are killing your birds. You can see the exact spread of the pattern, determine its density and ascertain if there are any holes through which a bird can escape. Sketch and cut out a life-size quail, snipe, woodcock or other small bird you are shooting and try to find some place in the pattern where the bird would have flown through. In this way you can tell at a glance if your pattern is dense enough, or if it is too dense for your usual range. If too dense you can open up the patent choke, or use scatter loads in the full choke gun or go to a larger shot size or both to eliminate mutilated birds. You want to kill them but you do not want to ruin them for the table.

Likewise, the man who is doing 60- or 70-yard pass shooting with a big ten-bore or a Magnum 12-bore, can shoot his patterns at that range and with a cut out replica of the flying fowl instantly determine the average number of hits he would have on said birds at such ranges when his lead was correct. Such pattern work is of inestimable value in learning how to hold for such ranges, both as to wind deflection and also for elevation and will show conclusively whether your shot are too large for an effective pattern or not.

Likewise the backing boards will tell you a lot about your penetration at such ranges and you will find the small shot often striking the paper but bouncing back from the pattern board instead of penetrating into it as they should. Whenever a pellet does not imbed itself into the wood at least, then you know instantly it was too small to carry pellet energy out to that particular range.

We once knew an old goose hunter who shot a lifter-action Parker ten-bore with his own black powder, handloaded, long brass cases. He had ground about all the forcing cone out of that gun in his earlier days, and had done a great deal of experiment with it and finally settled on a load of 1¾ ounces of No. 3 shot. We do not know his powder charge but was very heavy as he allowed us to kill some ducks with it in our younger days and the recoil seemed terrific, but it would kill single mallards at 75 yards almost every shot. He showed us many patterns he had run with it on news print paper and the bulk of the charge was almost always in about 24″ or less at 40 yards. He used no other shot than No. 3 for both big ducks and geese and had killed his full share for the market. He had also hunted bear with that gun in his spare time around Helena, Montana, and had killed a considerable number of grizzly with it and buckshot. We were shown the loads he used and the heavy buckshot loads were covered with wax. After loading the buckshot that went four to a layer he had poured melted miner's candle on them and then seated the over-shot wad. With this load he said he would pepper a grizzly as soon as he could get within about 40 yards and then when the bear came for him would wait until he was practically on top of him before giving him the other barrel in the face. He claimed it always shattered their skulls in great shape and never failed to stop them. In the early days around Helena there were a considerable number of grizzly and he hunted them when time permitted, especially in the Spring when the pelts were in good condition. Neighbors said he had killed plenty of them with that outfit. He also hunted the small whitetail deer, known locally as Fan Tails, over at Seven-Up-Pete's, on the stage road to the Blackfoot. Buckshot patterns he showed us made at 40 yards, had about all the charge always inside a 24″ circle and most of them inside a 20″ circle. Some 100 percent patterns were even smaller. It showed what could be done with the gun, and that buck load of his would have settled any deer to a full 50 yards. It held together better than standard buck loads and often several shot tore a big hole in the paper, no doubt held together by the candle wax.

Muzzle velocities usually affect the pattern and best patterns are usually secured by velocities slightly lower than maximum safe pressure requirements. However lower velocities also require more lead, and one will not do his best work when shooting shells of varying or different velocities unless the shooting is under 40 yards range. We had one lot of Magnum ten-bore Western shells loaded with 52 grains of Herco powder, that did not pattern well in our gun with 2 ounces of No. 4 shot, but when the powder charge was cut to 48 grains of the same powder they patterned very well indeed, going over 80 per cent both barrels.

Many times the over-powder wads which were made of some composition, drove through the pattern paper and dented the backing boards at 40 yards with the factory loads. When we cut the charge to 48 grains we saw no more prints from the over-powder wads on the target paper, and the lighter powder load seemed to kill considerably better than that particular factory load. With a later batch of the same make ammunition in No. 2 and No. 3 shot we were never able to even approach the factory patterns with any handload. We also tried several combinations of buckshot in that gun, never getting a good pattern with the full loads, yet Major Askins had one lot of Western loads going 20 buck to the two-ounce load that shot consistently 100 per cent into a 24″ circle. We would like some of those loads were they still available.

We did test a lot of Remington 1⅝-ounce Super ten-bore loads, 2⅞″ case, in the Magnum ten with its long 3½″ chambers and they shot very well indeed, giving very good patterns at all times even though jumped from the short shells in the long chambers. They were a smaller buck and counted 16 to the charge. Many of them went 100 per cent in a 30″ circle at 40 yards. Of the 5000 odd guns we test-fired at Ogden Arsenal during the war one Winchester Model 97 Riot gun with its short barrel would put the standard load of 9 pellets of 00 buck under the spread of our hand at 40 yards most of the time and was the best buckshot gun we ever saw. We would have liked to have bought that gun of Uncle Sam but it was not for sale and went out with a shipment of M.P.s for European service.

In conclusion, we would like to urge all shotgunners to pattern their guns and learn where they shoot as well as the most suitable loads for each game and purpose. We will reduce a bunch of patterns so that the reader can better grasp just what various good patterns look like on paper. By dividing the 30″ circle of the original targets into small squares and again dividing the much smaller 8″ circle into squares, we can thus place each pellet about exactly where it registered on the original 40-yard targets. Loads and guns are listed with each pattern for reference.

3″ 410-GAGE AND 28-GAGE, ¾-OUNCE

Shot Size	Pellets in Chg.	Cylinder 40%	Imp. Cyl. 45%	4¼ Chk. 52%	½ Chk. 60%	¾ Chk. 68%	Full Chk. 75%
BB	38	15	17	20	23	26	29
2	65	26	29	34	39	44	48
4	99	40	45	51	59	67	74
5	126	50	57	66	76	85	95
6	164	66	74	85	98	112	123
7	218	87	98	113	137	148	164
7½	259	103	116	135	155	176	194
8	300	120	135	156	180	204	225
9	526	176	192	222	256	290	320

20-GAGE, ⅞-OUNCE

Shot Size	Pellets in Chg.	Cylinder 40%	Imp. Cyl. 45%	4¼ Chk. 52%	½ Chk. 60%	¾ Chk. 68%	Full Chk. 75%
BB	44	18	20	23	26	30	33
2	75	30	34	39	45	49	53
4	116	46	52	60	69	79	85
5	147	58	66	76	88	100	120
6	191	76	86	98	114	130	143
7	255	102	115	133	153	173	191
7½	302	120	137	157	181	205	227
8	350	140	156	182	210	238	263
9	497	198	224	258	298	338	373

20-GAGE, 16-GAGE, ONE-OUNCE SHOT

Shot Size	Pellets in Chg.	Cylinder 40%	Imp. Cyl. 45%	¼ Chk. 52%	½ Chk. 60%	¾ Chk. 68%	Full Chk. 75%	Progress 80%
BB	50	20	23	26	30	34	37	40
2	86	34	39	45	51	57	65	69
4	132	52	59	67	79	90	99	106
5	168	67	76	87	100	114	126	134
6	218	87	98	113	137	148	164	174
7	291	116	131	151	174	198	223	238
7½	345	138	155	178	207	235	250	276
8	399	159	180	208	239	272	300	320
9	568	227	256	285	340	386	426	454

16-GAGE OR 12-GAGE 1⅛ OUNCES SHOT

Shot Size	Pellets in Chg.	Cylinder 40%	Imp. Cyl. 45%	¼ Chk. 52%	½ Chk. 60%	¾ Chk. 68%	Full Chk. 75%	Progress 80%
BB	56	22	25	29	33	38	42	45
2	97	38	44	50	58	66	73	78
4	148	59	67	77	88	101	111	118
5	189	75	85	98	113	129	142	151
6	245	98	110	127	147	167	184	196
7	327	130	147	170	196	222	245	261
7½	387	154	174	201	232	263	290	310
8	449	179	202	233	260	295	327	350
9	639	255	298	322	383	441	480	511

12-GAGE AND LIGHT 10-GAGE, 1¼ OUNCES

Shot Size	Pellets in Chg.	Cylinder 40%	Imp. Cyl. 45%	¼ Chk. 52%	½ Chk. 60%	¾ Chk. 68%	Full Chk. 75%	Progress 80%
BB	63	25	29	33	37	43	45	48
2	107	42	48	55	64	73	80	85
3	136	54	61	70	81	92	101	108
4	165	66	74	86	99	112	124	132
5	210	84	95	100	126	143	158	162
6	272	108	122	141	163	185	204	218
7	364	145	164	189	218	248	273	291
7½	431	172	194	234	258	293	323	345
8	499	199	225	255	299	343	374	399

MAXIMUM 10-GAGE LOAD, 1⅞ OUNCES

Shot Size	Pellets in Chg.	Cylinder 40%	Imp. Cyl. 45%	¼ Chk. 52%	½ Chk. 60%	¾ Chk. 68%	Full Chk. 75%	Progress 80%
BB	81	32	36	42	49	55	61	65
2	140	56	63	73	84	95	105	112
3	177	60	79	92	106	120	132	141
4	215	86	97	112	129	146	161	172
5	273	109	123	142	164	186	205	218
6	354	142	159	184	212	241	266	283
7	473	189	213	246	284	322	355	378
7½	561	224	252	292	336	381	420	448

MAGNUM 10-GAGE, 2 OUNCES

Shot Size	Pellets in Chg.	Cylinder 40%	Imp. Cyl. 45%	¼ Chk. 52%	½ Chk. 60%	¾ Chk. 68%	Full Chk. 75%	Progress 80%
BB	100	40	46	52	60	68	74	80
2	172	68	78	90	102	114	130	138
3	218	87	98	114	130	148	163	174
4	264	104	118	134	158	180	198	212

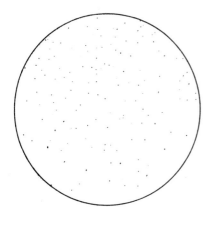

Martin Model 90 over-under, 410-bore, 3" Peters Hi-vel load No. 7½ shot. In the charge 259 pellets for ¾ ounce. In the 30" circle at 40 yards from the muzzle 159 pellets for 61%. This is a very good 410-bore full-choke pattern and while it would pattern well on big birds to 40 yards, it would be about all done on quail at 30 yards for certainty. No. 8 shot would be better for the smaller birds. The 28-bore with the same charge will usually count a few pellets higher and is the smallest gauge that should be used in our opinion.

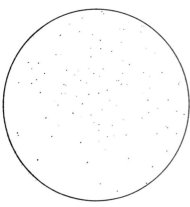

Right Barrel, Ithaca No. 4, 20-bore 26", quarter choke, 40 yards from muzzle. Peters Hi-vel No. 6 chilled. Pellets in the load of one ounce 218, in the 30" circle 113, or 52%, a very good quarter-choke pattern. The unusual dense center of this pattern would kill well to 45 yards, but again illustrates that No. 7½ shot is a much better size for the 20-bore as plenty of misses would occur outside that dense center. This pattern will take big ducks and pheasants to 45 yards but No. 7½ or 8 shot would be required for quail at 35 to 40 yards.

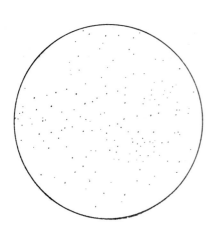

Full choke, left barrel Ithaca 26" No. 4, 20-bore. Peters, Hi-vel one ounce No. 6 Chilled. In the charge 218 pellets, in the 30" circle at 40 yards 164 pellets for an average of 75%. This is a very good full-choke 20-bore pattern, better than average. It also clearly illustrates why No. 6 shot are the largest that should be used in the 20-bore. This pattern will kill ducks and pheasants to 50 yards most of the time and is rather certain to 45 yards.

Ithaca 30" full-choked No. 5.
Major Askins' old gun. 16-bore.
1⅛ ounce Western Super X latest
folded crimp load of No. 4 shot. A
very high counting but irregular pattern. This is the best shooting 16-
bore we have ever seen with either
4s or 6s and this pattern illustrates
that No. 4 shot are too large for the
16-bore except for geese. In the
1⅛-ounce charge 148 pellets, in
the 30" circle 40 yards from muzzle
141 pellets for 95%. This gun shoots
crazy high percentages with No. 4s,
but makes a better killing pattern
with 6s. Serial No. of gun is No.
439410. We have never seen a 12-
bore handle 1⅛ ounces of shot as
well as this gun, any size shot.
Right barrel.

Ithaca No. 5 16-bore No. 439410.
Major Askins' old gun. 30" full
choke. Right barrel. Peters Hi-vel
folded crimp latest load of No. 5
shot 1⅛ ounces counting 189 pellets.
In the 30" circle, 40 yards from
muzzle 177 pellets for 93%. This
pattern is odd looking with the center
of pattern slightly to left of the 30-
inch circle but it enclosed most of the
shot. This is our old grouse and sage
hen load for the 16-bore. Open
country shooting from 40 to 55 yards.
Also good on mallards or pheasants
but not as dense as the usual 90%
pattern of sixes from this gun. Both
barrels pattern the same for average.

Right barrel B.H.E. Parker double
trap 32" full choke. Peters Trap
load 1¼ ounces No. 8 shot. In the
charge 499 pellets. In the 30" circle
419 pellets or 84%. A very exceptional long range trap pattern capable of handicap work if used with
heavier No. 7½ shot. For obvious
reasons we will not reduce any more
of these very dense trap patterns as
it is just too much work. Every
effort was made to place all pellets
where they landed, but mistakes are
possible as we are not infallible.

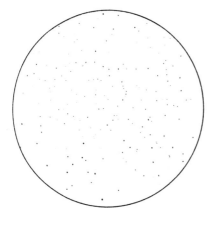

B.H.E. Parker 12 bore 32″ full choke right barrel, Remington Express No. 6 chilled. In the shell 272 pellets, in the 30″ circle 40 yards from gun muzzle, 244 pellets for a percentage of 89%. This shows No. 6 shot in the 1¼ ounce 12 bore load at its best as a duck load. It killed consistently to a full 60 yards on mallards and pheasants. In improved cylinder this load is deadly on big ducks at 45 yards.

Right barrel B.H.E. Parker double trap 32″ full choke. Western Super X—No. 6 Lubaloy shot, in the 1¼ ounce load 285 pellets by actual count. In the 30″ circle 40 yards from muzzle, 232 pellets or 81%. This is a poor pattern for this load as it averaged 85%. It is also a rather patchy pattern but killed ducks regularly to 60 yards. 12-bore.

Left Barrel B.H.E. Parker, 32″ full choke, Remington Express with top wad, 1¼ ounces No. 5 chilled. In the 1¼ ounce load by count 216 pellets. In the 30″ circle 40 yards from gun muzzle 184 pellets or 85%. A very good consistent duck killer on mallards to 60 yards, with ample pellet energy and penetration for that range. 12-bore.

B.H.E. Parker 32″ full choke 12 bore. Right barrel. Remington Express standard 12-bore heavy duck load No. 4 shot. In the charge 167 pellets, in the 30″ circle 40 yards from gun muzzle 158 pellets or 94%. It will be seen that only nine pellets missed the 30″ circle which gives one an idea of how near perfection the loading companies have come. Latest folded crimp load. This is an exceptionally good shooting 12-bore and this load regularly killed mallards for us to a full 60 yards. It would be hard on geese to 55 yards at least. This barrel averaged 90% with this load for ten shots. 12-gauge.

Left barrel B.H.E. Parker 32″ full choke. Remington Express No. 4 shot 1¼ ounces. In the charge 167 pellets, in the 30″ circle at 40 yards from muzzle 152 pellets or 92%. Only ten pellets were outside the 30″ circle indicating exceptional long range shotgun performance. This is a crazy shooting 12-bore with No. 4 shot, one of the exceptional guns. This load is good to a full 60 yards on big ducks.

Right barrel B.H.E. Parker 32″ full choke. Remington Express goose load 1¼ ounces No. 2 shot counting 118 pellets to the load. In 30″ circle at 40 yards 103 pellets or 87%. A very good pattern of No. 2 shot but clearly indicates No. 2 shot are too large to pattern well even on geese from a good gun and the factories should load No. 3 shot as their 1¼ ounce standard 12-bore goose load.

Ithaca super 10 bore 32″ full choke right barrel, Remington Super Ten bore load of 1⅞ ounce of small sixes counting 400 pellets in the one shell counted. Pellets in the 30″ circle at 40 yards from muzzle 333 for 83%. This pattern clearly illustrates why the super ten and magnum 12 bores are such deadly long range duck guns and the best of all around duck guns.

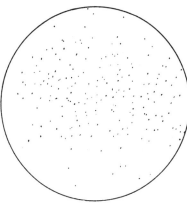

Left barrel, Magnum Ten bore Ithaca No. 500,000. Western Super-X 2 ounce No. 3 Lubaloy shot. 40 yards from muzzle of gun. Count was 218 shot, in the 30″ circle count was 211 shot. Average 96% plus. A very exceptional long range duck and goose pattern and will kill regularly to a full 80 yards on anything the size of a mallard or larger bird. One of the best patterns we have ever obtained from any gun. This barrel averaged 93% for a ten shot string. The poorest patterns with either barrel averaged 91%. The most consistent shotgun performance of our life.

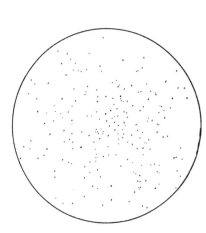

Right barrel, Magnum Ten bore Ithaca No. 500,000. Western Super-X 2 oz. No. 3 Lubaloy Shot. 40 yards from muzzle of gun. Count was 218 shot in shell, in 30″ circle 210 shot. Average 96%. Another exceptional pattern for long range duck and goose shooting, and will kill ducks or geese of mallard or larger size regularly to a full 80 yards. These two are the top patterns of a lifetime of work with No. 3 and smaller shot. Each barrel averaged 93% for ten shot strings and we fired 20 shots all told with each barrel and the average still stayed at 93%. The best shooting wildfowl gun we have ever seen or used.

Ithaca Magnum ten bore two ounces No. 2 Lubaloy, Western Super-X 40 yards from muzzle. In the load 172 shot, in the 30" circle 147 shot for an average of 85%. Not the best nor the poorest pattern with No. 2 shot but an average pattern and this gun went 85% both barrels for an average of ten shots for each barrel. It will be clearly seen the big gun does not handle No. 2 shot as well as No. 3 shot. This load would kill geese most of the time at 80 yards, however. Gun No. 500,000. Left barrel used for this target. With a 1⅞ ounce load of No. 2 chilled shot in the 2⅞" case this magnum ten shot 71%.

Left barrel Magnum ten Ithaca, No. 500,000. Western Super-X two ounce load of BB shot going 100 to the charge. In 30" circle 76 pellets or 76%. This pattern is an average one shot with BB shot in this gun and clearly illustrates why this size shot is about worthless even for geese at 80 yards. This pattern fired 40 yards from muzzle of gun. Shot scattered all over the paper, clearly indicating the big shot did not chamber right in the choke of the gun.

Right barrel Magnum ten bore Ithaca No. 500,000, Western Super-X 00 buck counting 15 pellets to the load. The only 100% pattern obtained of 25 rounds fired with this load that did not fit the gun at all. Most pattern had but ten to 12 pellets on the entire pattern paper. Even this is not a good buckshot pattern and does not compare with some 1⅞ ounce 16 pellet loads of Remington Express fired in the same gun. It does illustrate the best of 25 loads fired at 40 yards from the gun muzzle.

CHAPTER SEVENTEEN

Gun Selection

Upland Guns

SELECTION OF THE UPLAND gun depends entirely on your own ability to use a shotgun and the ranges and size game involved. The English in the main will have nothing but a 12-bore, even though they may have it made as light as six pounds and built for one ounce of shot or at most 1 1/16 ounce of shot. It may even be chambered for their short 2″ case.

Theoretically the larger the bore for the charge of shot, the less pellets will be deformed and also the larger will be the pattern spread. However there are many exceptions to this general rule of thumb and it does not hold water in many cases. We never could see any horse sense in shooting light charges from a 12-bore gun if a small bore were available. If one is going to need and use only one ounce of shot, then a good 20-bore will do the job about as well as anything larger and will be a trim, slim, light, handy little gun that you can lug all day and hardly notice you have a gun along.

If our shooting were to be confined to 40 yards range or even to 45 yards range, and under, we could be perfectly happy with a 20-bore gun and would need nothing smaller or larger for our own use. If the shooting is to be confined to 30 yards and under then a 28-bore will do the trick if you are an expert gun pointer and use it in full choke. We believe 410-bore 3″ and the 28-bore guns should be confined to full choke for use on game, so that their thin ¾-ounce loads will be well centered and insure either clean misses or clean kills. Thus we see that the small bores should be full choke or at least an improved modified choke for certain uniform killing. The real small bore, the 3″ 410 and the 28-bore are the guns for the expert, never the novice. The latter needs more spread of pattern to insure hits with reasonable certainty. The 2½″ 410-bore we never could see any earthly use for except possibly killing pack rats in the cabin or wood shed or similar usage. Likewise we have no use for the Magnum 3″ 410-bore. Its long shot column will very seldom deliver the patterns of a good 28-bore, so we believe the 28 should be the smallest shotgun gauge made or used on game, and this only for the expert shot.

Even for boys and ladies the 20-bore is a better gun, and it should be choked heavier than the larger gauges to insure certain killing patterns. Even for quail shooting, or woodcock or ruffed grouse at 25 to 30 yards the boring should not be less than 50 per cent or quarter choke. If the shooting is to extend out to 35 yards range in the one ounce 20-bore load then the gun should be half choke or 60 per cent and if the shooting is to be at ranges up to 40 yards then the three quarter or 69 percent choke is better and for shooting from 40 yards on to the limit of the 20-bore the choke should be full.

With an ounce of No. 7½ or 8 shot and a boring of 50 per cent or quarter choke the little 20 bore will handle snipe, quail, doves, ruffed grouse and woodcock to perfection at ranges of 20 to 30 yards and a bit beyond if the load fits the gun well and you do your part. The gun can weigh from about 5¾ to 6 pounds and be light enough for any one to carry all day and with a good soft recoil pad the recoil will not bother any lad or lady if the gun fits as it should. For larger birds such as pheasants and ducks the gun should of course have more choke and range and a three quarter or modified boring is very good to start the youngster or lady with for such game. It will kill well to 40 yards and very often to 45 also if proper shot are used; and we believe No. 7½ about the best 20-bore load except for heavy birds, when No. 6 shot might well be better and will kill well.

We believe the Poly Choke to be very useful on all single barrel 20-bores and it can be set to give about any pattern desired consistent with ranges involved. In the one ounce load of No. 8 shot there are 399 pellets, and the pattern will simply smother quail and similar game at proper ranges. If the birds are laying well to the dog then the shooting is usually close range and it is doubtful if very many more quail can be killed in a day with any larger bore gun by a good shot; certainly he would not get over 5 to 10 per cent more birds in a season. The 20 is a very sporting little weapon and absolutely deadly within its proper range if pointed right. The gun should weigh from 5¾ to around 6 pounds and have a barrel or barrels of 26″ to 28″ in length. The pump or auto-loader can well be 26″ and the double or single shot 28″ in length. If the upland shooting is confined to the smaller birds, nothing larger than pheasants and ranges up to 35 yards or even 40 yards, in full choke the little 20 will give a good account of itself in any company.

It is about three to five yards faster on the mark than a heavy 12-bore gun and you can take your birds that much closer in. The poor shot will of course do better with a larger bore that permits him to open up his choke and use a larger pattern but the expert can have a lot of fun with the 20 and he will often be amazed at the range the little gun will kill. Ammunition is also small and light to carry.

In the West a larger bore makes a better upland gun, because the ranges are usually much longer and the country more open.

Desert, and in fact most western quail, are shot at longer ranges as a rule than the Bob White of the East and South and the 16-bore is then a better tool. We have used the 16-bore gun as our favorite upland gun for a lifetime. Here our shooting is largely grouse, sage hens, pheasants and Huns and is apt to be fairly long range shooting a good part of the time so we have a far different problem than is presented in the South and East. Even our dove and snipe shooting is usually at much longer ranges, and we have no Woodcock. The ruffed grouse is usually the bird that gives us our closest range shooting, and the light one-ounce load of No. 7½ or No. 6 shot takes him very nicely. Huns and pheasants are both tough birds to kill and the Hun is an especially fast little devil, in fact of all my shotgun shooting we give the Hun the palm for being the most sporting game bird we have ever hunted. He will raise clean out of range a good part of the time and when he does get up in range you must be fast and get on him and shoot quickly or he is soon out of effective range. A winged Hungarian partridge will run the legs off a good dog at times and for some reason they neither lay well to dogs, nor do very many dogs ever master or handle them well. They are always prone to run on ahead as will wise old cock pheasants, then break cover out of range. For this reason very close shooting, full choked guns are in order and expert gun pointing as well if you would make a good bag on Huns.

We once killed six straight and thought we had mastered the little sage brusher, but then we missed some five or six before we killed another one which took most of the conceit out of us. We used to have an early season on them in Idaho when they acted much like quail and were not so difficult. Then later we would have another open season and then was when the trouble began and many gunners even went to the Magnum 12-bore with 1⅝ ounces of No. 6 shot in an effort to get in range of the fast turning, twisting, dodging little sage bullets.

For general upland work day in and day out in any country we know of nothing quite so nice as the 16-bore gun. It falls only about three yards short in range of the best 12-bore and a really good shooting 16-bore will often outshoot many 12-bores for range.

A good shooting 12-bore is in order, to beat our old No. 5 Ithaca, and even then it will have but 3 to 5 yards more effective range than that particular 16. We have long used the heavy 1⅛-ounce load of No. 6 shot as our favorite upland load for most shooting in this gun. If a bird raises under our feet we simply let him straighten out a bit and get out to 40 yards before busting him and if he raises at 30 yards we can still kill him before he gets beyond 55 yards. With 1⅛ ounces of No. 7½ we have a very good long range quail gun and with one ounce of No. 8 shot it is a good quail gun for lesser ranges.

The average shot will do well on quail with a good fitting 16-

bore with quarter choke to 35 yards range and with half choke to 40 yards and with three quarters or modified to 45 yards range. But for Huns give us 1⅛ ounces of No. 6, so we can reach out to 50 yards with certainty. It is also a good load on sage hens and ducks and we have even killed much larger birds to 60 yards with that gun. The 16-bore is also very good on decoyed ducks. The gun should weigh from 6½ to not over 7½ pounds and is about the handiest all-around upland gun any man could ask for, and equally good as a ladies' gun. Recoil is lighter than the 12-bore and ammunition lighter and less bulky to pack in the pockets. The recoil of the first shot does not raise the gun up out of alignment as much as does the recoil of the 12-bore, so the second barrel can be whipped in quicker should it be needed. Many times we have knocked wise old cock pheasants out of the air and seen them lower their legs for a running landing and have whipped in the second barrel to drop them in a crumpled heap.

In Montana we used to hunt the sharp-tail grouse a lot each fall and some later in Idaho. They are big, heavy grouse and often quite wary and raise at considerable range like blue grouse that have been hunted much. The 16-bore full choked double was the medicine for them and for many years we shot only 1⅛ ounces of No. 5 chilled shot from the old Peters Ideal load. It was good medicine for any big grouse, whether blue, sharp-tailed, or the still larger sage hens. Hunting right alongside good shots with 12 bore-guns we never did feel that they had any edge on us at all. What few yards they gained in range with 1¼ ounces of shot we made up for by faster gun mounting and more accurate gun pointing at the end of a long hard tramp. When the old hunting coat was loaded with fat heavy birds, the little slim 16-bore was easier to handle than any bigger and heavier 12-bore.

For a good shot, we seriously doubt if any better gun is to be had than a good fitting, good shooting 16-bore for general upland work. It is steadily becoming more popular and in time we would not be surprised to see the 16-bore take a much larger proportion of the total sales. While we use only exceptionally close shooting full choked 16-bore guns for our own use here in this long range country, we would advise the general use of the modified choke. It will kill nearly as far as the full choke gun and yet give you a more even spread of pattern and a slightly larger killing pattern as well. If we were shooting quail steadily, however, then we would want and need a more open bored gun, say 50 per cent first barrel and 60 to 68 per cent second barrel. The shooter who prefers the repeater will do well to have it fitted with a Poly Choke, then he can adapt his choke to any sort of shooting he is likely to encounter and this goes for all bores for upland use from the 20- to the 12-bore.

In eastern Oregon we hunted blue grouse a great deal in the fall and trained a little bay walking horse to hunt them and allow us to shoot from his back. He was equally good on pheasants and sharp tailed grouse and we had many pleasant days in the saddle shooting grouse with that Ithaca 16-bore from the saddle. Being used to the saddle and being more at home on a horse than on foot we had no trouble making doubles on many occasions.

Art Kirkpatrick on a Duck Pass with a 10-bore Model 1901
Winchester Lever Action Shotgun.

Shorty seemed to enjoy the sport as much as we did and seemed to simply smell them out as he poked along with his head carried low and his little stub tail sticking straight out behind. He carried his tail to the lift habitually and had been docked when a colt and was altogether the most ludicrous looking little jug-headed bay horse we have ever seen but he liked to hunt. Made no difference to him whether we were after grouse or later hunting coyotes. He would plug along at his fast walk and swing his head to the right and stop any time birds flushed. He would also stay ground-hitched for all day any time we dropped the reins and slid from the saddle. He was by all odds the best shooting horse we ever owned and though his ancestry was very doubtful, we would give a lot today for a week on that little 1100-pound nag again when the grouse were fat and plentiful. He had a long homely head and carried it low and his tail high, much like a good bird dog at work.

Time was when the 10-bore was considered the standard gun and was used as such even for upland work, but that is now long ago and the 12-bore is today considered the standard by which others are judged. More 12-bore guns are made than any other size. It is also the standard for trap shooting, but when only 1⅛ ounces of shot are used we would just as soon use our double 16-bore gun with its high percentage patterns.

The beginner can have a wider pattern with a 12-bore than any smaller gauge and it will give him more hits per number of shells expended. He can use a more open boring if he shoots 1¼ ounces of shot. For most upland work to 45 yards there is no need of the heavy duck loads and the moderate load of 3¼ drams bulk equivalent and 1¼ ounces of shot will kill all that any gun will at such ranges. He can well use trap loads for quail shooting and a load of 3 drams powder or equivalent and 1¼ ounces of No. 7½, the old standard trap load, is very very hard to beat for all small bird shooting, quail, wood cock, snipe, ruffed grouse and early Huns as well as doves. If he is just learning to shoot the Skeet boring or improved cylinder 45 per cent will be the ticket for work up to 35 yards at least and for longer range work he can use a quarter choke or 50 per cent to a full 40 yards and half choke for average work to 45 yards.

Upland guns can be had in 12-bore as light as anyone needs and the new featherweight Ithacas, Remington Wingmasters and others will give him as light weight a repeater as he could wish or would care to shoot with heavy loads. In the 16-bore we like 30″ barrels for our personal use on doubles but the pump gun should be 26″ to 28″ in 16-bore for upland work and in the 12-bore the same rule holds good; and while the double can well be 30″, the repeaters with their long actions are better suited with 28″ barrels for general upland work, and for close range brush shooting the 26″ would be even faster and handier. In repeaters weights can be had from about 6½ pounds upwards, so the man who favors a 12-bore gun can yet have a light fast gun to handle and carry all day.

If the shooting is pheasants or sharp tail grouse, sage hens or Huns that raise at considerable range then the three-quarter or modified choke is in order and for experts the full choke is even more deadly, but its centered pattern is usually too small for the novice to use regularly with effect.

In double guns you can have very light weight arms as made by many British makers, even when bored and chambered expressly for our heavy American duck loads, and we had one Wm. Cashmore with 30" barrels that weighed an even 7 pounds and was made and proved for our heaviest loads and is a whale of a good shooting gun. We also have a best quality Westley Richards double 12 with single trigger, ejectors and hand detachable locks for the 1⅛-ounce light 12-bore load with 2¾" standard case that weighs but 6¼ pounds, as the straight grip stock is well hollowed out under the recoil pad. It is a delightful little gun to use in the hills where hard climbs are in order for ruffed and blue grouse. Being bored improved cylinder and full choke with its light 26" barrels it would be a very deadly quail gun did we have the quail shooting here. It would also be excellent for early season Huns and pheasants but after they are hunted a bit we would then prefer our old heavy 16 that weighs 7½ pounds with its 30" barrels but will kill to longer ranges consistently than will this beautiful little 12-bore, with the same load of shot.

The 12-bore will give you a little more leeway in the matter of gun pointing and still make good consistent kills than will any smaller bore gun, and if you occasionally need long range, a good shooting 12-bore will outrange anything smaller. It will give you a wider Skeet pattern than will any smaller bore for the same pattern density, also a wider trap pattern as well if you could use 1¼ ounces of shot, but as long as trap loads are held to 1⅛ ounces we fail to see much advantage in the 12-bore over an equally good 16 with the same load except in the matter of pressures, for the 12 will handle 1⅛ ounces to very low chamber pressures, while the same shot charge in the 16-bore becomes a heavy load and with higher pressures in the smaller bore gun. The 12-bore gun is also a better all around gun for the average shooter, especially if he will also use it as a duck as well as an upland gun. When he turns to duck hunting, he has only to close up his choke a bit and go to heavy duck loads and be ready for the paddlers.

On the Continent of Europe, the 16-bore seems to be the standard upland gun, but in America the 12 has long been the standard and many men will not consider any other gauge even for quail shooting. Personally we prefer the 12-bore for duck hunting and especially if it is long range jump or pass shooting, but here again the Magnum 12 and the Super 10-bores are to be preferred and we could get along very nicely with a 16 bore for upland work and a big ten for duck shooting.

If a maximum number of hits per shell expended is the prime desideratum, then there can be no question but the man of average strength will do better with the larger pattern of the 12-bore than

he will with the smaller gauges. Big strong men will also be better
fitted out as to gun weight with the 12-bore than with smaller
gauges. There is a certain definite gun weight for each size man if
he is to handle it to best advantage. We vary a lot in size and bodily

Hugh Dunkin with Author's Dog Lunch on a Cold Day After Mallards.
Of Course the Guns Were Unloaded Before Resting Them Against the Car
Bumper. They Belong to the Author.

conformation, hence require different weight and length guns for
best fitting of the individual. Just as we can see little reason for the
410 gauge to be used afield, so can we see little reason for a big
husky man to carry a little 20- or 16-bore when he has the strength
to handle the 12 perfectly and probably needs the added weight
and length to properly balance his muscle reactions. The 12-bore
with 1¼ ounces of shot will also handle No. 4 shot very well in many
cases and these big shot will kill big birds to longer ranges than will
smaller shot when the gun handles them to best advantage. No. 4
shot are just too large for the 16-bore or 20-bore gun although they
would be effective on geese to 50 yards from the 16-bore, but the
fact remains the larger bore gun will handle them better, and with
a 1¼ ounce charge which works mighty well on the big sage hens
when wild and raising at long ranges. The very fact that you can
use the heavier shot charge in the 12-bore when needed puts it in
more of an all around classification and it is a better general pur-

pose gun than the smaller gauges. More 12-bore loads are loaded
yearly than any other gauge and you can always find 12-bore loads
at any local store while you might not be able to pick up 16- or 20-
bore loads as readily. Likewise trap loads will do for much of the
small bird shooting and are cheaper and more easily obtained than
any other loads. While our personal preference for upland work is
the 16-bore we believe in giving the devil his dues and the larger
gauge has much to recommend it especially for the one-gun man.

The 12-bore man can also use his gun for standard trap shooting. We believe however all 12-bore loads should contain 1¼ ounces
of shot even for trap and skeet and only the powder charge should
be varied from the light 3 dram or the medium 3¼ dram load up
to the heavy duck load with 3¾ drams equivalent of progressive
powders. Upland guns should have a bit more bend or drop at heel
to the stock, than trap or pass guns, as they must be mounted
quickly most of the time, likewise the stock should be a bit shorter
than trap stocks, just long enough for your thumb knuckle to clear
the nose in recoil. If you have a good Skeet gun that fits you, then
nothing is better for close range upland work and the practice you
get at Skeet will put you in good form for the upland birds. If it be
a single barrel gun, you can by changing the choke instantly adapt
it to much longer range shooting in the field.

The upland gun should not have too thick a comb as you mount
it quickly and may not have time to pinch the cheek down as hard
as you would when trap shooting. Usually just a good medium
thickness to the comb; and the cheek rest will also help you if you
have one on the gun, as the more of the face that comes in contact
with the stock the more apt you are to position your head on the
stock the same each time in this fast work. The better the gun fits
the better work you will do and when snap shooting quail or ruffed
grouse or cock at close range in dense cover you will need a gun
that fits you so well that you can simply throw it up and shoot where
you are looking without conscious effort or aim. For the close
range work the short barrel is also in order, and while not so' accurate as long barrels it is much faster on the mark and in such
close range upland work you often have no time to spare if you
would get the shot off before the bird dives around a tree or clump
of brush.

Duck and Goose Guns

When we select a gun for general duck and goose shooting,
we should take full cognizance of the requirements. Geese are
notoriously hard to kill, ducks also when full feathered and out at
long range. The 10-bore with the old 1¼-ounce load used to be the
standard duck and goose gun, but ranges were then as a rule shorter

than those shot today and the game much more plentiful. Today the game is many times scarce, much more wary and ranges are much longer as a rule, so the modern 10-bore usually called the Super Ten is still the best all around duck and goose gun in a double. Today it handles 1⅝ ounces of No. 4 shot for ducks or the same amount of twos or threes for geese and is a good consistent killer to a full 70 yards from the best close shooting full choked long barrelled guns.

When we come to straight duck and goose shooting at all ranges to 70 yards then the Super Ten-bore double has a slight edge on anything smaller in gauge.

It will deliver slightly higher patterns than will the best in Magnum 12-bores with the same load of shot. The Ten-bore having a shorter shot column for the same load naturally deforms less shot than does the long shot column of the 3″ Magnum 12-bore load. For the double gun man, no better weapon can be had than a nine pound Super Ten bore with 32″ full choke barrels for consistent clean duck and goose killing at long range. It is light enough to be mounted fairly quickly for jump shooting, and yet heavy enough to slow up the recoil of the big loads and what the 1¼ ounce standard 12-bore will do at 50 to 60 yards the big ten will do at 60 to 70 yards. The gun should pattern 80 per cent or better both barrels for long range work and when desired to be used for shorter ranges, then the old 1¼ ounce load can be substituted for the heavy loads. We have used two modern Super Ten bores for a good many years, and before that an old hammer ten bore L. C. Smith with the Super Ten 1⅝-ounce load, and before that an old lifter-action Parker with hand loads and the factory standard of that day. After all these years' use of the 10-bore on waterfowl, we have only respect for the big gun. It's a duck and goose killer to 70 yards, with the right size of shot. No. 4 shot seems to deliver the ultimate in pattern and pellet energy to 70 yards for all large duck but geese require heavier shot for certain penetration at that range and we believe No. 3 shot would be a better goose load in the Super Ten than would the No. 2 variety currently loaded for geese in both 12- and 10-bore guns. When shotguns must be used with buck for deer shooting, the Super Ten bore is also a good gun for that purpose with the Remington load of 15 No. 0 buck.

With No. 6 shot the big gun will also kill teal a bit neater than any smaller gauge or load to a full 60 yards. If we were shooting ducks every day for a month, and had to stick to one gun, we would select a good full choked double Super Ten-bore with ejectors and single trigger in preference to any other gun or load. For decoy shooting the big gun is not needed but can be used alright with the lighter 1¼-ounce loads. Jumped ducks practically always tower and always stay in sight for a time so they can be taken at about any desired range if they raise a bit close for the full choked gun and the gunner has only to swing with them and wait them out to 45 or 50 yards if necessary to avoid mutilation of his birds. While the Super Ten when properly bored will deliver a slightly better pattern than will the 3″ Magnum 12-bore, the difference in the field in actual game shooting is negligible.

We shot a Model 12 Winchester heavy duck gun one season with the 3″ 1⅝-ounce load and also shot an Eagle grade L. C. Smith Magnum 12 with the same load for three seasons and we never could tell the difference between these Magnum 12-bores with 1⅝ ounces of shot from the Super Ten in actual performance on game. On the pattern board, however, the ten bores gave the better and more even spread of pattern with slightly rounder edges and 3 to 5 per cent higher percentage count. Maybe we killed some of our birds with those ragged edges of the Magnum 12 pattern, but we seemed to do just as well and to just as great a range with the Magnum 12-bore load as with the Super Ten. Had we kept strict count of shells expended, however, we believe the ten bore would have shown a slight edge on the Magnum 12. If the hunter prefers an 8½-pound Magnum 12-double to the big Ten bore he can still have it and use the long Roman candle 3″ loads for the difficult shooting and the standard 2¾″ 12-bore heavy duck loads for shorter ranges. This works very well indeed and usually opens up the pattern to a modified choke and is one reason why so many duck shooters like the Magnum 12-bore for general duck shooting.

The Magnum 12 with 1⅝-ounce load is at its best on big ducks with No. 4 shot and on geese again we believe No. 3 shot would beat the thinner spread pattern of No. 2 shot, but both the Magnum 12 and the Super Ten will usually kill geese consistently to 70 yards with 1⅝ ounces of twos if you do your part. We have run a great many patterns with both the Super Ten bore and the Magnum 12 and both will deliver 80 per cent patterns or better and when the load fits the big Ten just right it will often go 85 per cent and sometimes 90. The Winchester Model 12 heavy duck gun has long been the standard Magnum 12 pump gun and Arthur Kovalovsky of 5524 Cahuenga Blvd., North Hollywood, Calif., has for some time been remodelling the heavy Remington and Browning automatics to handle the 3″ Magnum 12-bore 1⅝-ounce load. So the confirmed old duck shooter can have his choice of a Super Ten double, a Magnum 12 double or a Model 12 Winchester pump or a Browning or Remington autoloader, all guns to handle the full 1⅝-ounce loads and with a choice of lighter 1¼-ounce loads for shorter range work. Such guns are hard to beat.

We believe the barrels of all these guns should run to 30″ in length both double and repeater, and in the case of the repeater they should be at least 30″ long and all should be full choke. You

can open up your pattern with any of them by using the lighter
1¼-ounce loads and yet have the big loads and full choke available
at all times. We do not care much for any patent choke on these big
long range guns. They are intended primarily for long range waterfowl killing and that necessitates the use of dense well centered
long range patterns of heavy shot. They are also good turkey guns

Son Ted, Don Martin, and Our Dog Stub with a Couple of "Limits" of
November Pheasants.

to 60 or 70 yards with No. 2 shot, but turkeys are even harder to kill,
from what friends tell me, than geese; and the Lord knows they are
hard enough to bring down.

We once had a Super Ten old model Ithaca, another of Major
Askins' guns. The left barrel of that gun had been bored modified
originally but the Major had had it rechoked until it was an 80
per cent barrel but gave more of an even spread of the pattern
than did the full choked 85 per cent right barrel. It was a honey
for most jumped ducks and while the right barrel would kill a trifle
farther and we often wished the left was bored the same way the
fact remains we killed a lot of mallards with that left barrel. It had a
non-selective single trigger and we fired the left barrel first. Later it
was fitted with a selective single trigger but we never could see a

great deal of difference in the killing range of the two barrels, possibly 2 yards in favor of the right barrel. A mallard caught in the center of the pattern of 1⅝ ounces of No. 4 had very little chance and usually folded up a dead duck even out to 70 yards. Later we had a New Model Ithaca we bought from our old friend Capt. E. C. Crossman, also a Super Ten and with 32″ barrels like the old gun. This was a pound lighter going an even ten pounds and was an even better gun for long range duck killing. We shot these two Super Tens for a number of years and only quit them when we bought the Major's Magnum 10-bore. The Magnum ten is a better pass gun but is definitely not as fast to mount and get into action as those two Super Tens and is not as good a general purpose duck gun for that reason.

For the average man these Magnum 12s and Super Tens will give him more satisfaction for general duck and goose shooting than any other load or gun. Nine pounds is heavy enough for the Super Ten and the Magnum 12-bore can well be 8½ pounds to 9 pounds in weight. Then with a good soft recoil pad and a long barrel they are not unpleasant to shoot and the satisfaction of seeing big ducks crumple at long range and come down and bounce on the ground or splash high in the water is the cream of shotgun shooting.

Pass Guns

Pass guns are highly specialized weapons, intended only for taking wildfowl at long ranges. When the birds are flying regularly and you can mark off your range and find your lead there is no better sport to be had and we prefer pass shooting to any other form of wildfowl shooting. A man may kill twenty ducks over decoys from a blind, if such shooting were still to be had, and permitted, yet he would get a far bigger kick out of killing a half dozen fowl at 70 to 80 yards on a pass and would remember that day a lot longer than his mass killing at close range over decoys. Long range pass shooting is the college degree of shotgun work. The beginner has no more business trying such shooting than has the dub with the rifle to try long range big game killing with a scope sighted, long range weapon. However, when a man or woman has shot ducks long enough to be really good at judging distance and in following through with the swing and also in judging or finding lead, then the big pass guns and a good duck pass is tops in real sport.

The Super Ten and the Magnum 12 are most excellent pass guns and if shooting is confined to 70 yards and under then they will do very nicely. If however you want to extend that range to 80 yards, then nothing short of the 2-ounce Magnum Ten bore will turn the trick and an 8-bore with 2½ to 3 ounces of heavy shot would be even better but is not allowed by Federal law.

Contrary to popular opinion, judicious pass shooting of single or double birds at long range does not burn out the ducks and is far less injurious to the flights than the continued peppering of them at long range with an inadequate gun and load as we have all seen around a duck marsh. Many hunters will shoot at high flying ducks from 70 to 100 yards or more, with a standard 12-bore gun when they have little hope of ever killing a bird, and merely pepper them with spent ineffective pellets and wise them up and make them leave that section of the country. In comparison a good pass shot with a big Magnum ten bore who knows his gun and knows his range and lead will consistently kill his small limit and kill them clean as well and go home for the day.

If you can't hit them, then you don't hurt the ducks and you can always learn. We remember our first use of the Magnum Ten. We started shooting crows in the summer until we had them well figured out for lead to 70 yards with No. 4 shot, then when the duck season opened we switched to No. 3 shot and started in. At first all shots were clean misses at around 80 yards range. Finally we took up a stand over the Salmon river where every so often a stray merganser would come along. We had paced the range to the water's edge and knew exactly the distance out to where these big worthless fish ducks were flying. Being on a high bank over the water, we could clearly see the strike of the charge and found we were shooting way behind those ducks. We increased the lead until it seemed to us we were leading around 20 feet. Then business picked up and after splashing several of those mergansers, we hid out and awaited the next flight of mallards that came over very high but at about the same range. Using the same lead we killed eight in succession. We picked and killed the leader three times before we had the nerve to try for a double, but then we killed two doubles, cleanly, and had both birds falling at the same time. It was shotgun sport at its best. From then on we knew the 80 yard lead on Mallards when conditions were normal and had a great time down on the Snake River, hunting from a boat with Jim Wade of Peters Cartridge Co., and Collie Blevins.

Another time we were razzed unmercifully for bringing the Magnum Ten along for a duck shoot on the Snake River with Sol Spear and a friend of his. Sol shot a 12-bore and his friend a 20-bore. We helped put out a raft of decoys, and dug and crawled into a blind on the bank of the river at a shallow bend. As soon as it was light enough to see, the ducks started coming up the river; some small ducks but mostly high flying mallards. They did not come in well at all, probably having been shot out of just such a set-up many times. The limit was then 20 birds per gun. We tried several times to hit them from that cramped blind with the big gun and with no luck at all as we did not have room to swing properly.

Then we left our friends to their stand of decoys and their pits and went over to the center of the island as we had noticed flock after flock of mallards coming up the river and always passing high over that island. There was a good rose bush thicket in the center of it so we crouched there in hiding. The big ducks continued to come along, out of range of any 12-bore and at least 70 yards high. We would pick up the leader as he came in and kill him with a long lead just before he reached the vertical and then as the flock towered even higher we would pick another and kill him. We missed some shots but killed most of the time and cleanly and the big birds hit the ground in the open far behind us to often bounce six to ten feet in the air. Some had their breasts burst open from contact with the hard ground but it was great sport. When the day was over we all had a nice mess of ducks as I had killed 19 of the big fowl while my friends had one blue-bill to show for their efforts. Never again did they attempt to pan me and the big Ithaca.

Another time we made a float trip down the Snake River with some friends and used the Magnum Ten-bore with two ounces of threes. Our two friends both used standard 12-bore guns. As the day opened and it became light enough to shoot we found ourselves in a rather heavy fog. We could see ducks occasionally but we were unable to judge the range at all in that fog. The boys said they were 70 yards away and we tried the proper lead for 70 yards and hit not a single bird. Then one of them killed a mallard with the 12-bore and we knew it was much closer range than we had thought, so we took over the oars and steered the boat while they shot.

They did right well as those ducks were not over 55 yards away. Soon the sun burned out the fog, then the ducks really started coming up the river, but seeing us in that open boat they would swing wide and high out over the bank of the Snake River. Then we took our turn with the big gun and crumpled duck after duck to fall out on the land where we had to beach the boat to retrieve them. We killed nearly a limit each that day and had great sport, but after the sun came out and drove off the fog the standard 12-bore guns were useless as the fowl were from 70 to 80 yards away.

Ducks soon learn the effective range of any standard 12-bore and will fly just out of range the while they gabble and look you over. Geese are even more apt to keep well out of range and for pass shooting of either variety, the big Magnum Ten-bore is the best gun obtainable with two ounces of No. 3 shot. Its 93 per cent patterns are higher than can be expected of the average Magnum Ten-bore gun, but most of them will deliver 80 to 85 per cent, and such patterns of No. 3s will kill most of the time on flying ducks to a full 80 yards. Geese could be hit even farther if you knew the lead, but then No. 2 shot would be in order and the pattern would be too thin for over 80 yards; so today, with the law limiting the shotgun to 10-bore on wildfowl, the Magnum Ten-bore is the only 80-yard gun we have. Mighty few men can or will use it, as the big load has plenty of recoil and will rock the boat so to speak. An 8-bore will kill to 100 yards with a heavy dose of No. 2 shot but is not allowed and even if it were very few men would have the skill and strength to use it properly. Three ounces of No. 2 shot will from a full choked long barreled eight bore with 36″ barrels throw a consistent killing pattern to 90 yards at least and often to 100 yards. Such guns are still used in England, to some extent, for pass shooting. The English still have an ample supply of waterfowl, in spite of the use of all bores of guns, even to the devastating old swivel or punt guns mounted in the bow of a boat, for raft shooting of sitting flocks.

Pass shooting is the hardest of all shotgun work to master. Some days the birds will come down with a hard wind, then they require a lot more lead and last fall we missed some ten ducks in succession clean as a whistle at around 80 yards; not enough lead, as we found out later and we used the Magnum ten. At other times the fowl may be coming over very high, bucking a head wind and then do not travel as fast and though the shot are also drifted back some, they require less lead then than normally and we have killed them regularly out at 70 to 80 yards with Kimble's old lead of some eight to ten feet. Our reactions must be slower than Kimble's as he used but four lengths or eight feet lead on mallards at 80 yards, while we often have to use over double that amount for the same range. He shot in the Illinois river bottoms mostly and possibly the fowl did not fly as fast over that stretch as they usually do here in open country. More probably, his swing was a lot faster than ours and thus his perceptible lead was less. He used a gun with a much slower lock in his old six gauge muzzle loader and that also would give him considerable more lead after he pulled the trigger. At any rate, except on mallards bucking a hard wind and coming over fairly slowly, we have never been able to connect at 80 yards with Kimble's lead of four lengths of the fowl and usually found we were using a lead that appeared to be from 18 to 25 feet for 80-yard passing mallards.

Once a mixed flock came over us up the Pahsimeroi valley at around 80 yards. A big mallard was flying well to the rear of the other mixed ducks. We swung on him and then well ahead for an apparent lead of some 20 feet and killed him cleanly but the gun was actually pointing at a grey duck in the lead when it cracked and the lead or distance from that grey duck back to the mallard appeared a good ten lengths of the mallard to us.

Each hunter will have to find his lead himself and no man can tell him exactly what it will be as no two men have exactly the same mental reactions. What may appear as an eight foot lead to some men will appear as twice that amount to others. In all cases the best way to find your lead is to try and find some vantage point over a river where you can see your charge strike the water when shooting at low flying passing fowl. That is the way I learned and others should be able to do the same thing.

Recoil of the big Magnum Ten is very heavy and ammunition and gun are heavy to pack and the cost of ammunition is high, but more real sport can be had in the killing of five or six ducks per day on a good pass at 70 to 80 yards than is to be had from killing 100 at close range, at least for us. The day of flock shooting is long past and with our present small bag limits, the big pass guns can be used in a clean sportsmanlike manner and they afford a lot of real shooting satisfaction to their owner.

Any duck shooter who likes pass shooting and has a good pass available, should have one big gun in his battery, either a Magnum 12 or Super Ten or else the big Magnum Ten-bore; and used as it should be, and usually is, it is the most sporting of all shotgun shooting, also the hardest of all to master.

All-Around Guns

By the nature of things the all-around gun must be a compromise. Probably the most versatile compromise of all would be the standard 12-bore in either a double or a repeater equipped with a variable choke. If a double, one barrel can be more open in the choke than the other to better fit the gun for all purposes. The gun must be a good duck gun and also a good upland gun at the same time. It may also be used considerably as a trap gun or even a Skeet gun. While it may never be the ideal tool for any of these purposes it will be the best compromise we have today. Scatter loads can be used in the double gun for close range work, if it be choked too much for such shooting, while the repeater can of course be set for any desired range and pattern with its variable choke. You will be limited to about 55 to 60 yards maximum range even with heaviest duck loads for big ducks.

However, few shooters have the necessary skill to consistently kill that far out. But such shooting is far less difficult than many writers would have us believe and is merely a matter of studying lead and swing and getting far enough ahead of the duck before shooting.

If one contemplates doing more duck shooting than upland work and more trap than Skeet shooting, then the gun can well be a fairly heavy 12-bore around 8 pounds in weight, which will comfortably handle the heavy long range standard 12-bore loads all day without discomfort. On the other hand if the shooting is largely upland work and some Skeet shooting with very little long range work and little duck shooting then the lighter 12-bore running around 7 pounds or even less will do nicely.

A good full choked 16-bore will fall only about 3 yards behind the 1¼-ounce heavy 12-bore but it will have to be a full choked gun and is then far too close in its patterns for Skeet work or most close range upland work and is about hopeless for geese at beyond 50

The Author on a Duck Pass.

yards owing to the smaller shot being necessary to give it a killing pattern. If the shooting is largely upland work a good sixteen can be made to do the job. It will also take the ducks and even geese if we restrict our shooting to 50 yards on the big birds and not over 55 on ducks.

Nash Buckingham uses a Magnum 12-bore double for his all-around shotgun. He shoots standard loads in it for ordinary work and the 3″ Magnum loads only for long range waterfowl work. No doubt the gun weighs around 8 pounds. With the lighter 3¼-dram, 1¼-ounce or 1⅛ ounce load jumped from his long chambers he obtains a more open pattern for the closer range work. Such a gun if you have the strength to lug it all day can be made to work very well as an all-around gun. Most shooters however, will be better suited with a lighter standard 12-bore and we believe that is the best gauge to select for a general purpose gun.

When we were young the 10-bore was the standard all-around gun and it served very well, though it weighed from nine to ten pounds, but maybe we had better men in those days. We also had many times the duck shooting in those days that we do at present, and the standard 10-bore load was then 1¼ ounces of shot. No better than, if as good as, our present folded crimp heavy standard 12-bore duck loads with the same shot charge. Today we can throw the same shot charge to as high or higher velocity and with as good or better pattern from a 7-pound or lighter standard 12-bore. However, the all-around 12-bore should never weigh less than 7 pounds if you are to do much shooting with the heavy loads or a gun headache will be the end result. Remington has a heavy steel plug to fit in the magazine of the Model 870 Wingmaster, for use with the heavy loads, to increase weight, but it also completely destroys the balance of the piece and we can see no sense in such an abortion. The plug is fitted in the front end of the magazine and when in place gives the gun a very muzzle-heavy feel that would simply ruin one's shooting except for deliberate pass work. We are not likely to have a very big bag limit of ducks again in the forseeable future so we can dispense with some weight in the gun to make it more ideal for the usual upland work and the 7-pound 12 will do very nicely. The barrel length of the all-around gun must also be a compromise and while the long barrels are the best for long range work, the shorter ones are the handiest in the brush so it also should be a workable compromise and we would favor 30″ in a double and 28″ in a repeater. If more short range shooting is to be had than long range then the gun could have 28″ barrels in a double and 26″ in a repeater.

For mixed all-around shooting we probably shoot the full choked 30″ barrel double 16-bore more than any other gun as it is such an exceptionally close shooting gun, but we have very little close range work and it's mostly open country jump shooting. It does nicely for the upland birds for us and the occasional duck along small streams and out to 55 yards, but if much duck shooting is on the ticket then the old Parker 12-bore is more apt to accompany us. We firmly believe in letting every man kill his snakes in his own way, and do not like to be dictatorial on anything.

The standard 12-bore will give you the nearest approach to the all-around gun possible and you will find the widest selection of loads available for it of any gauge, suitable for almost any type of shooting from 25 yard upland birds with scatter or trap loads to long range duck shooting to 60 yards with the heavy progressive powder loads.

Boys' and Ladies' Guns

All boys should shoot and most of them want to do so. Many girls and ladies take to it also, and this is written primarily to start them out right. Neither the youngster or the lady should be given a heavy 12-bore gun to start. Such a gun is a bit too heavy for them to carry all day as a rule, also it has too heavy recoil for the beginner and they will learn shotgun shooting much quicker if given a light 20-bore gun. At the start the light ⅞-ounce loads can be used until they learn to point and swing the little gun accurately and lose all fear of recoil. Then when they become more proficient they can use the one ounce load and that will remain plenty of gun for many small women in the field. The youngster, however, as he grows can graduate next to the 16-bore and also the strong husky girl or lady as well.

The 16-bore will make them an admirable upland gun at all times with its heaviest 1⅛-ounce load. We have seen some ladies however who were big and husky and perfectly capable of handling a nine-pound ten-bore after they had learned to shoot, but such are in the minority. So for the average lady and boy a 20-bore is the best weapon to start them with.

It need not be an expensive gun at all but it should fit them exactly and have a good soft rubber recoil pad. We firmly believe the single barrel single shot weapon to be about the best gun with which to start the novice. They then learn to depend on killing with that single shot and know it's up to them to either miss or kill with it and better shooting will be accomplished, with a minimum of training, than if they were started with a pump or auto loader. Preliminary practice should be carried out with a 22 rifle, and safety rules learned and how to accurately point the little weapon, then they are ready for the 20-bore shotgun.

Formerly a great many really good shooting single barrel guns were to be had, but not so many are now on the market as formerly. The Winchester Model 37 is a very good gun to start them with. It is well stocked and if the butt stock is cut to proper length and a soft recoil pad fitted will fit out ninety per cent at least. It's a sturdy little gun with visible hammer, and we believe should be fitted with a Poly Choke, so the pattern can be opened up some at the start or if a fixed choke is used, then it should not be over a modified 60 per cent choke to start with. Formerly Stevens made some very nice hammerless single loaders that were also excellent for the purpose and Iver Johnson, Harrington & Richardson, Savage, Stevens, Western Field and others still make many excellent little single shot weapons that are about all ideal for the purpose. They should have an automatic ejector and most all of them are now so made. Another good training weapon is the 20-bore Mossberg 185-K. It is a three-shot, clip-loading, bolt-action repeater, but being a slow weapon for repeat shots is in reality almost a single shot weapon unless birds continue to rise one after another, giving time to work the bolt. These weapons all have either visible hammers or visible top safeties as they should to fit our needs. The Mossberg comes with an adjustable choke and all the others can be so fitted. These inexpensive little weapons will teach the youngster or the lady to handle the arm safely, to shoot accurately with it and will enable them to fully learn wing shooting and also the proper care of their weapon.

After that is all accomplished, there is plenty of time to give them a finer gun and either a nice little double or a repeater if they are fairly long armed and like the pump or auto-loader. Savage, Stevens and Mossberg all make bolt action repeaters, but we consider them only as a training weapon, for as soon as the boy or girl has really learned to shoot then they need either a good double or a repeater that will enable them to take doubles with speed and dispatch. Then also is the time to graduate them to a larger gauge.

The 20-bore should weigh around 6 pounds, not less, on account of recoil and should have not less than a 26" barrel and the longer 28" is usually better. Longer sighting planes are more accurate and the primary purpose of this weapon is to teach them safe gun handling and how to shoot.

In all cases the stock should be cut off to proper length to fit them out right. With the gun mounted and the forward hand in proper position the thumb should come over the small of stock grip a good half inch forward of their nose, so it will not hit their nose in recoil. As the youngster grows a slip-on recoil pad can be added over the regular one to give the stock more needed length and this little gun will teach them to shoot with proper instruction as well as the finest shotgun ever made. When they learn to properly take care of their gun and take pride in its ownership and care is time enough to get them a better, more costly weapon. The beginners should first hunt with an older instructor, or in the case of the lady with her husband, sweetheart or father or brother, someone who will take the time out from his own shooting to teach her. Give them all the breaks and the first rise of game and watch and coach their shooting and you will soon have a pal for life. We started both the wife and son, Ted, with a 20-bore, also our girl was fast becoming a good shot when she passed away.

If the shooting is very close range, say under 30 yards on quail or ruffed grouse and such, then open up the choke to improved cylinder and when they can handle the gun well with this choke it can be closed up to modified for the longer shots. To hit and kill clean will soon give them confidence and after they become really good shots or the shooting becomes longer range is time enough to close the choke to full.

Outfit the lady in proper hunting clothes that not only fit her but look well on her as she will never be satisfied wearing something that does not make her look well. The boy won't care a whoop what he wears so long as he is warm and comfortable and can get some game.

Study their stance and position and gun handling and give them all the help and pointers you can. If at all possible teach them to shoot with both eyes open, seeing the game clearly over the gun with the master eye but keeping both eyes open. If they have trouble at first, have them squint the other eye a bit until they master the trick and their shooting eye becomes the master.

After they have become really proficient with the cheap single gun, then look around and get them a good double of suitable gauge and boring or a good repeater with patent choke that can be set for the diversified shooting. Teach them to study the speed and angle of the bird and pick it up and swing with it and past it to the point where it will be when the shot charge arrives. Let them know from the start that they are only shooting at the bird on straight away shots and the rest of the time they must figure where that bird will be when the shot arrives and shoot ahead of it to intercept its course with their shot charge. A good shooting dog is also of inestimable value in training the lady or the youngster as he will hold the birds and allow them to walk up to certain easy range, before the flush and such a dog should be used at all times if available. If not then try jump shooting in good open cover where the game will lay well until approached. Running jackrabbit shooting, crow shooting, magpies, etc., will also offer much out-of-season practice and enable the lady or youngster to become proficient before the game season arrives. Ducks can also be jumped along small sloughs and creeks to afford close range easy targets. If a trap or Skeet field is available by all means take advantage of it and if not, you can get a good hand trap. Give them at first easy straight away shots and keep them on such easy shots as you stand behind them and check their gun mounting, stance, position and shooting until they master them, then give them easy angles with the same careful coaching until they master them, then is time enough to throw difficult targets and get in some game or pest shooting as the season dictates.

Put them up close to their targets and open up the choke until they are hitting regularly, for nothing gives confidence quicker than to see a target properly smashed over the gun. Once started, they will shoot and enjoy shooting most of their lives. Such healthy outdoor sport will do wonders for the youngster, and the lady as well, physically. Teach them how to clean and properly care for their gun and how to handle their game as well and take proper care of it.

The young girls and boys today will be our citizens of tomorrow and plenty of good healthy hunting and shooting experience will better fit them for the tasks ahead and so that they in turn can teach others for posterity.

CHAPTER EIGHTEEN

Care, Cleaning and Storage

Accident prevention.

A GOOD GUN deserves good care. If given good care and used as a gun should be it will last anyone a lifetime and should last out two or more lifetimes of shooting.

Never use a gun to pry down the wire on a barbed wire fence, or to poke rabbits out of a brush pile. The former will very soon ruin the foreend and badly scar the barrels as well, while the latter will sooner or later lead to a stick or some snow being lodged in the muzzle, when the gun will blow off the muzzle end at the next shot and ruin the gun. Never use a gun butt to tamp a rabbit or bird on the head. It is not only hard on the gun to thus jar it down on the ground, but is a very good way to suddenly wake up at the Pearly Gates and find old St. Peter has not yet gotten a place fixed up for you. Using a gun as a club to kill wounded game is also conductive to soft music and lillies o'er your brow.

In crawling up on geese or ducks or turkeys, where you must wiggle forward on your belly, never drag the gun along behind you, it's not only hard on the gun but dangerous as well. Keep that gun muzzle in front of you, where you can watch it and also avoid touching rocks that might give off a metallic noise that would not only alarm the game but scar the gun. If two persons are crawling forward together, then they should travel parallel or the one in the rear should reverse his gun and keep the muzzle well away from himself at the same time. Never load any gun until you first look through the bore and determine if it is clear. Cleaning rags may be left in a gun, an insect may build a nest in one or a mud dauber may seal the bore solid with mud.

An old timer that lived down the Salmon river below Shoup had a Remington 30 Express rifle, caliber .30-06 and kept it hung up on the wall at one end of the cabin. A neighbor who was out of meat dropped in and asked Elmer Purcell if he could borrow the rifle to kill himself a piece of meat. Elmer loaned him the rifle and loading the chamber he went merrily on his way. When he found a fine fat young mule buck he proceeded to take careful aim and let him have it. The deer was uninjured, but the rifle blew up the barrel which separated in two strips of steel the full length. The stock was shattered and one side of the barrel was bent back around the shooters neck in a tight, ill-fitting circle. He brought the rifle, or what was left of it back to Purcell, wearing it as a lavalier, and Elmer had to bend that long strip or half of barrel from around his neck to free him. His eyes were of course powder-burned and the rifle was a total loss. A mud dauber had sealed up the bore of the rifle as they later determined from careful examination.

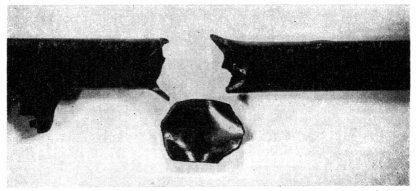

The Result of Leaving a Rag in the Barrel.

Never take a loaded gun into a car. It's unlawful to shoot from a car anyway. Treat all guns as loaded guns and never snap them without empty shells in the chambers or snap caps to cushion the fall of the firing pins, otherwise you will sooner or later find yourself with a broken firing pin, and usually when out on a hunt. At the ranch we used to keep several guns handy and loaded at all times in the house and everyone in the family knew they were loaded and we had no accidents. When we needed a gun around the ranch to kill predators in a hurry it was loaded and ready to use, but we made careful checks on the bores every few days and kept the guns where vermin could not get to them, either winged or other pests.

Father and a friend once stopped and crawled into an old corn crib to get out of the wind while eating their lunch on a quail shoot. Dad's companion watched a mouse crawl in the right barrel of his gun and grabbing it up told Dad he would eliminate that mouse, and before Dad could remonstrate he fired the gun out the corn crib window. Half his gun barrel was ripped wide open and the gun ruined, when the shot charge reached that mouse crouched in the bore. Never try to shoot any obstruction from a gun barrel. We once knew a sheep herder who stuck both a cleaning rod and a section of his shirt tail in his 30-30 and then tried to shoot it out with a bullet loaded cartridge. He died instantly from a piece of steel in his brain. One usually has a hard enough time trying to remain in this vale of tears without hurrying the matter of his decease by such foolish stunts.

Many hunters have died from using the butt of their gun as a club to kill a wounded rabbit, fox or coyote they had bowled over with the shotgun. When they swung the gun and struck the little beast the gun discharged into their chest. It happens every year and one would think that folks would learn from the sad experience of others, but as the old saying goes "a new crop of fools is born every minute."

Never carry a gun without having the safety on and never hunt with anyone who takes his safety off before he mounts the gun for the shot. There is always plenty of time to snick a safety button forward or to cock a hammer gun as the weapon is thrown to the shoulder and that is soon enough to cock or take the safety off.

If for any reason a load squibbs when you fire it or doesn't sound right with normal report, stop right there and look through that gun before you attempt to fire again; it may save your life to do so. You may have noticed the habit many old trap shots have of opening the gun, then blowing through it and also looking through it before they again load the piece. This is not foolishness, but common hard sense as all too many shooters have had a base wad pull out of the case head and be sucked half way up the bore of the gun, when the next shot ruins the gun and possibly the shooter as well. At some stage of a gun's firing there is a vacuum in the bore, and base wads have been known to pull out of the case and part way up the bore, and lodge there. It is something that may happen but once in a million shots but the possibility is there and it has happened. Only last year my friend, Don Hopkins, had such a thing happen even when he was very careful and in the midst of a string at traps. Some very experienced old trap shots even believe that at times an over-powder wad is sucked back into the barrel after discharge and we know no good reason why it could not happen as altogether too many guns have blown off parts of the muzzle end of the barrel right in the midst of a trap string when they had not touched the ground at any time during the string. We have one rifle that will cut off the front end of the case and pull it half way up the bore about one shot in three if we load more than the normal prescribed dose of powder in that particular Scheutzen rifle by Harry Pope. It has done that stunt time and time again. Many shooters have seen the case shoulders of rifle cartridges sucked in in deep dents, even though the load fired at 50,000 pounds pressure per square inch, especially if the chamber was short for the case.

We have seen many men with one arm gone at the elbow from dragging a gun out of a boat or car by grasping the muzzle end. The muzzle end is the one that will kill you, so endeavor at all times to keep it turned away from you and your friends. Likewise, never lean on the muzzle of the gun, be it rifle or shotgun. A dog may run up and jump up on you and hit the trigger and safety as well, of a hammerless gun with his toes and claws; or the hammer of a hammer gun. If the muzzle is turned away from you then it is not going to hit you if it is accidentally discharged.

When hunting with a pal, never take the birds on his side but shoot only at such that raise in front of you or on your side, unless he first shoots and misses. This is only common courtesy. Never shoot at a bird that raises between you and a companion until the bird has passed well out of line. Remember what happened to Bob Shook and the writer even when we were very careful to shoot only when the bird was going well away from us. Never shoot at high or low flying birds when another hunter or a ranch house is in line as shot will carry a long way at times and even a bunch of balled 7½ shot that are welded together can be dangerous at 200 yards. Large shot will carry a quarter-mile and still do damage if they hit; buckshot even farther when fired at an angle of 30 degrees or more. Never shoot toward any house or livestock, and never hunt in a field that is full of stock. Always keep the muzzle of your gun pointed away from yourself or any companion.

Never lean a gun against a tree or side of a car where a dog can knock it down. Better to lay it flat on the ground or stand it against a tree with limbs forming a secure crotch from which it cannot be easily dislodged. Never hang a gun in the house by the trigger guard. We have known of several firing when someone attempted to take them off such a nail in a hurry.

Never try to increase the factory load of shot and powder unless you are a very experienced hand loader and know what you are doing. Shotgun pressures run to around 10,000 pounds per square inch and the more smokeless powder you put in the shell the less barrel length it takes to consume the powder and the higher will be the breech pressures.

While the companies endeavor to hold pressures down to around 4 tons or 8,000 pounds, many loads go as high as 10,000 pounds or five tons and some such as the long Magnum loads in 10- and 12-bore may reach a breech pressure of as much as 7 tons or 14,000 pounds. Shotgun velocities, even with heavy shot are usually under 1,400 feet per second at the muzzle or at most 1,500 feet for buck shot loads; and fine shot such as 7½ are usually driven at 800 to 950 feet per second. The larger the shot the faster they can be driven within reason, but too much powder and trying to drive them too fast is always detrimental to good patterns. A heavy shot load is much better than a heavy powder load for good consistent killing patterns.

If you still use an old Damascus or twist barrel better stick to black powder. It fires much slower than smokeless and is safe in any reasonable load. While we have seen several cases of Super-X 12-bore put through an old shaky double hammer gun with Damascus barrels and several more cases through a very light Damascus barrelled

Greener 12-bore with no ill effect, nevertheless you are absolutely on your own when you shoot any modern smokeless load in any twist or Damascus barrel as all companies, both gun makers and loading companies as well, have long warned and refused to accept any responsibility for accidents occurring from such use of modern shotgun ammunition.

Even modern steel barrel will blow up just as quickly as will Damascus from an obstruction in the bore and some may have a longitudinal flaw and blow even quicker or rip apart from an obstruction in the bore. One of the most common of obstruction blow-

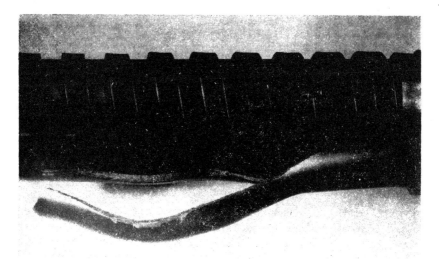

What Happened to An Autoloading Shotgun When Fired with An Obstruction in the Barrel.

ups comes from getting a smaller gauge shell into the chamber of the gun where it drops down until the rim catches in the forcing cone, when another shell can be loaded behind it. This always produces fireworks and a ruined gun as well as often causing serious injury to the shooter. 20-bore shell are dynamite around 12-bore guns and 16s will drop deep into a 10-bore gun. Never have two sizes of shells in your pockets or where they can become mixed.

Never shoot a handloaded shotshell or a muzzle loading shotgun that you did not load yourself unless you know the loader well enough to know what he had put in the load. We once shot an old muzzle-loading single barrel gun that some kind friends had loaded, at a passing flock of big, fat redhead ducks in Missouri. We killed three of the ducks but that gun blew all to pieces and why we were not killed is just one of the dim mysteries. The barrel split from breech to muzzle, the stock was shattered in our hands and the lock plate was loose while the hammer was blown back to full cock. The fact that the breech pin stayed in place alone saved us, but we were badly powder-burned and it was some time before we got all the powder picked out of our face and hands. We had a hard time explaining that at home that evening and finally came clean with the facts which our parents accepted but Dad admonished us never again to shoot a gun we did not load.

Once we saw a muskrat swimming up a slough under water and before that we had killed several by aiming into the water ahead of them when the shot charge would drive down and either concussion or some pellets killed them a good foot under water. On this occasion a friend who was with us was standing farther up the run and as the muskrat came along he simply jammed the barrel of his old '97 Winchester pump under the surface and fired. The barrel blew off completely at the water level and he was badly shaken up but the breech action held. The rat came to the surface kicking and his nose bleeding. We retrieved the muskrat before we knew what had happened to our friend's gun.

In one two-week session we spent in a hospital ward, the lad next to us had his right arm gone at the elbow from pulling an old hammer 10-bore from a duck boat by the muzzle. His folks were mighty nice people and between them we managed to cheer him up and keep him in as good spirits as possible until the stump healed and he was taken out.

A shotgun is a terrible weapon when fired at close range as many an old bartender had reason to know when he was forced to clean house with the old sawed off 10-bore that they usually kept laying just under the bar in many saloons of the west when we were a kid, and usually loaded with buckshot. They would simply saw a man in two at close range. We had a rancher friend at Winston, Montana, a widower, who had a tough kid. His Dad was working most of the time and did not have the time to devote to that lad and he went bad. He used to take his father's old Diamond Daly 10-bore double and hold up the hoboes that trudged along the railroad when his Dad was not around. One day he turned on his father after the latter had given him a taste of hickory tea that he richly deserved. He picked up the 10-bore and shot his father with it across the ranch house kitchen at about ten feet range. The heavy shot charge struck the old man in the right shoulder and though he lived, his right arm and shoulder withered away and was useless thereafter. The lad went to the reform school where he belonged.

Never shoot into brush unless you know that there is neither house, livestock or other hunters within range. One should always be able to see what is on the other side of his bird at least within gun range. Upland birds especially are notorious for turning and flying toward a companion that they may not have seen and each year many hunters are accidentally shot because their hunting companion saw only the bird and was so intent on killing it that he paid no attention to the course of the bird and shot his friend as well as the bird. Such men need their heads examined, and surely they should never be allowed to own or use a gun. Never allow your gun to point at anything you do not wish to kill. Handle all guns as though they

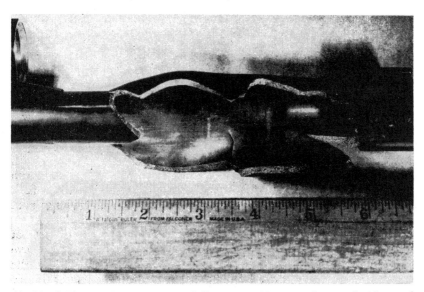

Result of Dropping a 20-gauge Shell Into a 12-gauge Gun and Afterward Firing a 12-gauge Shell.

were loaded. Empty guns are dangerous guns and if all guns were either loaded or treated as loaded guns far fewer accidents would occur.

When you come in from a hunt is the time to clean your gun. Clean it carefully inside and out and even though modern shotgun ammunition is supposed to be non-fouling and non-corrosive, clean that gun anyway. We have found from actual experience even when using Kleanbore ammunition that a gun can become leaded and after leading rust pitting will occur underneath the leading in the barrel. The latest Remington, Peters, Winchester and Western ammunition lead a gun very little as the two former makes use a lubricated expanding over-powder wad and the two latter use a cup-seal wad and a wax lubricant over the folded crimp. Both loads lead very little and often none at all but the bore should be cleaned. If leading occurs then remove it, as it will not only be a detriment to perfect patterns but will also leave a chance for rust to form under the lead coating.

When you buy your gun, also buy the best set of cleaning tools you can. The British usually make very fine outfits and in this country one of the best we have seen is the heavy Aluminum shotgun rod by Marble, of Gladstone, Mich. Get a good brass brush or better a Marble's Flexible cleaner with alternating washers of brass wire gauze and rubber or a Tomlinson cleaner that has an inner spring that expands two wooden halves of the cleaner and these in turn are covered with brass wire mesh. Of the three, the Marble's flexible cleaner is by all odds the best. First screw the cleaner onto the rod and work it back and forth through the bore and especially the first foot beyond the chamber where leading usually occurs. Next take the wool mop or some good strong square or round canton flannel patches soaked in Hoppe's No. 9, Fiendoil, Marble's, Winchester, Remington or other solvent oil or Borekleen. Scrub the entire bore with this solvent and leave it in the bore. The gun will then be clean and will stay clean. Rub off all metal exterior surface with an oily rag or chamois and lastly go over the stock with same or if it be an oil finished stock and you have been out in the rain, then go over it with a few drops of boiled linseed oil in the palm of your hand and rub it into the stock until all greasiness disappears and the stock feels hot to your hand. Take an old tooth brush and clean all traces of mud and grime from the checkering.

About twice a year the locks of the gun should be oiled but not soaked, just a few drops in the right place is ample and we have found nothing better to oil the gun locks and ejector locks or the mechanism of a pump or auto loader than Fulcrum oil. It is a very high-grade sperm that will neither dry and gum up nor run off and lasts a very long time. It is expensive but well worth all its cost.

When the shoot is over the gun should be put in its case so it will not be damaged in the car when being transported home. For long solid frame guns the conventional sheep-lined case is very nice for car use but a good trunk or leg-o-mutton take down type is much to be preferred and a great deal more protection to the gun in transit to or from the hunting field, or target range. Many fine guns are badly battered up each year by being dumped in that rear car seat along with decoys and sundry camp equipment. Ivory sights are thus knocked off, stocks scarred and sometimes barrels bent as well. A few minutes care in taking the gun down and putting it in a case that will afford absolute protection is time well spent.

There are many types of gun cases on the market today, both for carrying the weapon and for storage purposes. First we will take up the finer gun cases of Leg-O-Mutton and trunk type. The best of these are usually the fine English oak cases with solid leather covering and brass corners. These cases are almost indestructible and usually made for double guns, either shotgun or rifle and in some cases for full length solid frame rifles. While they cost around $75 upwards they offer maximum protection to any fine arm either in storage or in transit and are ideal for long trips by car or even pack horse when a fine gun is to be taken and fully protected. However they cost far too much for the average individual and are only to be considered for the fine gun that must have absolute protection. Nothing is better but they are usually quite heavy.

Next we have the fine Leg-O-Mutton type so widely made in this country by many different outfits, but some of the better known makers of fine cases of this type are Capt. A. H. Hardy, Beverly Hills, Calif.; S. D. Myres, El Paso, Texas; and Geo. Lawrence Co. of Portland, Oregon. When made of heavy cowhide they offer absolute protection and being fleece cloth lined or else soft chamois they do not draw moisture. However, in damp, wet climates the gun should never be left in a leather case or one made of tanned sheep skin as both draw moisture. We remember one fine bolt-action rifle that was packed in a sheepskin case on the way to Alaska and for some time up there while we lived in a fishing boat. When examined it was simply covered with red rust. The usual felt lining of the heavy trunk cases or the cotton or wool lining of most Leg-O-Mutton cases however does not draw moisture to such an extent and are safe to leave a gun in if stored in a warm dry house.

Next we have any number of canvas and full length leather gun cases for carrying the gun in a city or in the car to give it some protection. These are also very useful around camp to slip on the gun after it is cleaned from the day's hunt to keep rain or snow off the gun. The leather-bound woolskin cases so often seen offer about maximum protection to the gun in car transportation for their given weight and in dry climates are excellent but don't use them if you are in a damp or wet climate or they will soon rust the weapon.

We have also used very light cases made from waterproof oiled silk for carrying the weapon in the rain or wet snow and while they work well in warm weather they become brittle and break when it turns cold and are noisy. A soft case of water repellent cotton with canton flannel lining as made by Eddie Bauer, Seattle, is a better proposition for all types of weather in a light case for use on the trail or in camp. The best case of this type we have used is an old Moosehide case we bought from a Cree Indian on the Parsnip river in 1927. It has carried so many oiled rifles it is impregnated with oil. It has been soaking wet a hundred times but being smoke-tanned always dries soft, is light and pliable and when hunting in rain or wet snow we just leave the gun in the case until game sign makes its removal mandatory. It also offers considerable protection to a fine rifle.

For the general pack trip the best bet for rifles is a heavy saddle scabbard as made by Geo. Lawrence and others with a separate detachable boot to cover the butt stock. When on auto or train or plane trips the boot can be buckled over the butt of the weapon and when actually in the hunting country can be removed and the saddle scabbard used to carry the rifle on your saddle horse. Such an outfit is costly but well worth its cost on any hard, long pack trip. In the North the Indians practically all use the tanned moose or caribou fringed case and only remove the rifle when ready to shoot and it has proven most excellent for that cold climate.

A fine gun well merits a good case and should have one for its proper protection when not in actual use. For use along the Alaskan coast the gun case simply must be water-proof and should be of a material that will not draw moisture. A leather case up there will

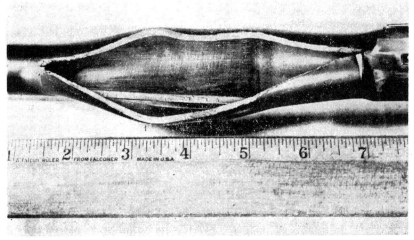

Another Case Where a 20-gauge Shell Was Dropped Into a 12-gauge Gun and Then a 12-gauge Shell was Loaded Into the Gun and Fired.

draw moisture as will a sheepskin case and waterproof cloth or canvas is to be preferred to cover the rifle when embarking in the sea dory or when it is standing around in a shore camp usually in the rain.

Storing Guns

When the season is over if you are not going to use your shotgun for another year then it should be properly prepared for its long storage. If it has been fired with corrosive priming it should be cleaned with boiling water followed by a brass bristle brush, then thoroughly dried and then cleaned with solvent after which it should again be cleaned for a day or two with solvent, then wiped dry and one of the better heavier greases swabbed generously through the boer and also over the outside, like Winchester gun grease, Rig, Gun Groom or some of the many other fine preparations for the purpose. The least messy of them all is the Gun-Groom made by John M. U'ren of Salt Lake City. That stuff deposits a hard thin film on a gun inside and out that seems impervious to rust if all traces of fouling are first removed or rust spots are carefully cleaned and removed. Never put a "rust rope" through a barrel and leave it there or cork up the barrel. You want a smooth, even film of grease or Gun Groom over the bore and metal outside but do not exclude the air or attempt to do so. Also a too thick and heavy coat of grease if not applied when the arm is warm may in turn draw moisture and cause rust. We have seen many bores rusted badly from a greasy "rust rope" pulled through and left in the bore—they are correctly named. Storage should always be in a dry room preferably in the attic or wherever the temperature is the most constant but never in the basement or cellar. Such places draw moisture. We have also noticed that stone or brick buildings as well as cement cellar or basement walls nearly all draw cold and condense moisture during the winter months so store guns in the driest place possible to find and if possible where an even temperature is maintained. If you are out in a hunting camp in cold weather, then leave your gun and especially the hunting scope far away from the fire, or condensation will rust the gun and cloud up the scope hopelessly.

Likewise if you must bring the gun from the cold into a warm room, then you should clean and dry it for several days until all condensation is over and it is thoroughly dry before rust-proofing for the winter months ahead. Most gun cranks like to periodically examine their weapons to make sure they are in perfect shape and it is a good rule for all to follow wherever possible. A little attention before storage may well save you the price of a fine arm or a new barrel, so make sure the weapon is perfectly clean and dry before greasing and then park it in a dry place until next needed.

If the weapon is to be examined every few months, then one of the finest oils for preserving the bore and action we have tested is Fulcrum oil manufactured and distributed by the Fulcrum Oil Co. of Franklin, Penna. This is also one of the finest oils procurable for periodically oiling the locks and ejectors of a fine gun, both as a lubricant and also as a rust preventative. It is not a solvent but one of the finest of lubricants and rust preventatives used on fine chronometers and similar instruments during the late war.

CHAPTER NINETEEN

Lead or Forward Allowance

WHAT OUR BRITISH cousins call forward allowance, is to us swing and lead, the swinging of the gun as you follow your target is just as important as firing at the correct instant, when the gun has swung ahead of the target for the correct lead. Practically all beginners shoot behind their birds or targets. They either fail to take enough forward allowance or else stop their swing when they shoot, either of which causes the charge to go behind the bird. The whole secret of swing and lead is to shoot where that bird is going to be when the shot charge arrives, never at the said fowl or bird unless it is going straight away and on a level with the gun. The rapid mental calculation as to speed and angle of the bird and range involved will in time become an automatic function of the subconscious, but until such a happy state is acquired through long practice, we must study the mechanics of swinging the gun and firing with it still swinging when it has passed the bird the correct amount.

There are two schools of shotgun shooters. One is the fast snap shot, who simply looks at the bird, throws up his gun and fires the instant it hits him, or her shoulder, at where he thinks the bird will be when the charge arrives. If the gun fits the shooter properly and he has had sufficient practice in this style of shooting he can be a very deadly shot, and the fastest of all shotgun shooters. However, if the snap shot gets out of form, or changes guns and starts missing, he will probably go right on missing, not knowing what is wrong, whether he is shooting behind the bird or ahead of it or if he is shooting too high or too low. The snap shot shoots with both eyes open, and keeps them glued to the target, usually not being conscious of seeing the gun at all. He must calculate the speed and angle of the flying bird, and simply throws the shot charge ahead of the bird for the correct amount of lead. This type of shotgunner is prone to take his birds at very short range, and usually uses open bored guns, killing the game as soon as it gets in the air. Its a very deadly system if practiced long enough with one gun to really become proficient at it, but never is as accurate a method for any long range work as the swing and lead method.

The fast snap shot can be very deadly on all upland game that raises close to the gun, and also in Skeet shooting, but when long range difficult shots have to be taken the snap shot usually comes out second best with equally good gunners, who have practiced the other method of picking up their bird over the gun and then swinging with it until the gun passes the mark and firing only when the correct forward allowance has been achieved and with the gun still swinging.

The aiming shooter has a very good chance to judge the speed of his bird as he picks it up over the rib or barrel of his gun, swings with the bird until its rate of speed is established and the gun is swinging with said bird, then swings ahead for the correct lead and shoots with the gun still swinging. This type of shotgun shot is not as fast as the snap shot, but he is usually far more accurate and if he misses, he usually has an idea, at least, of whether he was leading too much or not enough.

The writer used to be a very fast snap shot with a 30″ full-choked double 16-bore No. 3 Ithaca. We shot that gun for 17 years straight and became very fast and accurate with it by the snap shot method. Then we bought a 12-bore with straighter stock and went to missing and kept right on missing. Next we tried several guns and missed with them all, easy shots too, then by the time we went back to the old 16-bore, we were out of practice with it, and missed with it also, until we burned up a considerable quantity of ammunition during the summers on crows and magpies. In time we got back in form, but being a gun bug we simply had to try different guns, different drops of stock and different gauges and we soon found we also had to learn to shoot again and by a more accurate method, if we were to use different guns. Likewise the more one shoots, the straighter stock he will use, and we soon found the old standard stocked 16 with 1⅜″ at comb and 2¾″ at heel had now far too much bend for us. We went to straighter stocks, 1½″ at comb by 2 to 2¼″ at heel and learned to pick up our birds over the rib and double ivory sights and swing with them and business again picked up. However, it took time and ammunition. From all our own early experimenting, we learned a few fundamentals of shotgun work that should help the novice.

If possible, first procure the help of an old hand in selecting a stock length and drop that fits you or your particular shooting style. Remember the more drop or bend the harder the gun will kick, also too short a stock will cause your thumb to bump your nose in recoil and may induce flinching. Next take the new gun; if a pump or auto loader of modern persuasion, the chances are it will have very good dimensions, but alas, some of the doubles are still fitted with a stock of far too much drop, if you order a standard stock. When you get the new gun do some pattern work with it at 40 yards on a square of paper, 40″ each way.

This will enable you to know your elevations and how tight to hold your face on the stock and how high above the rear of the rib your eye should be, to throw the pattern to center for elevation. Next check also to see that the comb is not too thick for your face, or too thin, and that your eye is centered over the rib. Do plenty of shooting at paper squares or an old barn, until you know with certainty where your shot charge is going and what spread it will cover for a given range. Then and then only, are you really ready to try it on birds or clay targets. The stock should be straight enough, so that the line from the eye to front bead passes over the rear end of the rib about ⅛″ at least above the rib itself. Then the bulk of the pattern should also land over the top of the front sight. This automatically takes care of a lot of rising birds as in upland shooting. Next practice with that gun at every opportunity, either shooting or just throwing it up and catching aim on moving or still targets. Even when shooting at that square of paper, swing the gun up in line and shoot the instant the picture is right.

If you want to be a snap shot, then practice mounting the gun and firing when it hits the shoulder and keeping both eyes glued to the target. If the load goes high, or low, correct and try again until you know that particular gun. If you still want to be a snap shot, then for Allah's sake don't ever change guns, stick to that one for life. However if you want to do long-range pass shooting and more accurate pointing at varied game, then better learn to pick up your bird and swing with him and then past him for the correct lead and shoot as the gun is still moving. In this style of shooting the eye subconsciously picks up and sees the rib and the ivory sights and their relation to the bird for elevation, and the longer you use that gun and that drop of stock the more automatic will this aiming become and the less you will be conscious of aiming at all. This is our most accurate type of shotgun shooting and the style used by practically all good trap shots and most of the best game shots at varied targets. Practically all big ten-bore pass guns are used in this way. It is also the most employed system for duck shooting.

The fast snap shot usually works on upland birds and usually requires a more open boring and a larger pattern than the aiming shooter. He is fast at mounting his gun and shoots by feel of it alone when it hits his shoulder and when in proper form, kills his birds much closer than the aiming shooter. By the same token the aiming shooter needs a closer shooting gun, for his birds will usually be farther out when he shoots. For the aiming shooter, the stock should be straight enough or the rib pitch great enough to center the bird with the pattern, when the front sight is seen on a horizontal line with the bottom of the bird. If the bird is raising fast, then swing with him on course and shoot as your front sight blots him out.

Going-away shots, straight-a-ways are the easiest of all, you merely line the gun up with them and shoot when the front bead touches the bottom of the bird, but if climbing fast then swing faster and shoot as the bead blots them out. By the same token if you take a straight incoming bird, pick him up and swing with him until speed of swing equals that of flight then swing the gun upward even faster and shoot as soon as the barrels blot out the bird, the while you keep the gun swinging in an even follow through. Aimed shotgun shooting is not so much a matter of speed as smooth even timing. If you practice at traps, your birds will all be rising until they arc over and start their descent and then they are usually too far out. When a bird comes over you, as in ducks over a blind, aim and swing with the bird if he goes straight over and then swing faster until you have gained lead below the bird and shoot with that gun swinging.

Next take the quartering shots. You must lead them and strive always to shoot in front of them and not at them. They are moving fast and your shot charge only goes around 1000 feet a second and a fast traveling bird covers footage at the same time and you also require time for your mental processes to function and send the impulse to the trigger finger; and then the lock requires time to operate, though some like the Ithaca are very fast indeed. Remember, a bird quartering toward or away from you requires but about half the lead of one flying at right angles. Also the lead or forward allowance as the English call it, increases with the range. Where you may have to aim and shoot when the bead just passes the head of a bird at reasonably close range, out at long range you should figure lead in lengths of the birds and at 80 yards on a passing wildfowl you will need from 15 to 25 feet depending on your speed of swing. No two shooters will see lead as the same amount and no two shooters have exactly the same speed of mental and physical processes.

The easiest way to learn lead on a given range is to shoot from a high bank over water at passing fish ducks or mud hens, so that you can see where your pattern lands in relation to the flying fowl. When shooting at a string of passing ducks, always pick your bird and it is well to pick the first one in line, then if you should kill the next in line or a bird still further to the rear, you know instantly how much more you should have led that particular duck. Also if the lead bird flares up and begins to climb and you know he was in range, you can be reasonably sure you lead too much.

Some folks living in the west where the country is infested with worthless pest jack rabbits of the black tail or sage variety can also learn something of lead by shooting them running either with a rifle or shotgun. In all wing shooting, foot work is just as important as proper lead and swing. A good rule of thumb, is to always advance your left foot, if you are right handed, in the direction the bird is going; and vice versa for southpaws. With that left foot advanced you can take an easy stance and swing easily from the hips to cover the flight of your target, but get the wrong foot advanced and your swing is cramped and you will likely miss. Likewise elevations are effected on extreme swings if the wrong foot is advanced, through the head coming further to rear on the stock unless you have a Monte Carlo comb. Make it a rule to practice foot work, fast, and when a bird raises with a roar of wings, advance that foot even as you raise your gun, both in the direction of the bird's flight. We used to shoot grouse from a saddle horse and had to train that little Shorty horse to always swing his head to the right of rising birds, then hold his head down until the shot or shots were fired. It took some work, but was then a pleasure to shoot grouse from that horse and he seemingly enjoyed it as much as the writer. Shorty soon learned to swing his head and shoulders to the right whenever a bird or covey raised and then would hold still except for a slight trembling after the first shot, while he waited to learn if we were going to shoot again or not. Being practically raised in a saddle, we are still more at home on a horse than on foot and are awkward on foot in comparison. Those big sage and blue grouse were in fairly open, though sometimes steep, country, and it was extremely interesting to watch that little chunky bay horse bring his fore quarters around to our right, so that the bird would fly to the left when possible. He had, however been reined around a great many times with the help of my left spur tickling his left shoulder, until he learned to swing around almost automatically when a bird raised. Even out of season, when punching cows, that little horse would make his turn to the right and stop every time a grouse raised until I stopped him. The shotgunner must learn his foot work, as it is vital to proper stance from which proper swing can be had.

The body should swing from the hips, easily and surely and that left foot must be advanced slightly for the right handed shooter. On crossing birds at 35 to 40 yards the lead may be anything from one to three feet depending on the individual and each individual must learn his own requirements in this respect. Out at 50 to 60 yards the lead must usually be five to ten feet depending on the speed of the bird, as longer ranges require more lead. At one time we were consistently killing mallards at an even 80 yards, even attempted and made some doubles with the big magnum ten Ithaca and the lead seemed to us to be from 20 to 25 feet as near as we could tell, in proportion to lengths of the fowl. Several times we had two birds crumpled and falling in the air at once and this is the absolute tops in shotgun sport, but the hardest game of all to learn. We had been practicing on mergansers flying low over the water at the same range until we had the lead. Even then our first shot at Mallards killed the second bird in line, instead of the first one aimed at and we had to increase the lead. If your shooting is close range and your game is killed at 40 yards or less, you do not need a full choked gun, but are better off with improved cylinder to modified, but if your shots average 45 to 50 yards you need a modified bore and if some are at longer range then you need full choke. For close range work on woodcock and ruffed grouse in dense cover, it is problematical if any better boring can be had than No. 1 or No. 2 skeet boring. However the Skeet guns are close range timber guns only and totally out of place for shooting at 40 to 60 yards. If you use a full choke gun, then wait out a close raising bird until you are sure you will not blow him to pieces. But if using on open bored gun, then you must mount that gun and shoot fast while the bird is still in killing range of your rapidly thinning pattern. Remember your footwork, then swing with the bird and ahead for lead and shoot with the gun swinging. These tips may never make you an expert but they will help fill the game bag if adhered to and practiced religiously.

The British have a shotgun cartridge that incorporates a tracer pellet in the center of the charge and this tracer produces a very bright even light that can be clearly seen in bright sunlight. Those we tried seemed a great boon to any shotgun shooter desiring to learn the correct forward allowance on different game. We had but one box of them of Eley make and had a great deal of fun with them. When we lead too much, it was extremely interesting to see an old mallard flare up as that bright pellet flashed by in front of him. We shot a couple at a pattern paper and those tracers seemed to land right in the center of the pattern. However we believe they would also start fires in dry grass country. Just the same they were the greatest aid to accurately learning lead and swing and the elevation of your gun of anything we have seen to date and we could never understand why American companies do not load them. Long heavy guns swing more steadily and evenly than light guns, and once you get a big heavy duck gun swinging, it follows through much better and with less effort than does a light gun. This follow-through is vital to success, for no matter how accurately you judge the speed of your bird or how well you time your shot as the gun swings past for the correct lead; if you stop the swing, the pattern will usually go behind the bird.

While the snap shot usually likes a short light-weight gun, and this type of gun does very well for snap shooting, there is a definite gun weight ratio to the size and strength of the shooter for best results when the gun is shot by the swing method. The shooter will do his or her best work with a gun whose weight sort of balances their strength and reflexes. Too light a gun and they may swing too fast and speed up their timing, while too ponderous and heavy a gun may in turn slow their swing somewhat and more lead be required. It's the smooth even timing that counts and most all good shots have it. Watch a squad at the traps and notice how they will occasionally pick up a gun and swing it at different angles simulating actual shooting and notice the smooth even swing with which they move the gun. Then watch them shot and you will notice they are perfection itself on the art of swinging with their birds. It is well also to watch the doubles trap shot. Notice how he sort of winds up his body to take that first bird, then as he unwinds he swings over to the other and all seemingly in a smooth effortless swing that is grace itself.

More game and targets are missed by being in too much of a hurry than by being too slow, we believe. The roar of wings of a flushed grouse or pheasant is apt to make you want to hurry the shot, before you have attained the proper speed of swing or properly judged the course and angle of the bird. Such hurried shots unless you are a fast snap shot are apt to be clean misses. For one thing you may fire before the bird is out far enough for your pattern to open up and you have simply hurried the job and thus botched it as well. If the birds raise in reasonable range from five to 25 yards, you have plenty of time, on big fowl like grouse or pheasants in fairly open country. You should mount the gun rapidly but not hurriedly, then as you note the course of his flight and the angle, pick him up over the gun and swing with him until you have his speed, and then past, all in one smooth even movement, firing just as the gun appears to be far enough ahead for the given range involved.

It sounds simple enough but the roar of fast wings and the desire to make a kill will hurry you until you get onto them, then you will start killing them clean and keep right on doing so as long as you don't hurry, but maintain that even swing.

Another very important part of swing, is to note the angle of the bird's flight and start your gun swing on that same line of flight, then it is easy to keep on the bird's course as you swing ahead for lead. The swinging shot requires less lead than any other type, simply because the gun is moving on a line with the bird and is moving faster than the bird's movement from a straight course when it intercepts and passes the bird. For this reason the swinging shot requires less forward allowance than the snap shot.

With the snap shot, the bird's flight and probable location at the time of the shot are all mentally calculated in a fraction of a second, the gun is mounted and fired all in one continuous movement the instant the butt hits the shoulder. With the snap shot, there can be no change of pointing once the shot is started. The gunner notes his target and where it should be, all in the twinkling of an eye and has to throw his pattern farther ahead for any given range than if he had swung on the bird and followed it and then passed it for lead. This for the reason his gun is never swinging, but is simply snapped to the shoulder and fired where he has fixed his eyes as the probable location of the bird when the shot arrives.

If the bird changes course, while he is mounting and firing the gun, he will likely miss, for he has no chance to correct his point or aim in a snap shot. Close rising, fast flying game that is usually snap shot, is also prone to change its course and swerve and dodge around bushes, trees, etc. Quail and ruffed grouse are notorious for such swerves in their flight. Woodcock simply bounce into the air, level off slightly, and drop back to the ground again. When any of these birds changes course suddenly after the snap shot has made up his mind and is executing the shot he will miss unless at very close range and with a wide spread pattern. There is nothing he can do about it. He calculated the bird would be at a certain point when he shot, so he looked at that point and threw his shot pattern there only to have the bird swerve while he was mounting the gun and the net result usually is a miss.

Aiming is really a poor term for any kind of shotgun shooting, for the piece is really not aimed but pointed. The two hands, the cheek to the comb and the butt to the shoulder guide the pointing of the gun and the shooter should, if at all possible, always shoot with both eyes open. Two eyes can see more than can one, and binocular aiming or seeing is always better for range estimation than one eye. Thus the more deliberate shot who always sees his bird over the gun and who picks up the bird and follows through on its course in a swing, until he intercepts and passes the bird in his swing, has the better chance of correcting his gun pointing, should the bird dodge or turn in its flight than ever has the snap shot. Once the snap shot makes up his mind as to where the bird will be, he shoots there and if the bird turns he is lost and will miss.

At times the two very different styles of shooting seem to merge into one another, such as when the snap shot throws a pattern at a bird that turns and dodges the pattern, then he may well swing after the bird and kill it with his second barrel. The closer the range and the greater the spread of the pattern at said close range the more deadly is the fast snap shot, but as the yardage increases the more chance for error on his part as well as for the bird to change course. With birds like blue grouse, sage hens, and pheasants, which usually fly a straight course and are like a flying box car anyway, the snap shot can usually judge them and kill them very quickly, but with fast dodging twisting Huns, quail and even doves, he may well make many wild misses by the snap shooting method.

We have watched excellent snap shots repeatedly miss jacksnipe for the reason that they threw their pattern at them too soon and did not wait for old jack to straighten out his erratic course to where they would get full benefit of their pattern. When the fast snap shot tries jacksnipe for the first time with a full choke gun he is usually in for trouble. The bird is seemingly zigzagging back and forth and the gunner usually shoots just as the twisting little birds zigs off course. If he will but pick up the bird over his gun and let him go his zigzagging course until his pattern has opened up to a 30″ spread then he will usually kill them quite regularly. Thus we have tried to show what happens to the fast snap shot when shooting fast turning and twisting birds. The little ruffed grouse is very adept at dodging behind any tree near its line of flight and this also will cause many misses for both types of shooters.

When we were a boy in Montana almost every little mountain stream had its quota of ruffed grouse along its quaking aspen bottoms, and these furnished us a great deal of useful practice and experience. The ruffed grouse is a grand bird, none finer for its size, either as a sporting proposition when it has been hunted much, or for the table. However, when it comes to hard difficult shooting of upland birds the toughest one we have found is the Hungarian partridge. When much hunted, this bird is prone to raise at long range and is very fast, yet has all the tricks of the trade used by quail or ruffed grouse. He will tax the skill of the finest shotgunner. You must take him as soon as you can or he is out of range. We once killed eight straight with two doubles, and thought we had the world by the tail and a down-hill pull, only to miss the next six straight, which took all the conceit out of us. We tried both snap shooting and swinging, finally deciding that the follow up and swing was the better procedure on this little desert bullet. He seemed a much tougher target for us at least, than any quail we have shot.

All upland shots should master both styles of shooting, because many times a bird will raise in dense cover, when it can at once be noted he will be in sight but a brief second and the shot must be taken instantly or never. That is when he should snap shoot. At other times he may jump a pheasant or sage hen out in the open where the big bird gets up and under way and levels off on an even course affording the perfect target for the swing shooter. Such shots are easy if you know your gun, but the dodging twisting Hun or quail or ruffed grouse in dense cover will ever be a tricky target so you should know both styles of shooting and when to use them.

It is well to stretch out and measure various game birds after killing and then write down the average length of each. In long range pass shooting the only guide we have to the amount of lead is the length of the bird and so many lengths of a given fowl will give us so many feet lead. Long range pass shooting at ducks and geese, one of the very finest of wing shooting sports, also calls for the very highest degree of skill, and knowing the average length of the bird helps materially in mentally fixing the amount of lead for any given range. One good shot I knew figured out how many birds equalled the length of his gun and claimed he took lead by lengths of his gun. At any rate he was a very fine pass shot and claimed that at 70 yards, the maximum range of his Model 12 Magnum 12-bore pump gun he used about four lengths of his long pump gun in forward allowance on a big mallard for a full crossing shot. The gun was around four feet in length, so that would figure out around 16 feet of lead. At any rate he killed the ducks very regularly when within 70 yards with that load of 1⅝ ounces of No. 4 shot.

Another thing to consider in pass shooting is the effect of any strong prevailing wind, both on the flight of the fowl and also on the drift of your shot pattern. When mallards, canvas backs or other big ducks come in on a strong wind they are usually traveling much faster than normal and more lead is required, but when they are bucking a hard wind they are traveling much slower and at times simply float along. Then less lead is required for the birds but you must also compensate in your lead for the drift of your pattern. It does not take much wind to drift a pattern of No. 7½ shot clean off the 40″ pattern paper at 40 yards and by the same token a charge of shot can be drifted off the mark wing shooting on windy days. Large shot drift much less than small shot and are for this reason much better for long range work in a windy country. If the fowl are coming in on a hard wind or passing with a hard wind at their tails, they are then going much faster but the wind will also give you considerable footage in lead out at 70 to 80 yards, as it usually drifts your pattern enough to compensate for the increased speed of the fowl. Just as when the fowl are bucking a hard wind at long range, that slows them up, that same wind will drift your pattern and cut down your lead. However at closer ranges under 50 yards, your patterns are not effected nearly as much by the wind as the fowl's speed is increased or decreased by it so this must be considered.

Life is too short for any of us ever to learn all the answers, but intelligent study of the problems as they are presented helps materially in consistently taking fowl over difficult long ranges. Long range pass shooting is the college degree of wing shooting.

Fred Kimble, that legendary Illinois inventor of choke boring, shot mallards a lot for market in the early days with his big 6-bore and 1½ ounces of No. 3 shot. He considered the length of a big mallard with head outstretched as two feet. At 40 yards he swung one length of the bird or two feet ahead, and at sixty yards he used two lengths or four feet and at 80 yards he tried to lead four lengths of the bird and thus for an estimated 8-foot lead. He was shooting largely in river bottoms in Illinois and the big birds may then have been flying at a lesser speed than they do here, or Kimble and the writer probably swung with far different speed, as my lead seemed to always be around 20 to 25 feet when taking a crossing mallard at 80 yards. This proves nothing except the fact that no two men will see their lead as the same amount and each will have to learn from experience just how much he needs for different fowl at different ranges.

We have tried to estimate the amount of lead we use in killing cock pheasants. When the big birds are quartering away from us and at not over 40 yards we simply swing with them and shoot when the point seems to be about a foot ahead of their head. If they are crossing squarely across our front, broadside on and going full speed we try to swing about three feet ahead for the 40 to 45 yard shot and as the range increases we try to increase the lead, so that a pheasant crossing at 60 yards, requires for us at least about a 6-foot lead. The big cocks with their long streaming tails run anywhere from 30″ to 36″ in length depending on length of the tail and such lead is easy to figure for crossing birds in lengths of them from beak to tail and we use one length for the 45-yard shot and about two lengths for the 60-yard shot as near as we can tell.

For years we have tried to reason out why different good shots all apparently take a different lead on passing fowl or game birds at a given range, when they all use the same swing and lead system. No doubt different people see any unit of measurement differently at various ranges, but we do not believe this fact accounts for the wide discrepancies in their individual forward allowances. It would of course, necessarily make some considerable variation, but nothing to the extent of our own 80 yard lead on mallards and that employed by Fred Kimble years ago with his big 6-bore single barrel muzzle-loader.

We have finally come to the conclusion, that the great variation in speed of swing by different shooters is the factor responsible. We do not know the weight of Kimble's great duck gun but it threw an ounce and a half of No. 3 shot and he lead four lengths of the mallard for crossing 80-yard shots. No doubt the old boy was a far better judge of distance in the air than any of us now living will ever be, likewise, we now believe his speed of swing must have been at least double that of our own and probably three times as fast. If, as we surmise, his big six-bore tube caught up with that flying mallard and passed it at three times the speed of our own swing, then that could easily account for our apparent differences in lead. No doubt also, the lock time of his big muzzle loader was slower than that of our magnum ten bore Ithaca. This would in turn give him several more feet lead, from the time he pulled the trigger on a fast swing to the actual firing of the piece. Doubtless also, we are a much slower shot than Kimble was and we pick up the fowl and follow it to get its direction of flight before increasing the speed of our gun swing until we pass the big duck for our apparent lead of some nine to ten lengths of the bird. We have even laid out ten ducks in a row with bill and tail touching and paced off 80 yards from the row of dead ducks and that still looked to us like our apparent lead when we pulled the trigger and killed them cleanly. So, we must inevitably come to the conclusion that our swing is much slower than Kimble's was and our gun lock time is faster. This alone could account for the great difference between his lead of eight feet and our own of 18 to 25 feet depending on the speed the big fowl are flying. We killed eight one day at a full 80 yards in succession and with two doubles in the string, using the Western load of two ounces of No. 3 Lubaloy.

It was something to always remember, and on the doubles we had both fowl falling at the same time, though the first killed was of course much lower to the ground when the second duck crumpled. Such long range pass shooting is the absolute tops in shotgun shooting.

Since then we have often watched excellent duck shots work on mallards at long range, trying to see just how they accomplished their long range kills. We have seen many that seemed to swing at the same apparent speed we do, while others were three times as fast in their gun movement. They simply watched the fowl long enough to get its exact course before they mounted their gun, then they swung the piece in a straight line crossing the bird with the gun muzzles moving much faster than our own would have done and firing when the lead looked right to them. These men when questioned about the amount of lead, almost invariably gave much lower figures than our own, so that speed of swing we believe to be the answer to the wide variation in apparent lead for different shooters on the same fowl and at the same range.

There is also considerable difference in the speed of the various ducks and also in the speed of the same kind of fowl under different conditions. When a flock is coming down with the wind over a good pass and really going places, they are flying much faster than when they are circling and looking over the ground or water for a possible landing on some later circle. This fact must also be considered. Last fall we missed some eight or ten shots with the big gun at passing mallards without ever getting the lead or killing a single duck from those flights. They came over high and far out at an apparent 80 yards as near as we could tell, but those ducks had been jumped and shot at and were really clearing out of the country and coming with a strong wind. Whether we shot behind or in front of those single birds we selected we will never know, but the fact remains we had killed many ducks at that same range but for some reason never touched one of those fast flying fowl that particular day. The same day however we killed several mallards, that we had jumped and that crossed broadside at about the same range, getting our five limit, but we are still wondering just why we missed those that came up the river with the wind.

Such things are what makes pass shooting interesting and the greatest game of all duck shooting. If those big ducks could have flown low over the river so we could see the strike of the big shot, we would have found our mistake in short order and killed our limit.

We remember other days when hunting late season pheasants with Don Martin on his ranch with the big magnum ten-bore. The breaks in the bars along his ranch afforded excellent cover, but the pheasants would seldom raise at less than 50 yards and often at 60, due to the wide gulches and the fact we would shoot across them as the birds took to the air from the efforts of our little cow dog.

Martin had told us there was no use in hunting them there with anything less than the big ten bore and he was right. We usually managed to get a few birds, and often the limit, but it was long range very difficult shooting. Sometimes we figured the lead right and killed them cleanly at 70 to 80 yards and again we would get clean misses on a lead that looked right but certainly was not. The big gun with two ounces of No. 3 Lubaloy would always throw a killing pattern on such big birds to 75 and 80 yards, but figuring the lead and executing it in the short time available, as the birds jumped and then tipped down the steep mountain in full flight was often something else indeed.

Big ducks often appear to be going slower than they really are and for this reason we often miss behind them. Canvass backs which we seldom get in this section are probably the fastest of all ducks and really travel when going in high gear. Geese are so big they usually appear much closer than they really are, also their size makes them seem slow when in reality they travel from 80 to 90 feet per second. On the other hand a little green winged teal seems to fairly whistle through the air in full flight, yet his speed is considered by the experts to be just about the same as the Canada goose in full flight. Thus the size of the duck or goose makes the apparent speed seem much greater for the tiny teal than the big lumbering goose. With any species we have found you must get out and shoot them for a number of days at least before you really get onto their speed and the lead necessary to connect regularly. When that is accomplished the duck hunter is as near heaven as he is likely to get on this plane.

It takes time for the gunner's brain to send the mental impulse to his trigger finger when correct lead has been achieved by swing, then it takes more time for the lock to operate and still more for the load to fire and clear the barrel of the gun and all the time the fowl is flying steadily along. With the shot traveling at about 1000 feet per second, more time is required for the pattern to reach the bird. Men differ greatly in their own mental processes as well as in execution of them, so it is utterly impossible for any one man to figure the lead correctly for another individual. We can tell them what we use but it will only be a hint to them as to what they may require.

The effect of shot stringing on a passing fowl does give us a very slightly elongated pattern in theory. In other words even if our lead is too great there is a possibility of some of the last shot in the string striking the fowl and killing him. However the front of the pattern is the killing end of it and the straggler shot that string along behind are usually deformed and poor killers anyway and while the duck may well catch some of them, the possibility is too small to be considered, so we must figure on killing with that even spread of pattern from the front of the charge. Modern shotshell loading has greatly cut down shot stringing anyway.

Range estimation is just as important as correct lead and goes hand in hand with lead, so we must learn to estimate the distance to any passing fowl to have much chance of hitting it. This again can only be learned by careful observation and practice at every possible opportunity. When you kill a duck, then pace off different ranges from said duck. Put him up where you can see him clearly and note how far you can distinguish the markings of the feathers and the characteristics of the different kinds of fowl. If you make mental note of these observations, it will help you in judging the distance to a flying duck also and this in turn will give you an inkling of the lead required. Remember also that ducks passing over head usually appear farther out or higher than they really are, and birds passing out to the side are likely to be much farther away than they actually appear.

Short barrelled guns seem to swing faster than longer barrelled weapons and the arc is of course shorter. Light guns are no doubt faster than heavy ones, but in pass shooting the heavy gun swings more evenly and steadily once the swing is started and is prone to carry through in its swing much better than the light weapon. Thus the big heavy ten bore is really the pass gun for serious long range pass shooting. By the same token the lighter standard 12- or 16-bore is a much handier faster weapon for jump or decoy shooting. You can pick up your bird and swing ahead for the apparent lead much quicker with the lighter weapon for this type of shooting, hence gain yards in gun range in so doing. Long barrels, give greater accuracy of gun pointing than do short barrels, and one is more apt to maintain the proper lead with the longer barrelled weapon. The fact remains however, the lighter gun is much the better for fast close range jump shooting, usually 40 to 55 yards range. The gun that suits one man will not suit another, as a rule, as everyone has his or her own ideas.

Years ago Major Askins worked out a chart showing the comparative speed of about all the different birds and fowl, in feet per second, the average speed of them as well, the theoretical lead for crossing birds at 40 yards and the practical lead, as gathered from a compilation of all the best shots he knew at the time. It is doubtful if any man will ever come any closer to putting the 40-yard lead for various game birds on paper so we will append his chart to this chapter.

It will readily be seen that theoretical lead is practically double that of practical lead as given by a great many excellent game shots. This in turn is accounted for only by their speed of swing in passing the flying bird. Of one thing we can be sure, if the novice will practice swing and try to fire when he has this apparent lead and keep

Bird	Speed per sec. in feet	Average speed	Theoretical lead 40 yds. in ft.	Practical lead in ft.
Quail	60 to 80	70	8.7'	4 to 5'
Prairie Chicken	60 to 80	70	8.7	4 to 5'
Ruffed Grouse	65 to 80	72.5	9.	5'
Dove	70 to 90	80	9.8	5'
Jack Snipe	50 to 70	60	7.3	4'
Curlew	40 to 60	50	6.	3'
Mallard	50 to 90	70	8.7	4 to 5'
Black Duck	50 to 90	70	8.7	4 to 5'
Spoonbill	50 to 90	70	8.7	4 to 5'
Pintail	60 to 90	75	9.2	5'
Wood Duck	60 to 80	70	8.7	4 to 5'
Widgeon	70 to 85	77	9.5	5'
Gadwall	70 to 80	77	9.5	5'
Redhead	80 to 90	85	10.4	5 to 6'
Bluewing Teal	75 to 95	85	10.4	5 to 6'
Canvassback	90 to 100	95	11.66	6 to 7'
Canada Goose	80 to 90	85	10.4	5 to 6'
Brant	80 to 90	85	10.4	5 to 6'

his gun swinging in an even follow through, he will score enough hits to give him an inkling of the correct lead he should use and this will help him no end in becoming a good wing shot. He will still have to observe the speed of the bird under different conditions, and remember also these figures that Major Askins compiled are for passing birds at just 40 yards.

CHAPTER TWENTY

Practical Shotgun Shooting

MANY FACTORS ENTER into the technique of becoming a good wing shot. We must have a gun that fits us. It must also be of a weight that best balances our strength and muscle reactions. The barrel length should also be somewhat in proportion to our height and arm length. A tall person can best handle a long gun and a short person is better fitted with a shorter weapon.

In trap and skeet shooting the shooter has ample time to get set in any position that suits him or her best, and to wind up for the doubles targets, so that they can take the first target and simply unwind and find their gun pointing on the second target. Not so the game shot, for no two birds ever raise at exactly the same angle or travel exactly the same. The game shot must be on the alert at all times when expecting birds to flush. When using good well trained dogs, the game shot can relax until the dog makes game and he knows a shot may soon follow, but when rough shooting, walking up birds without a dog or jump shooting ducks along some creek or slough, then the gunner must be on his toes and the game may well flush just as he is astraddle of a barbed wire fence or wading to the very top of his boots and endeavoring to keep from filling them with cold water. To anyone desiring to become a good trap and Skeet shot, we can heartily recommend Fred Etchens book, "Commonsense Shotgun Shooting." It will teach them the fundamentals of the sport and also carry them along to a finished shot at either game. While hints may help, the good game shot is usually the person who has hunted game a lot and studied their flight and his or her mistakes.

Many beginners are apt to be startled by the sudden roar of wings as a pheasant or grouse breaks cover at some unexpected angle and then shoot too quick, before either the bird has straightened out in flight or they have had time to properly judge the speed and angle of flight. When shooting quail, Huns, ruffed grouse or cock, the birds are often in sight but a short time if the cover is heavy, and one must be on his toes and ready to mount the gun and shoot with the least delay before the bird whips round some tree or clump of brush. Sage hens and pheasants are big birds and while they travel at a fair rate, they also usually assume an even angle and once their direction is started it is maintained, and they do not twist and dodge as do doves, quail, Huns and ruffed grouse.

A big, powerful man or woman seldom does the best work with too light a weapon. They tend to be too fast and shoot before they are on the mark. By the same token the small person of moderate strength seldom does his best work with too long or too heavy a gun in upland work. The weight should balance the size of the person to some extent for best results. In pass shooting, gun weight makes little difference, as we have ample time to watch the fowl approach,

The Author Demonstrates the Old-timers' Carry— the Best Walking Position for a Heavy Gun. This Gun is a Magnum 10-bore Ithaca Weighing 10½ pounds.

and mount the gun for the shot. Likewise the longer the barrel the more accurate the gun pointing in this phase of shotgun shooting. Any man of average strength has ample time to mount a ten to 12 pound gun for such work and shoot it well, but in the uplands such a gun is totally beyond the strength of the average person for the quick fast work that such shooting usually demands.

The comb of the stock should adequately support the base of the thumb, neither too far forward so there is not sufficient room, nor too far to the rear so it does not support the thumb base properly. The thumb and fingers should be at least three quarters of an inch forward of the nose, and better an inch to an inch and a half with guns of heavy recoil. This with the head in a normal position, but dropped slightly against the comb of the stock. The right elbow should be high and the butt of the gun held well into the hollow of the shoulder, never out on the arm. The top of the butt plate or pad should be about level with the top of the shoulder. The left arm should be in a comfortable position, not extended too far. Prefer-

The Author Demonstrating the Taking of a Left Crossing Bird. The Gun is a No. 5 Ithaca 16-bore.

ably the left shoulder for right handed shooters should be slightly advanced toward the target. That is, we should move that left foot slightly forward and the feet should be about 15 to 18 inches apart as a rule. When the gun is mounted and the face glued to the stock, but with the eyes seeing well over the length of the barrel, then the arms, head and shoulder as well as the gun should be held in one unit and should swing and aim as a whole. Swing can be started from the knees and the body should do the turning from the knees and hips upwards, keeping that gun, head and arm unit swinging as a whole. This makes for fast even swing and perfect follow through that is equally important. One should stand naturally when possible and with the body erect but not leaning back. Except for that head, gun, arm and shoulder being simply glued together in one unit, the rest of the body should be utterly relaxed. Never fight recoil or brace against it or tense your muscles, just relax and let the body roll with it exactly as a ball player catches a fast ball. While one should lean into the gun slightly, he should never brace himself or tense his mucles in any way. Pull the gun tight against the shoulder and hold it so with hands and head and then utterly relax every other muscle so the body is free to swing easily as if on a pivot.

In the field, fast foot work is often called for and we move our feet into position as we mount the gun and snick off the safety. Right handed shooters should be facing slightly to the right of their target and left hand shooters slightly to the left of the target. Some big heavy men we have observed seem to shoot abnormally short stocks and place them almost against their chest rather than their shoulder, and face their targets squarely. This has never been as comfortable or as natural a position for us, and we cannot do as good work in such a position as when we advance the left foot and shoulder slightly toward the target and face slightly to the right of the target's line of flight. The feet should never be spread too far apart as this puts the body in a strained position and while a wide foot position may be of some assistance in shooting off-hand with a rifle in a strong wind, it certainly is detrimental to fast, smooth, even gun swing with a shotgun.

The head should not be pulled back or stretched too far forward; just a natural stance for the length of your neck. Too much emphasis cannot be placed on the importance of placing the gun the same on the shoulder each time, or on the holding of gun, hand and shoulder together as one unit. Let the body do the turning and twisting but maintain that gun and head and shoulders as a single unit.

If a bird flies to the right for a right handed shooter then he should advance the left foot toward the bird's flight or bring the right foot back to throw that left foot and shoulder more towards the bird's course as he mounts the gun. If the bird swings to the left, that is the easiest of all shots for the right handed shooter and of course vice versa for southpaws. Unless the bird is flying straight away and at about the elevation of the gun, it requires lead. If you can see the bird's head at all it always requires lead. You are endeavoring to shoot where the bird is going to be, not at it, except in level straight-a-ways. The amount of angle of flight and the range determines your lead. Keep the gun swinging even after you shoot and if the first shot does not score you are still in proper position to whip in the second barrel.

When a bird flushes or you call for a target at the traps, the weight should be a trifle forward on your feet, the shoulder should be up as well as the elbow when the gun is mounted, and the stance should be without any tension whatever. The gun should come up with the top of barrel almost level with the eyes as you pick up your bird and follow and swing ahead for lead. What you want is a smooth effortless coordination and stance, without any strain or tension, that will permit swinging with said birdie until you have passed him for the lead and the gun has fired. Many of the best wing shots have a

The Author demonstrates his "ready" or "walking-up" position. The gun is a 16-bore No. 5 Ithaca.

stance with the forward knee slightly bent and the rear leg straight. This seems to help them in their body movements of swing. Good form with a shotgun, is just as important as good form and follow through at golf. Mastering it requires practice until in time the subconscious takes over, then you move your feet and body into position and the gun comes up and in proper alignment without any conscious thought on the part of the shooter. Only then are you a finished shot and able to do your best work.

You must swing your upper body, smoothly and freely, just as if you had your favorite gal on a good dance floor and the orchestra was playing a smooth waltz. Smooth even swing, a knowledge of correct lead and ranges and timing are the secret of good wing shooting. One must also know something of elevations of his pattern at the longer ranges. Guns with sufficient rib pitch usually throw the patterns high enough to take care of this angle out to the maximum effective range of the shot size used as small pellets drop a great deal more than do heavier pellets. One should shoot the gun

Photo by John Bishop

The Author Demonstrating the Taking of a Right Crossing Bird. The Gun is a No. 5 Ithaca.

on pattern paper or an old barn or at a snag in the water to different ranges to know his elevations as well as the lead required.

Wing shooting combines split second timing at fast moving targets with perfect body control and the coordination of mind and body. Whenever possible have an expert check your gun and body movements and tell you your faults and what you are doing wrong, then strive to improve these defects.

You will never be a finished wing shot if you try to move only the gun and your arms without proper body swing and movement. To move the gun with the arms and hands alone destroys the control of your head on the stock and your shooting eye in relation to the top of barrel or rib; your movements become jerky and the smooth even rhythm is lost. That is one good reason it is so difficult even for an experienced shot to do his best work from a cramped sitting position in either boat or duck blind. Control of the body alone is not sufficient, but the gun must also be controlled and as near an integral part of the upper body during the gun movements as is possible to

Photo by John Bishop

Georgia Bishop Demonstrates Taking a Straight-away Bird. The Gun is a Browning Superposed 20-bore.

achieve. When you mount the gun, clamp down on it with hands and cheek and make it an intergral part of the upper body, then swing from the hips and knees and you will have the correct swing and follow through. The boxer watches and trains his foot work and the gunner must do the same, so that when a bird flushes he automatically gets his feet in proper position, just as the boxer shifts his feet and stance to either dodge or give a punch.

While the very fast sixgun shot trains his hands to coordinate with his eyes and brain to point the weapon accurately, the finished shotgunner must train his upper body, head and arms to do the pointing, with the gun held snugly as a part of the body.

One must be able to clearly see his bird or target over the barrel at all times, in order to anticipate and correct for any turn or swerve in the course of flight. As the eyes note any turn, the body, being in perfect coordination with the eyes and the gun simply a prolongation and an integral part of the body naturally follows the bird in its course as the brain dictates.

When one knows which way a bird will fly or a duck will pass then he can place the feet in accordance and sort of wind up his body, so that when the gun is mounted and the swing started, he simply unwinds his body as the gun follows the bird. This fact is far more important than most amateurs realize and the finished old hunter who makes a high average of bird killed per shots expended unconsciously winds up for such shots when he can pre-determine the course of the bird. He then makes a pivot of his upper body. If you know the bird is going to the left then face the bird and twist the upper body slightly around to the left. When the bird flushes and proceeds on its course to the left you simply unwind from the hips as it were in a smooth even follow through. Some shooters face their expected target squarely while others do best including this writer, by facing slightly to the right of the expected rise. In pass shooting you have ample time to note the course of the bird, when it will pass in range and have the gun ready and your body in proper position, before you rise to your feet for the shot. Practically all good and experienced shooters do this unconsciously, but the novice will do well to study such positions.

Most of the weight of the body, over half in fact, should always be on the forward foot or left foot for right handed shooters, or the right foot for left handed shooters. This in turn helps you to handle recoil correctly and to quickly recover from recoil for that second shot should it be needed.

Field shots seem to pivot the upper body from the knees up, while trap shots seem to pivot from the hips up, and they certainly do have a most beautiful even swing. However field angles are apt to be much wider than trap angles. Keep that gun shoulder high at all times. When a bird flushes, do not jerk the gun up into position. Bring it up smoothly and in line with the bird, no hurried movement and no jerking, just smooth even rhythm. Never hurry the shot, nor dwell on your aim or point, once correct lead is achieved. Remember the gun must be a part of the upper body, so coordinate both gun and body movements in a smooth even rhythm of movement.

The position you carry your gun when afield and expecting game is also very important. We never could see this Skeet stance, that most top notch Skeet shooters assume when in the field. It is necessary for the very minimum gun movement and getting the shot off in the Skeet game but out of place in the field. We usually carry a light or moderate gun with the shooting hand grasping the small of the stock and the barrels cradled in the crook of the left arm when walking up birds. If we expect a rise then the left hand goes out to the forestock and barrels and the gun is carried with barrels pointing downward toward the ground. When a bird raises we simply bring the gun up in line with his course as we shift the feet

Photo by John Bishop

The Author Demonstrates His Gun Position with Guns of Heavy Recoil. Here He Swings to the Left with a Magnum 10-bore Ithaca.

to proper position and all in one smooth movement. There is no unnecessary movement of the gun and one has only to stop his walking stride and place his feet, as the gun is mounted. It comes up in line with the course of the bird and the body is wound up for the shot all in one smooth movement. If we are with a partner, then the barrels point to the left if we take the left hand side and if we take the right hand side the gun barrels point down in front of us. If a right and left hand man hunt together, it is always well for the left hander to take the right side and vice versa for the right hander. The gun is then never pointing near your hunting partner.

When a heavy duck or goose gun is carried afield we still prefer the old timer's method of carrying the gun with the shooting hand grasping the small of the stock and the gun upside down on the shoulder with barrels pointing slightly upward. One has only to bring the gun over and into his forward hand in line with the duck or bird's course and it is the best method of packing a heavy ten to 10½ pound weapon all day and still not tire the arms unnecessarily

John Bishop Illustrates an Excellent Gun Carry for the Left-hand Man of a Pair of Hunters—Fast to Get Into Action. The Gun is a Magnum 10-bore Ithaca.

and be ready for a reasonably quick shot. A gun packed on the shoulder with the shooting hand grasping the butt plate is a slow awkward gun position and requires too many movements to bring the gun in line with a fast disappearing target. Over the years we have found these three positions best for walking up game. One: the gun gripped across the body with the shooting hand grasping small of stock and the barrels cradled in the left or forward arm, barrels pointing to left for right handers and to right for south paws. Two: the gun grasped with shooting hand at small of stock and butt back under arm, and between arm and body and the left or forward hand grasping barrels or forestock at their proper place for a quick shot and the barrels pointing downward to the front. Three: gun if a heavy gun, or any gun for that matter, as one must shift positions to keep from tiring certain muscles, grasped by the shooting hand and upside down on the shoulder with barrels pointing slightly upward. These three positions are comfortable and while No. two is fastest and No. one next, even the No. three position is far from slow and these positions enable you to carry a gun all day afield and be ready for action at any and all times.

With the No. one position the gun is brought around across the body with a smooth even movement in line with the bird's flight. In No. two position the gun is simply raised in line with the flight of the game, and in No. three position you simply bring the gun on over the shoulder and drop the barrels in the left or forward hand in line with the flight of the game. Practice, of course, makes perfect and makes for speed. Carrying a gun under the shoulder and resting in the hollow of one arm is comfortable but takes several movements to get the gun in action and is far too slow when expecting game. Avoid any strained gun carrying positions, just be comfortable and use one of the three above outlined positions and you will be ready when the game flushes.

Those who prefer the pump gun will soon learn to pull the gun down out of recoil from the first shot while they work the action and with the new Savage, Remington, and Ithaca pumps as well as the fine old '97 and Model 12 Winchesters, one can select as light or as heavy a gun as he wishes. The same is true in autoloaders and the new Remington is as light as anyone will want for the loads involved. Select a weight commensurate with your strength, then get afield with it as much as possible, Crows, hawks, horned owls, magpies, etc., will furnish plenty of summer shooting and you will be in trim for the game when the season opens. Remember stock length can be compensated for to some extent by the position of the forward hand on the action slide or barrels. If the stock is a bit long grasp farther back with that forward hand and the gun will come up smoothly and if short then grasp farther out on the barrels with the forward hand. A recoil pad or even a slip-on pad will add length to the stock when needed and also soften up the recoil a bit.

Confidence is half the battle and confidence in your ability can only be secured by doing a thing over and over again, so you must practice at every opportunity. After a time when you have killed enough game you will know beyond a reasonable doubt that you can kill the next bird that flushes; then you have arrived as a wing shot. You will have your off days when you are not in proper form and your brain and muscles do not work in accord as they should. Maybe you have been up too late the evening before or have a hangover or are sick, but off days will come when you cannot seem to hit even easy shots. At other times you will find you simply cannot miss—so it goes.

In pass duck shooting many arguments occur as to how best to take incoming birds. We used to hunt with the late Jake Lindner. He shot an old hammer, lifter-action Parker 12-bore with the heaviest loads of No. 4 shot he could get. Jake always allowed the birds to pass over, then killed his double quickly and with dispatch. Have seen him do it so many times there was no argument as to this being the best system for him. He knew just how far to hold under those birds that had passed overhead in range and practically always made his double.

We preferred to take the birds when still coming in and kill the first one well out in front of us by simply getting on the duck and raising the barrels until he was blotted out in a smooth even swing and firing the instant the duck was blotted out by the barrels, then twisting and taking the second fowl when it was almost over or directly over us as they towered up higher from the killing of the first duck. This worked for us but we never did master that going-away shot to suit us when the fowl had passed overhead. Sometimes we killed them and sometimes we missed them clean and when we did kill them they fell a lot farther out and were harder to retrieve. Jake and the writer used to argue about the merits of the two systems, he claiming that the duck was much easier penetrated when going away which is perfectly true, nevertheless we continued and still continue to take them as they are coming in and the second bird almost over us as they tower. Jake has now gone to a better hunting ground, I trust, but we had a lot of fun together in our early Montana days.

Select the system that suits you best and that you can kill the most ducks with and to hang with what the other fellow does or thinks; for after all it is you that is killing the ducks and what may be duck soup for him may be all wrong for you.

We got started killing incoming ducks at a pond with an old 40-inch barrel cheap single-barrel 12-bore and No. 3 shot. We learned that incoming lead and swing perfectly and to this day prefer to take incomers when well out in front and have used the same shot on pheasants many times that other gunners had flushed and it worked with them also. There can be no question, however, that heavily feathered late ducks or geese are harder to penetrate with a frontal shot than a going away shot, but we mastered that incoming shot so prefer to take it and if the shot are heavy enough for the birds involved they will penetrate all right as many day's bags have proven for us. If one were shooting very small shot like 7½ at 50 to 55 yards, then there would be sound logic in waiting for the birds to pass over as such small shot are about spent as to pellet energy at such ranges.

Try both systems of taking incoming birds or taking them after they have passed overhead and stick to whichever system you prefer or that produces best results. Always pick a single bird and concentrate on your lead on that one bird until he is killed or missed. Forget all about the others even though there may be a hundred more in the flock. Pick that one bird and kill him, then when the gun cracks swing onto the next nearest bird and try again. We have

Ted Keith Illustrates the Taking of An In-coming Bird.
The Gun is a 20-bore L. C. Smith.

seen shooters that were so excited they shot at the flock as a whole with the usual result, nothing was hit. A bevy of quail or Huns is even more startling to the novice when they roar up from under your feet, but you must pick one bird and even though it may be the bird that offers the toughest shot of any in the entire flock, stick to the one bird until you have killed or missed him.

One should never walk too close to a hunting companion when expecting birds to rise. We have had them swing our way so sharply when a grouse or pheasant flushed under foot as to hit us with their gun barrel and we once had a fine double gun struck with a fellow shooters gun so hard he bent the muzzle of our gun out of round and it had to be reshaped. You should keep constant check on the position of your companions, if in sight and if not in sight then by low whistles or other signals such as shaking a small tree or bush so each of you know the other's position. Never take a chance or shoot in the direction of a companion. All the birds in Christendom are not worth the taking of one single chance that might lead to an accident. Most accidents, so-called, are not accidents at all but pure carelessness.

While an eye opener is allright when you get up on a cold frost morning or a small drink to warm you at lunch time when sitting in a cold blind, do not try to mix liquor and gun powder, for the combination is dynamite and just as dangerous as whiskey and gasoline. We do not like to hunt with the type of man who seems to think his very life depends on getting the game, and who will take any chance to score. Such fellows also beef a lot if they miss and we prefer the hunting companion who goes about the business with a smile and is just as happy if the bird gets away unscathed as if it were killed.

Of course any good wing shot takes pride in his work, but he must remember a bird missed today may form some sport and good eating another day. We have been on the spot, so to speak, most of our young life due to having written so much on long range rifle and sixgun shooting and have had to demonstrate both on game and targets time and time again, but a lot more fun and enjoyment can be had if you simply go out and take the shots as they come and hit or miss come in in a good humor. If you are a lousy shot, or are doing badly, just charge it up to lack of experience and go on trying. We have hunted with men who habitually shot the same time we did and who always claimed the credit for the kill. The only thing to do in such cases is move off to one side on your own and then see which of you are doing the killing. One, of course, knows where his gun pointed and the range of the bird and has a very good idea if he killed or the other fellow. Never claim any bird that there can be a shadow of doubt about, better to let the other chap have it and be happy unless he proves a hog, then the best thing is to not go with him again.

At times you may be off form in your shooting, simply cannot get the swing and lead right and the aim or point will appear very close to right but the bird goes on unscathed. Remember the size of your pattern as taken on paper or old buildings at a given range and remember also you have half the width of that pattern and no more to err in and also remember, if a full choked gun, that that center of the pattern is what kills, not the laggard deformed pellets on the outer fringe. The aim may appear to have been very close but yet not close enough or you shot too quick before your pattern had opened up. If this is the case try slowing up a bit and riding your bird or target out a trifle farther and you will usually get results. In pass shooting it is always well to pick the lead bird. If you kill him you know your lead is right, if you kill a bird back behind the leader, then you know your shot was not right and more lead was called for. Also if the birds are in range and all tower and flare up at the shot, then you can be very sure you lead too much and shot in front of the fowl. You must concentrate on that one fowl

Photo by John Bishop

The Keith Family—Ted with a L. C. Smith 20-gauge; Lorraine with a Browning 20, and Elmer with his Magnum 10.

to the exclusion of all others until you see it crumple, then is time enough to swing onto and try for a double.

Many times in a rise of upland birds or even jumped ducks we have picked a bird that rose first and well out only to have others rise much closer to the gun and presenting much easier shots; but the thing to do is to stick to that first bird you are after and kill him, then try for the second. Never switch from one to another because a later bird may have raised at closer range. When you start your gun movement, follow through and concentrate on that one bird until killed or missed and the devil take the others. Over-anxiety spoils many a shot. If you get too anxious to make a kill you will probably do something wrong and miss.

We well remember coming back from the National 30 Caliber Matches in 1925 and taking our girl friend out for pheasants. We were in perfect training with the rifle then but picked up her father's single barrel 16-gauge and jumped and missed several pheasants at very close range. Too close in fact and we snap shot without letting them get out far enough for the full choked pattern to open. Though the lady later became our wife, we made a very bad showing that day. She laughed uproariously at those easy misses and that tamed us down until we finally got in the groove and killed a mess of pheasants for the table. We had been shooting a rifle steadily for over three months, but were simply way off the beam with a shotgun and could probably have come closer to those chinks with the rifle. Nothing is so good for the soul, as to have the conceit knocked out of you on occasion. We shot completely in front of those pheasants and as soon as we allowed them to get out to 35 and 40 yards, killed them cleanly with exactly the same lead we had been missing them with at 20 to 25 yards. Had we centered one at the closer range he would have been ruined anyway. The lady's laugh at our expense was just what was needed to slow us down and make us concentrate a bit on the range and pattern spread.

Watch the good trap, Skeet or game shot at every opportunity and analyze his stance and gun movements, but do not necessarily try to imitate him. Your own stance may be different and rightly so, but you can learn much from him and apply it to your own problems.

Two of the main reasons for missing, if you have the lead right, is flinching or stopping the gun when you fire. Both are fatal to good shooting. If you get to flinching, better load the gun with empties and follow and lead and snap on several before you again load the gun. Do the same thing if you are stopping your gun swing when you shoot. Usually the two go together and the shooter who is flinching is also stopping his gun swing. You must keep those eyes open, preferably both of them, and see exactly where the gun pointed when it raised in recoil.

If you get a case of flinching and stopping your gun swing, then try the empty cases on the next bird or birds and in fact any bird that comes along will do for this practice until you are again sure of yourself, then load the gun and go to work on the next bird. Some methodical shots may wait out their bird too far, being over-anxious on their point or aim, and this again is all wrong. Shoot the instant the gun swings ahead for the correct lead and do not hesitate or dwell on your aim unless the bird is too close for the pattern of the gun, then keep swinging with him until out far enough, then cross him and fire the instant the lead appears right. When pheasants raise under our feet, we often deliberately bring the gun up slow in a smooth slow movement allowing the bird to get out to 40 yards before crossing his path for lead and shooting. This is more deadly than mounting the gun hastily and following the bird too long. If you follow him too long you may in turn cramp your style and miss. In time one acquires a certain timing and rhythm and that should be maintained at all costs even though you wait the bird out a bit before raising the gun to the shoulder. Each shooter must analyze his own mistakes and try to correct them. None of us are perfect and none of us will always perform the best at all times. We all have our off days and we may even get into a slump in our shooting and be off for days. At Camp Perry in 1940, we served on the Idaho Civilian 30 Caliber Team and had shot continuously for months. One day the Team Captain ordered us all out for additional practice. We could feel we had shot enough so told him we were going to lay off that day while the rest of the team shot. We did and our scores went right back up where they belonged the next day simply because we relaxed and got all thought of match rifle shooting out of our heads for the day and rested up.

Trap and Skeet shooting will help you for field work but they can never be made to give you all the angles and problems of field shooting. Practice both trap and skeet if you can. It will help, but as all angles are pretty well known in advance and the shooter can take his stance and get all set for the shots, these are both games and will never make a finished game shot, but they will help a great deal and be of inestimable value in learning lead, stance etc. In trap shooting, even doubles shooting, you know the widest possible angle that can be secured and about where to expect the birds. At Skeet though the ranges are short the birds are also fast and require an exacting technique if you would make a good score. Though the gun must be held with butt below shoulder it is in almost as advanced a stage of gun mounting as in trap where it is mounted before the bird is called for. In field shooting you will usually be caught off balance by a rise of birds unless you have a good gun dog and know in advance of the birds presence and exact whereabouts. Practice on clay targets at every opportunity, it will help. Also practice on predatory birds and stray house cats and other vermin during the summer months. You will not only gain gunning experience but will also help the game supply greatly. Be satisfied with less than a limit and help preserve the game supply for posterity.

To all who have read through the pages of this book, we wish good hunting.

This special edition of

SHOTGUNS BY KEITH

BY ELMER KEITH

has been privately printed for members of The Firearms Classics Library. Film was prepared from an original 1950 edition. The book was printed and bound by Quebecor Graphics/Sherwood. The text paper was especially made for this edition by P.H. Glatfelter Company. The binding is genuine pigskin Saderra leather, Himalaya grain, furnished by the Cromwell Leather Company. Endleaves are 300-denier silk moiré. Edges are gilded and spines are brass-die stamped in 22-karat gold. Cover stampings and design of the edition by Selma Ordewer.